W9-CDS-064

BENCHMARKING

A Tool for Continuous Improvement

The Coopers & Lybrand Performance Solutions Series

C. J. McNair, CMA
and
Kathleen H. J. Leibfried

HarperBusiness
A Division of HarperCollinsPublishers

HarperCollins books may be purchased for educational, business, or sales promotional use. For information please write: Special Markets Department, HarperCollins Publishers, Inc., 10 East 53rd Street, New York, NY 10022.

FIRST EDITION

Library of Congress Cataloging-in-Publication Data

McNair, Carol Jean.
    Benchmarking:a tool for continuous improvement/C. J. McNair, Kathleen H. J. Leibfried.
        p.   cm.
    Includes bibliographical references and index.
    ISBN 0-88730-548-2
    1. Management audit.   2. Organizational effectiveness.
    3. Organizational change.   4. Total quality management.
    5. Competition.   I. Leibfried, Kathleen H. J.   II. Title.
HD58.95.M36   1992
658.5'62—dc20   92-6932
                                                                        CIP

93   94   95   96   PS/RRD   10   9   8   7   6   5   4   3

Each project brings its special friends and active supporters. To each of you my heartfelt thanks. To George and Jason, my appreciation for taking me through the highs and the lows of writing. And to Mike. Where would I begin the list?

C.J. McNair

To my mother, who was *always* there when I needed encouragement; to Mike, who believed in my ability and challenged me; and to Charlie, who gave me benchmarking.

Kate Leibfried

CONTENTS

CONTENTS

CONTENTS

CONTENTS

ACKNOWLEDGMENTS

Although everyone involved deserves thanks, both authors want to extend their heartfelt gratitude to Mike Gleason. He is a nurturing, yet demanding, mentor who has had tremendous impact on every one of his "students." His classroom is the real world; his exams are the challenges he places in each of our paths. He asks for one thing only: that you do your best. Always. There is no other option, no other path to graduation. Thank you, once again. Where would we be without you?

...AND REMARKS

The following page lists all of the contributors to this book, from Coopers & Lybrand, Babson College, and from other settings. The complete list of acknowledgments for this book would make a book in and of itself. For those of you mentioned, thank you once again. For those overlooked in our joyous rush to dot the final *i* and cross the final *t*, we apologize.

Creating a book is a major undertaking. It brings with it stress, anxiety (hopefully creative), and joy. The product is never perfect, but always serves as one more step in the learning process of everyone involved. Authors, then, are in many ways students of their own work. Often keen insights come from having to explain to others exactly what that nagging demon inside is trying to say. At other times, it becomes clear that what seemed like inspiration was just a mild case of heat exhaustion.

The final judge of whether or not this book accomplishes its mission is you, the reader. If it does, the thanks will go to the people listed in the following pages, because their patience, support, open sharing, and wisdom were then put to good use. Should the project fall short of the mark in the eyes of you, the ultimate customer, then only the two authors can take responsibility. We hope that the lessons we have learned can be put to good use in your own company, and that this book is but one step on your own journey toward excellence.

LIST OF CONTRIBUTORS

Project Sponsors

H. Michael Gleason—Coopers & Lybrand, MCS
Tom Walther—Coopers & Lybrand, MCS
Robert King—Coopers & Lybrand, MCS
Gary King—Avon Products, Inc.
David Sheffield—Janssen Pharmaceutica
Daniel Marie—Exxon Chemical
James Meenan—AT&T Communications
Irv Krause—Mertius

Contributors

Bill Band	John Lin
Jerry Benison	Ian Littman
Joseph Barba	Richard Luettgen
Russel Barss	Alan McNab
Carl Benner	Ron Mastrogiovanni
Michael Blum	David Miller
Gerry Briley	Stephen Parkoff
Keith Brown	John Patberg
Charles Bunstine	Clive Pyne
Peter Cohen	James Raney
Dennis Conroy	Craig Roberts
Joe DeSalvo	Jeff Rosengard
Jack Dunleavy	Rod Roy
Dan Elron	Carl Schroeder
Winslow Farrell	Mal Schwartz
Judy Faucett	Art Sciarrotta
Richard Greenberg	James Warner
Howard Harowitz	Doug Watters
Jim Hom	Bill Wheeler
Richard Huot	Graham Whitney
Randi Johnson	David Wilkerson
Vijay Kumar	Chris Wood
Chuck Kachmarik	Ed Woroniecki
Robert Lage	Ron Zimmerman

ACKNOWLEDGMENTS

C&L Support Staff

Annamaria Cucuzza
Marilyn Charles
Carol Desouza
Julia Dictter
Niki Girvin

Katrina Greene
Doris Grillo
Lyle Spelowitz—graphics
Susan Steiner
Connie Yee

Babson College Support

Sandra Texeira
Elli Gross
The Word Processing Group

General Encouragement and Cheerleading—C&L

Hank Johansson
David Carr
Ed Kostin
John Pedlebury

Bruce Townsend
Nancy Stagg
Susan Storch

General Encouragement and Cheerleading—Babson & Elsewhere

Larry Carr
Mike Fetters
Lou Jones
Bill Lawler
Larry Ponemon
Bob Stasey
Dick Williamson

Kelvin Cross
Fran Gammel
Chris Karas
Rich Lynch
Gordon Shillinglaw
Walter Stasey

And others too numerous to mention.

PREFACE

Each book has a point of inspiration, a moment when thoughts begin to crystallize and momentum is gained. For Kate, this happened three years ago when she met Charles Christ. He was a new partner at Coopers & Lybrand but an old hand at benchmarking. He had been instrumental in creating benchmarking while he was president of Xerox Reprographics in the 1980s. The concept of benchmarking was new then.

Many companies contacted over the next few years maintained that they were already the best, that they had nothing to learn from others. After all, they were profitable and successful competitors in their markets. The state of crisis that had propelled Xerox into the benchmarking process was absent. Without this competitive pressure, there was no perceived need to do benchmarking.

Although some decided to do some preliminary benchmarking using databases and other publicly available sources, many simply turned a deaf ear to the message. Those who took the time to use benchmarking found out, in graphic terms, that they weren't ahead of the game—they were behind the eight ball. One by one, major corporations began to understand the differences between this word *benchmarking* and traditional operation improvement programs, and Kate began to see that it was more than a fad. It justified change and was a tool for continous improvement.

Today there is an ever-growing interest in benchmarking and the lessons it has to teach in the United States, Europe and Australia. Good companies know they have to get better; poorly run ones are clinging to straws. This realization is occurring along with an increasing awareness of global competition and its impact on the quality of life and future prosperity. No message could be clearer: the United States is lagging behind its competitors. As this performance gap grows, it becomes increasingly difficult to stop the flow of resources and wealth from the economy.

Benchmarking is an early warning system of impending problems. If its siren sounds, change is needed. Through the use of objective, market-oriented measures of performance, it focuses attention where attention is needed and rips away the blinders that prevent learning. It is more than a one-time measurement; it is a tool for creating the learning organization.

BENCHMARKING

1: BENCHMARKING—THE COMPETITIVE EDGE

It is not always by plugging away at a difficulty and sticking at it that one overcomes it; but, rather, often by working on the one next to it. Certain people and certain things require to be approached on an angle.

André Gide, 1924

Gaining—and maintaining—a competitive edge is the key to success in all walks of life, both on the playing field and in the boardroom. In sports, the scoreboard continually flashes information on the winners and losers of the contest. It is a clear signal of success or failure. For the businessperson of today, though, no readily available scoreboard exists; the rewards go to the manager with the best intuition, or "gutfeel," of the vagaries of the customer and marketplace and how to capitalize on them.

Yet tradition and intuition are really no replacement for objective external comparison and analysis, or *benchmarking*. Benchmarking is emerging in leading-edge companies as a tool for obtaining the information needed to support continuous improvement and gain competitive advantage. Initially employed by Xerox Corporation to meet the Japanese competitive challenge of the 1970s, benchmarking embodies the pursuit of excellence, the desire to be the "best of the best."

What is benchmarking? Benchmarking is *an external focus on internal activities, functions, or operations in order to achieve continuous improvement*. Starting from an analysis of existing activities and practices within the firm, the objective is to understand existing *processes*, or activities, and then to identify an external *point of reference*, or standard, by which that activity can be measured or judged. A benchmark can be established at any level of the organization, in any functional area. The ultimate goal is quite simple: to be better than the best—to attain a competitive edge.

David T. Kearns, CEO of Xerox Corporation, states that benchmarking is "the continuous process of measuring product, services, and practices against the toughest competitors, or those companies recognized as industry leaders."[1] Both definitions suggest an external focus, a movement away from a concern with cost reduction and budgets to an understanding of what activities customers value and what level of performance they expect.

Through the use of benchmarking concepts and techniques, an increasing number of companies, both in the United States and abroad, are realizing that future success will require more than gutfeel, and more than just doing what they've always done a bit better. Success in the 1990s and beyond requires fact, not fiction, and analysis, not guesstimates, with a clear, ongoing focus on meeting and exceeding customer expectations.

SUCCESS IS MORE THAN PROFITS

The continuous pursuit of excellence is the underlying and ever-present goal of benchmarking practices. The starting point in achieving excellence is the customer. Whether external or internal to the organization, the customer sets the expectations for performance and is the ultimate judge of its quality. "Customers" populate the corporate landscape. A customer is anyone who has a *stake*, or interest, in the ongoing operations of the company. Richard J. Schonberger, in his recent book *Building a Chain of Customers*,[2] notes that

> ...world-class performance is *dedicated to serving the customer*. ...The wide-awake now see the final customer as just the endpoint in a chain of customers. Everybody has a customer—at the next process (where your work goes next). Making the connections along the chain is our common task.

The "customer," then, can be internal or external to the organization. It is anyone who receives the output of our labor or is affected by its quality and timeliness.

Another way to view the demands placed on the modern organization is in terms of corporate stakeholders. *Stakeholder* is a broader concept than *customer*, which indicates that a service or product is being provided as an endpoint in a value chain. A stakeholder has an interest in the corporation that extends over time; it doesn't end when a product is shipped or a service delivered. Stakeholders, then, are intricately tied to the organization and dependent upon its survival. Who are the corporate stakeholders?

Stakeholders include suppliers, owners, employees, and customers (see Figure 1.1). These four groups are dependent on the corporation for their physical and financial well-being. In turn, the organization could not function without their ongoing support. Maintaining all of these relationships consumes a significant amount of a company's resources. In fact, it is hard to identify a cost incurred by a company that isn't in some way caused by a stakeholder relationship.

Reacting to stakeholder needs is a basic requirement for corporate survival. Survival isn't the goal, however; competitive excellence is. To attain excellence a corporation has to move far beyond the basics, looking for ways to improve upon existing products and services. Faced with a broad range of competing opportunities for improvement, management has to choose those that will provide the most benefit to the stakeholders in total. The challenge facing management is deciding how to increase the value of the firm without sacrificing the interests of any of its stakeholders.

Benchmarking provides management with the tools needed to make the hard decisions about resource allocation and the

Stakeholders

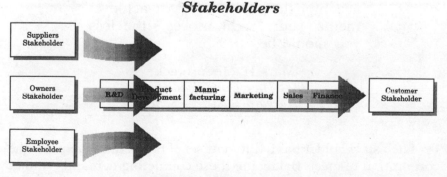

Figure 1.1   Stakeholders.

strategic focus of the organization. It does this by providing objective measurements, or scorecards, of the company's efforts to meet stakeholder needs. Benchmarking develops a series of objective measures of the success of the corporate game plan as set against internal goals as well as against external organizations performing at recognized levels of excellence.

In a free market, every stakeholder has other "investment" options. The game that management is playing, therefore, is not getting product to market faster or building it a little cheaper. These are important ways to gain competitive advantage, but they are only part of the challenge. In reality, managing a corporation is a brutal competitive struggle to secure and expand the resources committed to the corporation by its various stakeholders. Only by benchmarking the company's performance against the expectations of these stakeholders can this game be won for the long run.

MEETING THE NEEDS OF STAKEHOLDERS

Business is a competition, and any high-level sophisticated competition is almost exclusively a head game. The Inner Game of Business, as this could be called, is understanding the Business Paradox: the better you think you are doing, the greater should be your cause for concern; the more self-satisfied you are with your accomplishments, your past achievements, your "right moves," the less you should be.

Mark H. McCormack
*What They Don't Teach You
at Harvard Business School*

Each stakeholder has a different set of needs that it expects the corporation to meet. Balancing these competing demands cannot be done without information about what those needs are, how well they are currently being met, and what options exist for improving on current performance. Unfortunately, many of these questions cannot be answered by a manager sitting in an office. That may be an approach open to academics, but managers operate in the real world, where answers are difficult to identify and implement. Brainstorming may help water the internal idea crop, but when nutrients are added growth is faster and stronger. Beating the competition requires looking outside the organization by using benchmarking and related techniques to peel away the layers of "difference" to make valid comparisons against other organizations, and to learn from them.

The Owner as Stakeholder

Management is well aware of its obligations to the owners of the corporation. In the United States, pressure from the financial markets is an ever-present specter that drives corporate decision making. The dominant measures used to gauge a company's success in meeting shareholder (and debtholder) needs are dividends, share price, return on investment, and related financial measures (see Figure 1.2). These traditional measures are based on the numbers generated by the company's accounting system and are reported through the various media.

Even though accounting profits are justifiably part of the corporate scorecard, adding value to the shareholder does not stop there. Why? Because the owner of the firm, whether on-site or absentee, has invested funds that are used by the other stakeholders to support the company's value chain. These funds, or the underlying cash flow they generate, are the lifeblood of the organization. Although accounting gurus have only recently focused their attention on reporting cash flows to external users of accounting information (that is, "the market"), any businessperson can tell you that running out of cash is a death stroke. The list of large

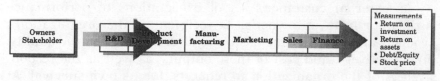

Figure 1.2   Traditional measurements.

corporations that looked good "on the books" yet were felled by a lack of cash is long and replete with familiar names such as retail giant W. T. Grant. Alfred Rappaport[3] suggests the pervasive role cash plays in maintaining stakeholder relations:

> If the company does not satisfy the financial claims of its constituents, it will cease to be a viable organization. Employees, customers, and suppliers will simply withdraw their support. Thus, a going concern must strive to enhance its cash-generating ability. The ability of a company to distribute cash to its various constituencies depends on its ability to generate cash from operating its businesses and on its ability to obtain any additional funds needed from external sources.

Shareholder value, then, is dependent on a healthy cash flow that keeps the other organizational stakeholders involved.

Increasing market values and maintaining sound cash flows are only two of the demands the owner places on the organization; the third is a long-run concern that the company survive and grow. Of any group of stakeholders, owners have the greatest interest in the company's survival. The resources invested by the owners can be recouped only if the company continues to operate successfully. Owners are vitally concerned with the long-run creation of value (that is, growth) of the organization.

This is one of the most challenging areas facing management today. Incessant pressures from the financial markets often drive myopic, short-run decision making that in the long run spells disaster for the corporation. As company after company faces the prospect of corporate decline, there is an increasing number of attempts to find ways to fight these unseeable, yet powerful, forces. Management teams are taking companies "private" to shake off these pressures and focus on long-run value creation. Ongoing growth is in the best interest of all stakeholders.

Customers as Stakeholders

An external customer's set of expectations of performance is different from an owner's. As recipient of the organization's products and services, the customer directly relies on the quality, timely delivery, and cost of these outputs, as well as the responsiveness of the organization to requests, for its own survival. At all times looking to maximize the value received for its purchases, the customer will look elsewhere if corporate performance does not meet (or exceed) these expectations

Whenever the customer has repeated contact with the organization, the situation becomes more complicated than a simple market transaction would suggest. When a company is providing a raw material for another firm, it is effectively setting boundaries on the quality, cost, and delivery that organization can offer to its customers. Recognizing this, many companies have established preferred vendor networks. These networks erase the clean boundaries between the two organizations, creating a new entity with a linked destiny. At this point the customer becomes an active stakeholder in the organization, often to the point of participating in redesigning the processes and products of its "supplier."

This form of direct control by the customer-stakeholder is still more of an exception than a rule. Instead, most customers retain the right to vote with their feet (and their dollars), changing allegiances as events unfold, seeking to get the most value for every dollar spent on goods and services. Value, though, does not necessarily mean cost alone; even the transient customer expects quality, timely delivery, and responsiveness. In fact, "value creation includes all the quality, service, and customer satisfaction tools that have been evolving in different areas of North American business, but it combines them in such a way that the whole is greater than the sum of its parts. A truly integrated philosophy of competition will be required if businesses are to cope succussfully with the myriad challenges that business leaders are facing today. Myopic business concepts and strategies will no longer suffice."[4] To succeed in the competitive arena today, a company has to know whether it is meeting customer expectations on all of these dimensions. Benchmarking is one tool for getting this information.

Suppliers and Company Survival

Looking at the organization from the supplier's perspective is the flip side of the previous discussion. Although the company can exercise its options as a customer (for example, it can change suppliers), this is not a costless alternative. Over the past ten years many companies have established "preferred vendor" relationships to support just-in-time (JIT) processing. These relationships blur the boundaries between the companies, making the supplier an integral part of the delivery mechanism. Even if this isn't the case, changing suppliers can have an adverse effect on the people who actually run the machines, provide the service, or otherwise participate in the value creation process.

Suppliers have a significant stake in the success of a company. They may be creditors of preference in a liquidation, but that doesn't mean they'll ever see their money if the company fails. It is therefore in the supplier's best interest to make sure that its customers are successful and are generating enough cash to pay for the goods and services they purchase. Both sides of the vendor-customer relationship have vested interests in the well-being of the other.

Employees: The Ultimate Stakeholders

People are the most important resource an organization has. They are the eyes, ears, and minds that develop plans and execute them, adding to the value of the firm. They also protect the interests of the other stakeholders on an ongoing basis. In fact, Michael L. Dertouzos et al. suggest that employing the whole worker means that participation, both in decisions and rewards, is a prerequisite to success.[5]

> In the most successful firms today the role of production workers is shifting from one of passive performance of narrow, repetitive tasks to one of active collaboration in the organization and fine-tuning of production.... The objective should be continuous learning on the job.... If people are asked to give maximum effort and to accept uncertainty and rapid change, they must be full participants in the enterprise....

Employee participation has been an active topic of discussion since the 1950s, when the development of formal budgeting procedures made it clear that individual participation was a requirement for gaining commitment to the organization's goals. When participation was lacking, individuals would either ignore the preset goals or engage in various types of games both before the budget target was set and during the actual reporting of results, to make sure that the goal could be attained. Additionally, the development of individual and departmental goals provided a fertile ground for parochialism—the pursuit of what's best for you or your department, no matter what the consequences for others.

Parochialism, or turfmanship, is nonproductive, non-value-adding behavior at best, destructive at worst. In any setting it is at odds with the type of cooperative effort needed to beat the competition on the global front. It places unnecessary roadblocks in the path of productive change, creating perpetual "do loops" that add little value, in the customer's eyes, to the organization or its products and services. Undoing the traditions and culture of individualism is one of the major challenges facing companies today.

The participative organization is based on cooperation; the adversarial relationship that has long characterized the management-labor issue has no place in a company pursuing excellence. Each individual throughout the organization is vitally important to its overall performance and success. These individuals are on the front line, protecting the interests of each and every stakeholder; management, staff, and labor fight the daily battles that spell victory or defeat for the organization as a whole.

Value creation is the heart of organizational activity. Benchmarking provides the metrics by which to understand and judge the value provided by the organization and its resources. The measures developed during the course of a benchmarking project point the way to continuous improvement and competitive excellence, enhancing the interests of the organizational stakeholders and the long-run competitive position of the enterprise. One must remember that, although the measures may point the way, it is the individuals who populate the organization that turn measures into action and action into value.

ESTABLISHING THE BOUNDARIES FOR SUCCESS

There is something that I don't know
    that I am supposed to know.
I don't know *what* it is I don't know,
    and yet am supposed to know,
And I feel I look stupid
    If I seem not to know it
    and not know *what* it is I don't know.

Therefore I pretend I know it.

   This is nerve-wracking

   since I don't know what I must pretend to know.

   Therefore I pretend to know everything.

   I feel you know what I am supposed to know

      but you can't tell me what it is

      because you don't know that I don't know what it is.

R. D. Laing
Knots

Every individual needs to have a clear idea of what goal is being pursued in order to make the decisions along the way that will ensure this goal's being reached. As suggested by the poem, ignorance is seldom admitted. If people don't know what is expected, they'll set off on their own path—a path that may or may not coincide with that of the organization.

In the past, a significant amount of management effort has gone into setting out clear action directives, telling employees exactly how to do a specific task but never letting them know why the task was necessary in the first place. The resulting misdirected action was often worse than no action at all. Anyone who has stood in a long line trying to get a vehicle registered, a tax issue resolved, or any number of other frustrating details attended to understands the concept of tight action controls with absolutely no results. Its familiar term is *bureaucracy*—the mindless pursuit of precise action that frustrates, rather than promotes, goal attainment.

When employees are actively participating in an organization, they are empowered with the right to make decisions, instead of simply following prescribed courses of action. To attain world-class competitive capability, then, everyone must know of and work toward desired results. The individual is trusted to use appropriate means to get to the ends; management focuses on clearly communicating both an underlying set of ethics (for example, culture) and the mission, or objective, that is being pursued.

Today, world-class organizations are looking for ways to integrate activities both horizontally and vertically through the organization; they are turning their efforts toward clear identification of objectives at every level and the linkage of these goals to the corporate mission statement. This integration down through the communication of goals, balanced by timely information and feedback systems, lays the framework for excellence.

Proactive Management

Fixing mistakes and reacting to changing conditions is a losing proposition. To achieve world-class competitive capability, management must constantly be looking forward, adjusting the organization's activities and goals to respond to perceived shifts in customer needs. Planning, or focusing constantly on the next play, the next challenge, is the critical dimension to ongoing success. In fact, a philosophy that spurns acceptance of the status quo is essential to compete successfully in today's world. Benchmarking can be the cornerstone of that philosophy.

The Japanese are well known for their forward-looking approach. Looking backward is valuable only if it helps make future plans more successful—if it promotes learning and continuous improvement. As product life cycles continue to shorten, proactive management of next-generation products and processes will come to dominate management's time. The key is to plan well so that mistakes are minimized and opportunities maximized.

Measuring Performance

All of this brings us back to the role of measurement in setting clear objectives and goals that ensure competitive excellence. Benchmarking is becoming the basis for this measurement process; it is forward-looking, holistic, participative, quality focused, and above all, stakeholder driven. The process of benchmarking forces a clear communication of goals to all involved, the active participation of every employee in establishing current practice and identifying best practice, and the identification of the type of results or change needed to match and exceed best practice.

In establishing externally driven benchmarks, or performance measures, many of the problems associated with traditional control systems are countered. First, in order to establish a benchmark, or performance target, individuals or departments must both identify and communicate with their customers. This directed interaction mitigates the effects of years of turfmanship;

it attacks parochialism at its roots, forcing a clear recognition that everyone is part of the team.

Second, the ability to manipulate the system both before goals are set and after action occurs is greatly diminished, as is the motivation for doing so. Individual managers do not control the input, or data, used in the evaluation process—these are generated and reported by an external agent, such as the customer. The individual does have control over the elements or tools necessary to achieve a strong performance evaluation, but these are driven by the customer's needs, not gaming the system.

Communication or direction setting,[6] is enhanced through the process of establishing internal and external benchmarks, reducing another control problem. The benchmarking process is predicated on clear, two-way communication and participation. Benchmarks cannot be established without a comprehensive understanding of current practice, desired results, and the recognition and acceptance of the changes that will need to occur to meet and exceed those goals.

Finally, in establishing active two-way communication and participation, benchmarking processes dampen negative attitude problems. Specifically, people who know what is expected, are fairly evaluated against agreed-upon objectives, and have sufficient control over the tools necessary to attain those results are motivated people. Negative attitudes are the result of many of the traditional management philosophies—of autocratic command structures that never asked for advice from subordinates, just effort.

The Goal: Continuous Improvement

The process of communicating, setting goals, and working toward world-class competitive capability never stops. The process of continuous improvement, or *Kaizen*, means gradual, unending improvement, doing little things better, and setting—and achieving—ever-higher standards.[7] Masaaki Imai makes the following observations:

> The essence of KAIZEN is simple and straightforward: KAIZEN means improvement. Moreover, KAIZEN means ongoing improvement involving everyone, including both managers and workers. The KAIZEN philosophy assumes that our way of life— be it our working life, our social life, or our home life—deserves to be constantly improved.[8]

In the end, those who do not change and who do not improve gradually face extinction or radical upheaval. This fact can be observed in nature and in a long history of evolution in society and its social institutions. Governments that fail to respond to the demands of their "stakeholders" are eventually overthrown; species that do not evolve as their environment changes disappear.

Unfortunately, as suggested by Imai, few individuals or companies are open to continuous change and improvement. Instead, people strive to hold on to the present, to put protective tariffs and other fences around themselves to keep change away. When a company or an industry places blinders on the truth, tricking itself into believing that "business as usual" mentalities will work, it magnifies the chance that it will ultimately die. Avoiding change in the short run, putting it off until a competitive crisis threatens the organization, decreases the opportunities for long-run survival. Yet, time after time, companies turn toward *Kaizen*-based approaches only when they have exhausted every other bluff or change-avoiding tool. When the patient is in intensive care, radical surgery may be done, but the chances for success are greatly reduced.

Benchmarking is an excellent vehicle for developing a *Kaizen* culture in a company. It is a continuous process of evaluating current performance, setting goals for the future, and identifying areas for improvement and change. It is a dynamic, ongoing effort by management and workers alike. It contains the seed of organizational and cultural change that must occur if survival, let alone competitive excellence, is to be achieved. The goal is to put benchmarking to work to help you and your company achieve world-class competitive capability.

Setting the Stage

This book is about benchmarking. Using examples from companies adopting benchmarking practices in many different areas of their organizations and the successes and lessons gained along the way, the text will explore benchmarking from many different perspectives. The ultimate goal is to provide you, the reader, with the tools necessary to embark on a benchmarking project of your own, or to decide whether benchmarking is the right tool to use. Practical examples will be used throughout the discussion to clarify issues, provide insights, and illustrate why benchmarking matters to every organization.

Part One will set the conceptual framework for the benchmarking process, including the issues involved in benchmarking internal operations. Part Two will expand the focus to include competitive and industry benchmarking and the issues raised in these settings. Part Three will illustrate one of the more promising aspects of benchmarking, providing a detailed examination of "best in class" benchmarking projects, their costs and benefits, and clues on when to use them and how. The final section of the book brings implementation issues to life. It may be interesting to read about benchmarking, but its greatest value comes from its application. Detailed discussions of how to put benchmarking to work will provide the impetus for actually doing, not discussing, benchmarking techniques.

Throughout the discussion, the goal will be to provide the tools needed to begin the benchmarking process and to use it to reap short-term and long-term continuous improvements. Only by knowing what the goal is can a course be plotted to get there. Benchmarking provides the compass readings and navigational details for attaining competitive excellence. What is needed to put them to work is a sound understanding of the tool and a desire to improve.

"Success" is never merely final or terminal. Something else succeeds it.... The world does not stop when the successful person pulls out his plum; nor does he stop, and the kind of success he obtains, and his attitude towards it, is a factor in what comes afterwards.

John Dewey
Human Nature Conduct

2: THE MANY FACES OF BENCHMARKING

Whatever helps us to visualize things as different from what our intellectual sleepiness shows them to be, ought to be gladly welcomed.

Ernest Dimnet
What We Live By

Benchmarking provides a new vision or perspective on traditional management concerns. Traditionally management has relied on internal expertise, bolstered by occasional outside intervention, to establish strategic objectives, and monitor performance. Relying on experience, or a "real feel for the business," might make sense if the playing field were level and no one were allowed to change the rules once the game was in motion. Unfortunately, companies are not playing on a level field today; they are fighting an uphill battle against competitors who have redefined the rules. The marketplace today expects, and is receiving, constantly improving products and services at an ever-decreasing cost per function.

This litany appears in almost every trade book available for modern managers. It doesn't take much imagination to figure out that continuing current practices is not a viable option if long-term success is desired. The path forward, though, is littered with debris. It takes intelligence, common sense, and patience to wade through the plethora of "solutions" that are popping up everywhere. In a time of "have acronym, will travel," the wary manager has to carefully evaluate and choose among the opportunities available for improvement and growth. Since fads are not cheaper by the dozen and have been known to wreak havoc on the corporate psyche, it is critically important to be able to distinguish those projects that will yield benefits for the long run from those that will only chew up resources with minimal benefit.

Benchmarking: Know Thyself

Everybody thinks of others as being excessively human, with all the frailties and crotchets appertaining to that curious condition. But each of us also seems to regard himself as existing on a detached plane of observation, exempt (save in moments of vivid crisis) from the strange whims of humanity en masse.

Christopher Morley
Pipefuls

Gaining the knowledge needed to choose among these competing opportunities starts with understanding your own organization. Looking at it from a different light, taking a step backward and questioning existing practices, and tracing the value chain through the organization's myriad functional areas are the techniques for gaining this understanding. Even if a company believes that it *really knows* its business, there are surprises around every bend when a *horizontal perspective* is taken (see Figure 2.1).

What is a "horizontal perspective"? It is the value chain, which starts with the receipt of a request from a company stakeholder and terminates when that request has been answered to the satisfaction of all. To actually deliver product to a customer, for example, individuals in almost every part of the organization have to get involved, whether on the plant floor making the units or

2: THE MANY FACES OF BENCHMARKING

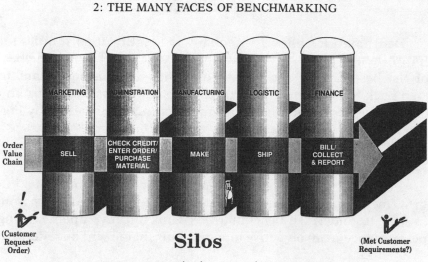

Figure 2.1   The horizontal perspective.

in the back office processing the invoice. Each value chain is made up of tasks that are linked across the organization. Orders are not filled by one functional silo, but rather by the cooperative efforts of individuals in different departments, functions, and perhaps divisions.

While it is a technique for looking outward to gain measures of excellence, the process starts by understanding the organization itself, its work flows, and the value added at each stage of the process. This is because benchmarking is a *comparison* of existing practices in your company to those used externally. Comparison means that some baseline of similarity has to exist. Benchmarking is an "apples to apples" exercise that starts by understanding what type of apples are in your bushel. Only then can valid comparisons and identification of improvement opportunities be achieved.

BENCHMARKING BASICS

Man's highest merit always is, as much as possible, to rule external circumstances and as little as possible to let himself be ruled by them.

Goethe

Benchmarking allows a company to identify opportunities for improvement and to proactively direct efforts to become the best of the best. To put the tool to use, though, it is important to step back for a moment and think through the assumptions and characteristics of the benchmarking process, as suggested by Figure 2.2.

Seeking Continuous Improvement

Benchmarking is based in the philosophy of continuous improvement: it is a change management tool. The only reason, in fact, to undertake benchmarking is to improve upon existing performance in an objective manner. This theme will be reiterated

Philosophy   **Continuous Improvement**

Perspective   **Stakeholders**

Objectives   **Identify Best Practice (in order to)...**
- **Support Value Creation Process**
- **Prioritize Opportunities for Improvement**
- **Enhance Performance Against Customer Expectations**
- **Leapfrog Cycle of Change**

Targets   **Strategic Issues**
Roles
Processes
Effectiveness & Efficiency

Critical Success Factors

Defining Features   **Purposive**
External Focus
Measurements-Based
Information Intensive
Objective
Action Generating

Figure 2.2   Benchmarking basics.

throughout the book because it sets the tone, and also underscores the need for and value of the benchmarking process. Benchmarking identifies gaps in performance and opportunities for improvement, and it sheds new light on old methods. It is difficult to conceive a benchmarking project that does not have change as the outcome.

A second major issue noted in Figure 2.2 is that benchmarking takes a "stakeholder" perspective. As suggested earlier, the company is serving many different constituents at all times. Benchmarking succeeds best when everyone's interests are understood and considered in the chosen solutions. Placing customers ahead of employee interests may seem to be a formula for success, but the employees are the ones who will make that customer happy, not the "organization." Conversely, placing employees above owner interests can also lead to downstream problems, resulting in the withdrawal of the capital essential for supporting the organization's activities. Finally, responding to a customer demand at the cost of suppliers can make the next "crisis" impossible to manage.

In reflecting on benchmarking, then, recognize that there is always room for improvement. Be willing to learn from others and remember that the changes must take into account all stakeholders' interests. The advantage that benchmarking offers is that it objectifies this process of change, clearly laying out the types of solutions external organizations have used and providing a global perspective on how parts of the company affect the whole. It helps focus the improvement efforts to arcas where gains can be made; gains translate to value added for everyone involved.

Objectives of the Benchmarking Process

The overriding objective of benchmarking is *to identify best practice*. Knowing is not doing, though. For benchmarking to have value, therefore, it has to be put to work to support the value creation process, helping to prioritize opportunities for improvement, enhance performance against customer expectations (which increases sales), and to leapfrog the traditional cycle of change.

During the 1980s, Xerox Reprographics Manufacturing Group had a continuous improvement program that was achieving an

8 percent productivity increase over a period of years. One Sunday afternoon, however, Charles Christ, president of the group, saw an ad in the *New York Times* for copiers that were essentially the same, in terms of function and performance, as the ones he was building in Webster, New York. These copiers were selling at retail for less than he could manufacture them! At about the same time there was an article in *Fortune* that quoted the president of Cannon claiming he was going to wage total war on Xerox and was going to win.

This was a turning point. "It made me realize we had greater problems than we had anticipated," Christ recounted. "We had been very successful [in the late 1960s Xerox developed a flagship product—the 914 copier—and had 80 percent of the marketshare by the mid 1970s]; we had lost that and now we were fighting, in a sense, for the market that we had established." Xerox stock was at an all-time low and marketshare had dropped to the low 30s.

In response, Christ sent a team of manufacturing people to Japan to study, in great detail, the process, the product, and the material. His parting words to the team were, "I need a benchmark, something that I can measure myself against to understand where we have to go from here. This competitive benchmarking resulted in specific performance targets rather than someone's guess or intuitive feel of what needs to be done—which is the real power of the process." Quality went from 91 defects per 100 machines to 14. Line fallout (defined as bad parts on the line) went from 30,000 per million parts to 1,300 per million. There was a 50 percent reduction in manufacturing costs, a 50 percent reduction in unique parts, and a 66 percent reduction in development time.

Christ, who is now vice president of Digital Equipment Corporation, concluded that "the purpose of benchmarking is to gain sustainable competitive advantage. Specifically, know yourself. Know your competition and best-in-class. Study them. Learn from them and be ready to adapt their best practices—how they do things—to your process."

Value is created whenever the same outputs are made with fewer inputs or more outputs are obtained with the same inputs. Value is the premium paid to the organization for transforming raw materials into a package (whether product or service) that the market values more than the raw materials themselves. Value creation is the test of a company's worth; whether that value is stated in dollars or in other terms is unimportant.

Prioritizing projects is the most difficult part of managing the scarce resources of an organization. While this is clearly discussed by capital budgeting experts, decisions are made every day that divert resources from one use to another. Benchmarking makes these decisions more objective, providing an external reference that each new opportunity can be judged against. Choice is easier when the desired endpoint is understood.

Enhancing performance against customer expectations has become the rallying cry for an entire group of management techniques that suggest that keeping an eye on the customer, whether internal or external to the organization, is the key to growth and competitive excellence. Given that the customer is one of two stakeholders who provide the working capital or cash used to support the entire organization, it is important to keep the customer's needs in mind. But the "customer perspective" actually means much more than this: it sets the performance targets, or definition of what the outputs of any task, or organization, need to be. By factoring the "customer" into discussions about how a specific job is done or the way a product is designed, downstream mistakes and unpleasant surprises are minimized. In other words, the person who receives the output is the best judge of its quality, timeliness, and value (for example, its cost versus functionality).

Quantum leaps are revolutionary changes that bring a company to a new and higher level of operating effectivness and efficiency, thereby creating competitive advantage. Benchmarking helps a company redefine its objectives, shedding new light on old issues. It short-circuits the "do it a little better, a little faster" evolutionary approach, placing in its stead a critical reexamination of what is being done in the first place. In this respect, benchmarking focuses attention on the core issues, suggesting creative, novel ways to approach them, while highlighting value-added activities and eliminating non-value-added activities. Continuous improvement is "tweaking" the existing process; benchmarking may result in throwing away existing practice and starting all over.

One of the most well-known examples of this "leapfrogging" in response to benchmarking information is Ford Motor Company's experience in the accounts payable area. As described by Michael Hammer,[1]

In the early 1980s, when the American automotive industry was in a depression, Ford's top management put accounts payable—along with many other departments—under the microscope in search of ways to cut costs. Accounts payable in North America alone employed more than 500 people. Management thought that by rationalizing processes and installing new computer systems, it could reduce the head count by some 20%.

Ford was enthusiastic about its plan to tighten accounts payable—until it looked at Mazda. While Ford was aspiring to a 400-person department, Mazda's accounts payable organization consisted of a total of 5 people. The difference in absolute numbers was astounding, and even after adjusting for Mazda's smaller size, Ford figured that its accounts payable organization was five times the size it should be. The Ford team knew better than to attribute the discrepancy to calisthenics, company songs, or low interest rates. In fact, Ford found that complex, cumbersome, and unnecessary procedures, or non-value-added activities, accounted for much of the discrepancy in relative size and cost of their accounts payable function. The solution, or quantum leap, required elimination of non-value-added work, . . . and reduced head count to 75 staff.

Targets for Benchmarking

It is a good plan to aim a little higher than your target so as to make your shot sure, but not so high that you overshoot the mark.

Baltasar Gracian
The Oracle

Benchmarking can focus on roles, processes, or strategic issues in the quest for best practice. *Roles* are the essence of what a person, or function, does for the organization. What tasks, responsibilities, and services are offered by the customer service group? How do these stack up against the structure, processes, and service capabilities of other companies? Are we getting the most for our information system dollars, or are we wasting resources in some way? Each of these questions springs from a concern with the role the customer service group plays in the organization. Roles, then, are bundles of services provided by a group to either end customers or other parts of the organization.

While roles can be a focus, it is also possible to question *how* the work is performed. Questioning roles means asking, "Are we doing the right things?" (in other words, effectiveness), while examining *processes* triggers a concern with "Are we doing things right?" (in other words, efficiency). Every process consumes resources. To garner the most value possible from these processes, a company has to squeeze out waste and inefficiency in the process itself. Benchmarking targets for elimination those processes that are constraining the organization or using excessive resources with questionable value creation. While every process can be improved, the overriding concern remains getting the most benefit out of each dollar spent on process improvements.

Strategic issues focus on the plan for creating value in the company one to five years in the future. The establishment of goals, new projects, or new ventures is critical to the success of the company. As Xerox discovered, cost reduction targets are relative; 8 percent may be adequate if the game is left unchanged, but, if assumptions are questioned, 30 percent savings become possible. Benchmarking, then, can be used to target strategic issues, to gain enough information to prioritize competing projects, and to establish an overall game plan that will enhance stakeholder value.

As Figure 2.2 suggests, benchmarking targets the *critical success factors* for a specific company. What needs to be done to ensure long–run success? Where does top management see a potential for competitive advantage? Each company has a different mission, a unique way of combining its resources into outputs, and a defining culture or social system in which action occurs. For example, research and development and time to market for new products may be a critical issue to one company, whereas manufacturing cycle time may be important to another.

Benchmarking helps identify those features, or areas, that are supporting ongoing success (that is, are *critical* for success) as well as those aspects of the organization that are far less important overall or where resources may be misdirected. (Remember: there aren't any bad people in companies, just good people being asked to do the wrong things.) Improving on areas identified as critical to ongoing success provides the basis for quantum leaps in performance: the ultimate goal.

Defining Features of Benchmarking

We should have no regrets. We should never look back. The past is finished. There is nothing to be gained by going over it. Whatever it gave us in the experiences it brought us was something we had to know.

Rebecca Beard
Everyman's Search

To benchmark is to shrug off history and to embrace the future. What are the defining features of benchmarking that lead to these changes? It is a process of improvement that is

- Purposive
- Externally focused
- Measurements based
- Information intensive
- Objective
- Action-generating

Benchmarking is, above all, a purposive exercise in which information is collected from external sources to provide the basis for measuring existing performance against some objective target. *The purpose is to generate action, some form of improvement, that will enhance the value of the organization to its stakeholders.* Benchmarking should not be done just because it is in fashion or has become the latest rage in corporate "programs." It is not merely an intellectual exercise. It is done because there is a clearly identified desire to get better, to improve on existing practice. Before any benchmarking is undertaken, the ultimate objective or target has to be very clearly understood and the potential costs and benefits assessed. Without this analysis, benchmarking is simply a resource drain that reduces stakeholder value.

Whatever the underlying purpose, or target, of the benchmarking process, its ultimate goal is to *generate action*—to trigger the process of improvement by changing the way a role is performed, processes are undertaken, or strategic issues are defined. Benchmarking, then, is used to focus the organization on the opportunities for improvement; to benchmark is to explicitly decide that the organization is going to change. The changes undertaken are done carefully, using objective, externally based information that pinpoints weaknesses and suggests solutions. Benchmarking replaces gut feeling and tradition with facts and the future.

THE WHO, WHAT, AND WHY OF BENCHMARKING

I had six honest serving men;

they taught me all I knew.

Their names were where and what and when

and why and how and who.

Rudyard Kipling

Benchmarking, or the use of externally defined quantitative and qualitative performance measurements, provides the foundation for meeting and exceeding stakeholder expectations. Understanding its potential benefits, though, requires understanding the purpose and type of benchmarking project that will provide the desired results. In other words, the basic questions that must be answered in a benchmarking project are those put forward by Kipling above: when, why, how, what, where, and whom do you benchmark?

When Do You Benchmark?

While benchmarking can be performed at any time, it is most often undertaken in response to information needs that arise from some other major project or issue in the company. Examples of these "triggers" include

- Quality programs
- Cost reduction/budget process
- Operations improvement efforts
- Management change
- New operations/new ventures
- Rethinking existing strategies
- Competitive assaults/crises

Benchmarking in any of these settings is a logical step in developing new procedures, establishing new objectives, and creating new performance measurements. For instance, when any form of quality improvement program is instituted, the first question that must be asked is, "What is the best we can do?" This question can be addressed by looking at the best the competition has to offer or, even better, by looking across different industries to find the company or product that embodies excellence in form and function. When evaluating the performance of a lawn mower engine, the important question is not what the best lawn mower engine can do but what the best engines can, no matter what their application.

Likewise, when management is developing budgets, there is a clear need to establish objectives throughout the organization. One approach is to simply take last year's numbers and goals and "tweak" them a bit. This is called incremental zero-based budgeting, and it is at the heart of most budget cycles in Western companies. An alternative is to turn everyone's eyes outward, to look for improvement potential outside of current practices. Otherwise business as usual can end up in no business at all.

This search for facts extends from the private sector to government. For example, when the CFO of a large consumer product company was put in charge of the corporate information services department (IS), he looked for a benchmark for the role of corporate IS in a decentralized environment. This information provided a reference point and supplemented his knowledge base. In government privatization efforts, such as the telecommunications and cellular industry, benchmarking helps eliminate bureaucracy, focus on the customer, and create a roadmap for streamlined value-added processes.

As a company pursues operations improvements such as those arising out of business process re-engineering or just-in-time manufacturing approaches, what types of improvements others have been able to attain, and how, become critical questions. While improvement ideas can come from the inside, it is quite likely that scanning the external environment will provide insight, break down barriers to change, and establish a clearer definition of what types of improvement can be expected. Once again, benchmarking provides a way to change the game, to step outside the boundaries of tradition to make major improvements possible.

Finally, any time an organization is planning, or undergoing, major changes to its management structure or its operations, benchmarking becomes critical. Since current practice is obviously not good enough, there is a very real need to look for information that will help reshape the organization. Innovative solutions come from identifying and integrating effective techniques used by others. A general, plotting a campaign, looks to the best and worst strategies in historical battles, and also culls every available shred of information on the enemy. All of this effort is focused on providing a competitive edge...the battlefield success on which lives depend.

While the military analogy is perhaps a bit overdramatic, there can be little doubt that faulty planning and poor execution of strategy and structural changes can also spell disaster in a corporate setting. And when management fails, many lives are affected. Survival and growth depend on getting and using the right information at the right time. Benchmarking provides the first step in this vital process.

Why Do You Benchmark?

This is the most important question of all, one that has been focused on throughout this chapter. Specifically, benchmarking:

- Signals management's willingness to pursue a philosophy that embraces change in a proactive rather than reactive manner

- Establishes meaningful goals and performance measures that reflect an external/customer focus, fosters quantum leap thinking, and focuses on high-payoff opportunities

- Creates early awareness of competitive disadvantage

- Promotes teamwork that is based on competitive need and driven by data, not intuition or gut feeling

A company should benchmark, then, because it wants to attain world-class competitive capability; because it wants to prosper in a global economy; and because it wishes to survive.

The question to be asked, then, is not "Why should we benchmark?" but rather "How can we afford not to?" In an age of accelerating cycle of change, increased competition on a global scale, and reduced tolerance for inefficiencies and ineffectiveness, benchmarking is not an optional activity; it is required at every level of the organization, every day.

Whom Do You Benchmark?

Benchmarking can focus on diverse internal functions or processes, competitors, industry performance, and "best-in-class" targets (see Figure 2.3). *Internal benchmarking* is the analysis of existing practice within various departments or divisions of the organization, looking for best performance as well as identifying baseline activities and drivers. *Drivers* are the causes of work; the triggers that set in motion series of actions, or *activities*, which will respond to the requests or demands by the stockholders.

In doing internal benchmarking, management is looking downward, examining itself first before looking for outside information. Significant improvements are often made during the internal analysis stage of the benchmarking process, as questions such as "What do we do that for?" trigger decisions to remove unnecessary, non-value-adding steps from the process, eliminate practices that are historical artifacts rather than value-creating events, and help identify areas where the handoffs between one unit and another are resulting in fumbles. Internal benchmarking is the first step in any benchmarking exercise because it provides

2: THE MANY FACES OF BENCHMARKING

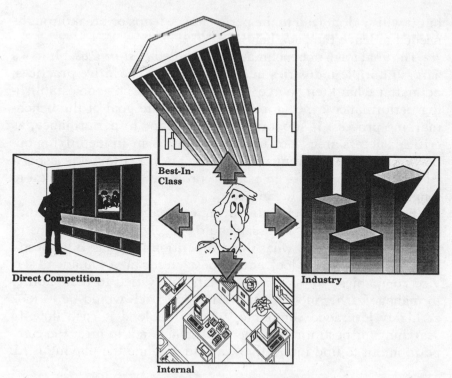

Best-In-Class

Direct Competition

Industry

Internal

Figure 2.3   Whom do you benchmark?

the framework to compare existing internal practices to external benchmark data.

While internal benchmarking focuses on specific value chains, or sequences of driver-activity combinations, *competitive benchmarking* looks outward to identify how other direct competitors are performing. Although it reflects a fairly narrow view of benchmarking, knowing the strengths and weaknesses of the competition is an important step in plotting a successful strategy. In addition, it can help prioritize areas of improvement as specific customer expectations are identified and current relative performance against them measured. Competitor-based information helps to level the playing field.

Industry benchmarking extends beyond the one-to-one comparison of competitive benchmarking to look for trends. Yet industry benchmarking is still limited in the number of innovations and new ideas it can uncover. Why? Everyone within the industry is basically playing the same game with the same set of rules. Analyzing industry trends can help establish performance baselines, but it will seldom lead to the performance leaps or breakthroughs needed to leave the pack behind.

The final form of benchmarking is called *Best-in-Class*. It looks across multiple industries in search of new, innovative practices, no matter what their source. This broad perspective on establishing performance expectations is the ultimate goal of the benchmarking process. It supports quantum leaps in performance, as critical success areas look up toward the "best" in identifying opportunities for improvement. Choosing any other target is a short-run solution: it may fix an existing problem, but it won't lead to long-run competitive advantage.

For example, if a manufacturing company wants to optimize its cash management process, it could conceivably talk to industry experts to understand what the competition is doing. But doesn't it make more sense to look at the "best" in the area—financial service companies whose success is intricately tied to their ability to manage cash? Another innovative approach would be to look at highly leveraged companies whose lifeblood is cash flow. In searching for best practice, then, the goal is not to meet the competition but to find innovative ways to redefine the playing field.

The best of everything is the only individual of that thing. We should ignore the rest.

Louise Imogene Guiney
Goose-Quill Papers

What to Benchmark?

Benchmarking can focus on roles, processes, or strategic issues. For example, in the case of roles, benchmarking can be done to establish the function or mission of an organization and how that is reflected in its operations and services. The actual structure (in terms of degree of centralization, location of specific functions, and clustering or divisions of departments) of a competitor or "best-in-class" benchmarking target can be analyzed and evaluated. Benchmarking can also be used to examine existing practices as it looks across the organization to identify the practices that support major processes or critical objectives. Specific attributes can be examined, such as credit terms, quality of specific products, delivery procedures and practices, or customer service levels. The key is first to understand what elements of performance the customer values and then to identify what aspects of the organization affect them.

In the case of strategic issues, the objective is to identify those factors that are of critical importance to competitive advantage, to define measures of excellence that capture these issues, and to isolate companies that appear to be top performers on these measured attributes. Once this analysis is complete, benchmarking can look for the practices and roles that lead to excellence. For example, in a chemical company excellence in research and development (R&D) is a critical success factor. Taking this position, management might decide to undertake a benchmarking study to identify the world-class performers in research and development, based on such criteria as the percentage of R&D projects that are successfully commercialized or the contribution of R&D to the profitability of the company. Benchmarking would allow the sponsoring company to look into the roles, processes, and practices used by top performers, helping it translate strategy into action by learning from companies that have already mastered these concepts.

Focusing benchmarking on specific processes, activities, or functions is only part of the answer to the "what" question, though. A second issue to be resolved is the depth of the analysis to be performed. Benchmarking studies can focus on specific departments or functions (vertical benchmarking), or they can instead focus on a specific process or activity (horizontal benchmarking). While early studies may be confined to departmental or functional performance, the ultimate goals of the benchmarking process require a cross-functional focus on the value chain—the linking of activities across the organization to meet customer expectations in the most efficient and effective manner possible.

Where Do You Get Benchmarking Information?

Benchmarking builds off of existing sources of information. Informally, benchmarking can be done by using published material, insights gained at trade meetings, and conversations with industry experts, customers, and others. Keeping an ear to the ground, marketing representatives can serve a vital role in keeping everyone in the organization apprised of competitive opportunities as well as potential threats. Creating and effectively using a "grapevine" can provide signals of changing events and expectations, buying management much needed time to craft a response.

Structural benchmarking includes culling through established databases for information (such as Value Line tapes, LEXIS/NEXIS, or published industry data). It also elicits specific external information by establishing a consortium of benchmarking partners, or through some form of survey, which can be conducted by mail, over the phone, or in person. Each approach has both pros and cons associated with it, including availability of information versus its accuracy and applicability to a specific question.

Databases are cheap and quick to use, but they often have old or imprecise data elements. On the other hand, doing in-person interviews can yield accurate, current information, but completing this type of benchmarking project will consume time and money. The final choice depends on the type of benchmarking project being undertaken, the degree to which an immediate answer is needed, and the overall importance of the project to the long-run competitive performance of the organization. Quick solutions may be good enough for short-run, highly focused analysis, but the changes needed to obtain continuous improvement and gain a competitive advantage require sound data that directly applies to the questions at hand.

How Do You Benchmark?

This entire book is about different ways companies have used benchmarking to gain competitive excellence. How it is done, though, will depend on available resources, deadlines, and the number of alternative sources of information that can be identified. While countless words could be used to describe the benchmarking process, the best teacher is experience. To guide the learning process, the experiences of many different firms that have used benchmarking in traditional and unique ways is presented in the pages that follow (see Figure 2.4).

Benchmarking focuses on continuous improvement and value creation for stakeholders, utilizing best practice to focus improvement efforts. It can look at roles, processes, or strategic issues and is best thought of as a purposive, information-intensive, externally focused measurement process that sets objective goals

2: THE MANY FACES OF BENCHMARKING

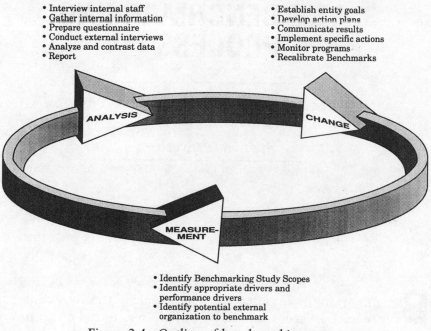

- Interview internal staff
- Gather internal information
- Prepare questionnaire
- Conduct external interviews
- Analyze and contrast data
- Report

- Establish entity goals
- Develop action plans
- Communicate results
- Implement specific actions
- Monitor programs
- Recalibrate Benchmarks

- Identify Benchmarking Study Scopes
- Identify appropriate drivers and performance drivers
- Identify potential external organization to benchmark

Figure 2.4   Outline of benchmarking steps.

for developing action plans. The steps noted above reflect all of these characteristics.

In reality, there is more than one way to do benchmarking. The final implementation path chosen will be based on the information needed to address the organization's critical success factors.

The most effective way to ensure the value of the future is to confront the present courageously and constructively.

Rollo May
Man's Search for Himself

3: THE BENCHMARKING PROCESS

Three helping one another will do as much as six men singly.

Spanish Proverb

Benchmarking is an effective way to query the root cause of problems, or issues, raised by either an external or an internal customer. The core issue is defined by listening to the customer. Listening means more than responding to the initial request or a specific complaint; the focus has to be on understanding the underlying message or intent of the complaint. Understanding the customer's needs naturally leads management to question its own assumptions about the goals and objectives of the organization. Responding to customer needs does not mean adding more structure, rules, or departments to handle the problem; it requires a complete reexamination of the core issue of how the company provides value-added services to its customers.

Benchmarking establishes a reinforcing cycle of change that drives out inefficient practices by creating an objective way to evaluate them. Contrary to the age-old belief that people don't like to change, in reality they happily embrace change if it addresses a problem that has nagged at them for a long time. There are very few individuals who enjoy working on a product, project, or service only to see it end up in the corporate "trash pile." Most would rather put their effort into value-creating activities. Change is only threatening, then, when it is poorly understood, miscommunicated, or unneeded. Changes that create value are seldom a problem—zero-sum games are.

3: THE BENCHMARKING PROCESS

Harnessing the Cycle of Change

> We all know how Adam said to Eve: "My dear, we live in a period of transition."
>
> Vida D. Scudder
> *The Privilege of Age*

Focused on a specific workflow or activity chain, the benchmarking process seeks first to understand what is currently done, and then to obtain objective evidence or information about what level of performance it should be pursuing—the gap. The final goal is to develop an action plan (see Figure 3.1).

The action plan focuses on implementation steps to close the gap, or the difference between what the company is currently doing and what is perceived as "best practice." Best practice can be defined by looking at competitors, industry, or best-in-class firms from a customer perspective. The dimension selected will be dependent on the issue being addressed, with the ultimate goal of achieving a higher level of performance. Setting any other objective will leave the company behind before it starts.

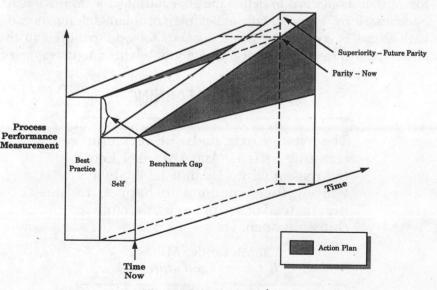

Figure 3.1   Action plan.

Parity, though, is not the key to long-run competitive success; superiority is. While closing the benchmark gap improves a company's competitive capability in the short run, the ultimate target is to meet and then exceed best practice as it currently exists. In the face of global competition, the baseline of excellence is being constantly raised. Standing still is equivalent to losing ground; losing ground accelerates into a headlong freefall to competitive crisis.

The larger the gap identified in the benchmarking process, the more important it is for the company to implement far-reaching changes. If the gap is slightly positive, celebrations should be delayed—the competition is closing fast. A large gap on the positive side signals that the company has a competitive advantage that can be exploited or an area under control for now; management can turn its attention to less adequate areas of performance. If the gap is slightly negative, management can look to continuous improvement methodologies to reach parity. A large negative gap has only one meaning—radical change is required. The advantage of the benchmarking process is that the size of this gap is clearly identified and labeled for all to see; the problem is, good news is not guaranteed.

Benchmarking is a tool for harnessing the cycle of change, which is constantly modifying the corporate landscape. Because it looks forward and outward to define the expectations for improvement, benchmarking helps create a flexible, problem-solving organization that is constantly on the lookout for opportunities in the environment, rather than worrying about reacting to its vagaries.

A FOCUS ON LEARNING

The average man finds life very uninteresting as it is. And I think I know the reason why . . . is that he is always waiting for something to happen to him instead of setting to work to make things happen.

Alan Alexander Milne
If I May: The Future

A logical sequence to the learning process is embedded in benchmarking (see Figure 3.2). Starting from an understanding of an unmet customer need or performance gap, the company reviews the key processes and related measures, moves from the concrete physical reality of its day-to-day operations internally and externally, analyzes and revamps these processes on paper and then uses this information to change reality through the implementation cycle.

By analyzing existing workflows and the performance measures currently in use, the company identifies the boundaries of the problem. The output process mapping can provide a form of learning and improvement in and of itself. Very seldom does a company look at how it does its work in such detail. Laying it out in black and white can reveal some obvious problems, raise awareness of opportunities—and the need—for improvement, and underscore the level of waste present in existing operations.

Simple Questions, Difficult Answers

> In developing our industrial strategy for the period ahead, we have had the benefit of much experience. Almost everything has been tried at least once.
>
> A. Wedgwood Benn
> *Observer,* 1974

When one deals with complex organizations and activity chains, it can be quite difficult to identify the primary characteristics of a process. One way to tackle this problem is by tracing the path a product or service request takes through the organization. The path is a flow of work that leads to some final output or product that is valued by the customer; it is a value chain that knits the organization together. In detailing this flow, a series of questions need to be asked that can help unravel the complex sequence of events that results in the delivery of a product or service

Figure 3.2 A framework for benchmarking.

Phases: Identify Core Issue → Internal Baseline Data Collection → External Data Collection → Analysis → Change Implement

	Identify Core Issue	Internal Baseline Data Collection	External Data Collection	Analysis	Change Implement
Input:	• Issue – Unmet Customer Needs – Performance Gap – Problem Areas – Strategic Advantage	• Overview of Process • Current Measures • Potential Drivers & External Organizations	• Benchmark Questionnaire	• Compare & Contrast Benchmark Data	• Implementation Plan • Issues

Output:	• Defined Benchmark Area
	• Overview of Key Process to be Benchmarked
	• Selected Performance Measurements
	• Identify Potential Drivers and External Organizations
		• Process Flow Mapping
		• Validate Drivers
		• Benchmark Target Companies
		• Short-term Operational Improvments
		• Benchmark Questionnaire
			• External Company(s)
			• Process Analysis, Performance Assessment and Measures
				• Gap
				• Process Improvements/ Reengineering Opportunities
				• New
				  – Flows
				  – Policies
				  – Procedures
				• Implementation Plan
				• Outstanding Issues
					• Plan to Close the Gap
					• Actions to Close the Gap
					• Recalibrate Benchmarks
					• Additional Analysis/ Benchmarking to Address Issues

to an internal or an external customer. Some of the preliminary questions that need to be addressed are the following:

- Who is involved in delivering the product or service?

- Why are they involved?

- What are they doing?

- Why are they doing it?

- Is what they are doing adding value in the customer's eyes?

Answering these questions results in a *process flow diagram*, which links the tasks performed by individuals *across the organization* into an activity chain. Each activity chain is a *customer service delivery system* (whether the service includes a physical product or not). These delivery systems are what the customer sees and evaluates in each and every contact with the company.

While many different types of process maps can be developed, it is often quite informative actually to develop a form of "road map" of the organization and then simply trace the product or paperwork from one area to the next. Companies implementing cellular manufacturing usually keep these maps to remind themselves to pay attention to the total process flow rather than the output of any one machine. The result of this exercise can be shocking, but when this shock passes there is seldom any lingering doubt that improvements can be made.

Figures 3.3 and 3.4 illustrate a process flow diagram for a common decision (make versus buy a component) as it was studied at a large industrial firm, MLB.[1] The objective in developing these two maps was to analyze the full "real" cost of making versus buying a nonstrategic component for one of the company's major products. Even a casual glance at the diagrams underscores the fact that making the component, as shown in Figure 3.3, is far more complex than purchasing it, as shown in Figure 3.4. Each task performed brings with it a chunk of cost, or resources consumed. The more tasks (or activities), quite likely the more an activity costs. This is exactly what MLB discovered. Making the component costs more than buying it. Arriving at the decision to outsource the component was

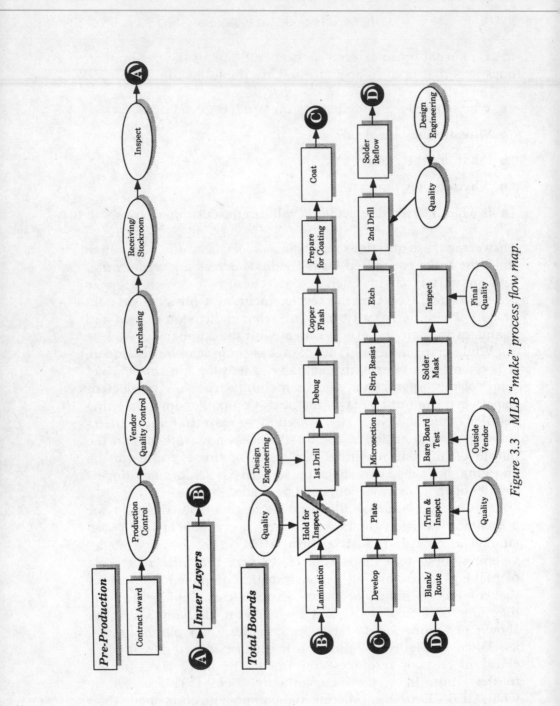

Figure 3.3 MLB "make" process flow map.

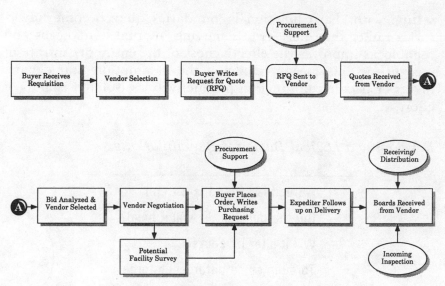

Figure 3.4.   MLB "buy" process flow map.

not based, then, on a simple labor savings model but rather on the cost of the complete activity chain caused by the two alternative approaches to obtaining the component.

In the "buy" scenario MLB is the customer of an external supplier. In the "make" situation, though, there are a series of internal customers, ending with final assembly. Each "handoff" between different functional areas in the organization's activity chain establishes a customer-supplier relationship. For example, the group performing "pre-production" analysis hands off to production. If pre-production is poorly performed, then the "customer" (manufacturing) either has to reject the product (the design specifications), ask for or receive changes to the initial design (engineering change notices), or alter its own processes to accommodate the product (process redesign).

Any of these alternatives results in waste, or non-value-added activities. They use resources, delay the final delivery of a product to the end customer, and can create dysfunctional consequences, such as ongoing battles between design and manufacturing. In reality, these two groups actually depend on each other for their continued existence, but in an "over the wall" traditional setting with sharp functional boundaries, they become adversaries rather than partners. Removing internal boundaries and roadblocks improves the effectiveness of the entire organization; recognizing this means removing the assumption that departments or people can function productively as isolated islands of effort.

Developing a Logical Basis for Benchmarking

A trend is a trend is a trend

But the question is, will it bend?

Will it alter its course

Through some unforeseen force

And come to a premature end?

Sir Alec Cairncross
1969

The detailed set of process flow maps and listing of current performance measures are used to understand what drives the process as it currently exists—why are things done the way they are? what causes or triggers the workflow? Answering these questions is the key to unlocking the mysteries of "history"—the "we've always done it this way" comments that can drive a change agent insane. Processes emerge for a reason; understanding this reason is crucial to gaining the momentum for change that will be needed over the long haul.

This analysis is performed *before* the benchmarking process or external information-gathering process. In addition to the drivers, or causes for current workflow patterns, operational improvements are detailed and non-value-added activities identified, using existing criteria. One goal is to come to a complete understanding of existing routines and obvious targets for improvement efforts; the other is to identify the core features of the work performed in the area so as to support the choice of benchmarking targets and draft the preliminary benchmarking approach.

In choosing the benchmarking targets (such as the sample of firms or departments that will be used as the basis for developing best practice), it is important to eliminate the unique features of the way the work is done at your company. The benchmarking process is only valid to the extent that an "apples-to-apples" comparison is made. While each organization has unique features, there is an underlying core of activities that are generic to all organizations (for example, accounts payable operations). The focus is on identifying a set of generic "activity clusters" that lead to value-added output for the customer. Once again, it is the customer's perspective that is key, not management's.

Developing the "generic" activity grid is one of the hardest parts of the benchmarking exercise. The issues that have to be dealt with include the following:

- What aspects of the work performed in an area cannot be changed due to regulatory or corporate constraints?

- What does the customer see as the "product" of this service delivery system?

- What are the essential tasks that need to be performed to meet customer requirements as we are currently structured?

- What things are we doing that seem to have no real basis in concerns for the customer, or control? Where does "history" begin?

- Where are the hidden barriers to change as we move from one task to another or from one functional area/department to another?

- Who will be the winners and the losers if we change different parts of the process?

- If non-value-added work is to be eliminated, what are we going to do with the resources that are freed up?

- Do we want to worry about "best-in-class" comparison, or should the project focus on industry practice first?

- What are we going to do if our performance is even worse than we imagine? (Who's going to tell the boss?)

- What are the long-run implications of the benchmarking project? Do we need to consider changes in our structure, our products, our services, or marketing strategy?

While the list could go on, the point should be clear. Simply detailing the existing workflow and opening up an internal dialogue around core issues can lead to constructive change as well as potential discord. Which one occurs will be determined by the way the information is gathered and used. The objective is not to identify problem people, or non-value-added positions; it is to improve the company's ability to meet customer requirements and to support the long-run attainment of continuous improvement goals. It is not the tool that will cause problems, but rather how that tool (and the information it uncovers) is used.

Whether internal, competitive, industry, or best-in-class, a critical success factor in the benchmarking process is conducting an effective external interview. With the popularity of benchmarking growing, companies are beginning to be more discriminating about the number and type of studies in which they participate. Some companies are reportedly receiving over 50 requests to participate in benchmarking studies per day. With such added interest, obtaining benchmarking participants has become a competitive process. In this setting an effective benchmarking questionnaire is the key to gaining support.

Target benchmarking companies should be able to understand what is being benchmarked and who should be involved, and be able to assess the value of the study from the questionnaire. This implies that the questionnaire is focused, with relevant, direct questions presented in a succinct manner. Good questionnaires are normally between 10 and 15 pages in length, using large, easy-to-read formats and typefaces and clear instructions for the participant.

A second factor critical in the external data collection process is the *exchange* of information. A target benchmarking company expects to give *and* receive information. Therefore, do not ask for something that you are not willing to provide to others. Finally, the actual collection of the data (in person, by telephone, or by mail) will affect the design of the questionnaire. In-person data collection allows for the greatest exchange of information—an apples-to-apples comparison—and minimizes potential misinterpretations. However, this approach is expensive and time-consuming. Telephone interviews allow for some clarification, but can miss subtle distinctions. Mail surveys, on the other hand, are the least expensive but are also open to the most misinterpretation.

Benchmarking Done—Analysis Begins

The conclusion of the external data collection tasks moves a company out of the third step of the benchmarking process, taking it into the realm of analyzing and interpreting information from the field. The benchmarking process in the first three steps involves the following:

■ Indentification of core issues

■ Internal baseline data collection

■ External information data collection

Once this information, which serves as the heart of the benchmarking process, is compiled, the company can begin to evaluate its own structure and processes against best practice guidelines. The objective of the analysis stage is to develop new workflows. The changes are explored in detail in documents and through discussions, resulting in reengineering of current operations to bring them into line with benchmarked best practice.

While earlier steps of the process may have limited their focus to current ways of doing business, looking for the "easy" opportunities for improvement, the analysis step actually examines new ways of organizing the work and defining the objectives of the workflows. In the process, both the strengths and weaknesses of existing practices are detailed. If existing practice in your firm is already "best-in-class," there is no need to go further, or to force change for change's sake. Improvements are always possible, but given limited resources, only the most critical weaknesses can be addressed immediately.

When a major UK retail chain acquired a similar company a third of its size (1,200 to 400 outlets, respectively) the CEO recognized that significant differences existed in management style, organization structure, systems, and outlet profitability. Prior to the companies' integration, he had both organizations examined for the following specific reasons:

- To understand the overhead cost base
- To evaluate the effect of the different levels of control, direction, and mangement on outlet profitability
- To identify the optimal systems strategies of the merged organization

The first step was to identify the key areas of comparison such as staffing levels, volumes, and product mix. Interviews with all levels of management in both organizations were conducted to understand assignment of responsibility and operations. Finally, the relative performance of the key areas was measured, and best practices were identified.

As a result, the merged organization focused its integration efforts on achieving best practice, which improved performance and increased profits.

Implementation: Fighting the Power of Tradition

So that the river of tradition may come down to us, we must continually dredge its bed.

Henri De Lubac
Paradoxes

Completion of the tasks in the "analysis step" result in an implementation plan to change the process. While the task is simple—namely, putting the plan into action—entire books have been written on the challenges, pitfalls, and problems that can be encountered during implementation. Even if everyone agrees that change is needed, the real frictions begin when individuals realize the personal implications facing them: change is good, as long as it is someone else doing the changing. Whether we admit it or not, each of us seeks the comfort of tradition. Within the corporation, these traditions become inbred, accepted ways of doing business that are never questioned. Anyone who has ever asked the fatal question "Why do we do it this way?" and been greeted with the rapid response "Because we've always done it this way" knows just how much tradition can blind an individual or an organization.

To effect an implementation, a company has to shatter the myths of tradition, creating the need for a new solution, a new path, to fill the void. Shattering a myth means it has to be recognized and discussable. Yet acceptance remains as the major roadblock to change in organizations; broadcasting that the ship is going down with all hands aboard is not a popular task. Many of the destructive performance loops in organizations are locked into their culture, incentive systems, planning and control cycles, and performance measurements. In some companies, the truth is so carefully masked behind a wall of accounting magic and reporting mumbo-jumbo that few even grasp that problems exist. Implementation of a new idea starts with a felt need; getting to that felt need can be aided by the objective identification of a performance gap.

Is there really any alternative to tradition, that established pattern of acting and communicating that can be found in every organization?

Thus, for the kind of vital organizations we want, we need to nurture and extend the reach and power of tradition. But to deal openly and intelligently with the realities of changing circumstances, we need to fight off the hold tradition has on our vision of things. To build real commitment, we must have effective tradition. But to avoid holding the horses, we must expose the

artifice through which tradition works. We can enlist deep loyalty only by allowing genuine tradition to flourish. But we can
go behind our father's saying only by allowing ourselves to see
that that saying is relative and contingent, a partial view of the
world from which our awareness of artifice has drained away.
For reasons of community, we must have tradition organic and
whole. For reasons of judgment, we must know it to be a thing
"built" or constructed.[2]

The dilemma is evident in this paragraph. In order to remain com-
petitively viable, organizations must constantly look for ways to
improve. Improvements translate to shaking up the status quo—
to seeing the world in terms of "what if" instead of "what is." Yet
organizations base their very survival on being ultra-stable; the
constant flurry of change in the environment leaves them essentially untouched. Being untouchable translates into being resilient
to the highs and lows in the marketplace; it means shipping product every day even if half the corporate staff is out with the flu
(although some might add, with a smile, that things ship better
in that case).

Benchmarking provides the basis for prioritizing opportunities for change and for providing ostensible proof that change
must occur. The push to change is always supported by one
undisputable fact: while corporations may pursue profits, they
fight for survival. It is no coincidence that more radical forms
of change occur when a company is on the "critical list" than
at any other time. When survival is threatened, only one goal
remains: do what is necessary to plug the gaps and get the
ship back on course. Unfortunately, the probabilities of failure
increase exponentially as companies approach the brink, being sucked down into the swirling maelstrom of corporate decline.

Not a pleasant thought, but an avoidable one. Ongoing benchmarking provides early warning that competitive problems are
emerging. Being forewarned, management can plan a gradual
implementation process that can move everyone toward the
new goals and objectives at a reasonable pace. While change
may still be dreaded, if handled carefully, it can be quite rewarding.

The reasonable man adapts himself to the world: the unreasonable one persists in trying to adapt the world to himself. Therefore, all progress depends on the unreasonable man.

George Bernard Shaw
Man and Superman,
Maxims for Revolutionists

AN IMPLEMENTATION SEQUENCE

While any number of lists of implementation sequences could be developed, several characteristics are critical:

1. *Initial problem solving:* A team, or task force, is created to study the problem and develop a preliminary list of possible avenues for the company to take.

2. *Open communication:* Once the preliminary definition of the problem is completed, the task force needs to open the lines of communication to key individuals who currently are or will be affected by the problem. Alternative perspectives on the issues are pursued.

3. *Analysis and justification:* Having assembled a broad sample of thought and fact about the problem at hand, the task force begins to search for ways to prioritize the alternatives.

4. *Communication and education:* The task force arrives at a preliminary action plan for the change process. At this point, meetings are conducted to determine if a consensus can be reached on the change to be undertaken. In conjunction with this stage, the first round of education about the procedures and implications of the proposed action plan is undertaken.

5. *Pilot test:* A representative pilot site is chosen to test the full-scale implementation plan. Progress and problems are monitored. Concurrently, large-scale education is undertaken for the entire organization.

6. Detailed plans for complete implementation are developed. The resources needed and the timetables for each major portion of the implementation are created; commitments and accountabilities for results are established.

7. New performance measures are developed to "lock in" the change.

8. Recalibrate performance, and then benchmark to determine parity and superiority.

Factors that must be kept in mind during this process are the urgency of the proposed change, the level of agreement on the objectives of the change process by key individuals, resources available, the temperament of managers and other employees, accepted mores and traditions that may hinder the implementation process, and the need to build a new stability to guide the ongoing operations of the organization into the change process.

As anyone who has spearheaded a major implementation can attest, the sequence followed may look logical, but it feels like shifting sands to those involved. Converting to a new management system, or a new way of defining and performing work, takes time. The time is not spent in actually designing the new system; it is instead directed at obtaining and maintaining commitment and momentum. Open communication and trust are what separates a successful implementation from an unsuccessful one. Finally, the role played by top management support is an ever-present concern.

The objective is to get the affected individuals to pick up their roots and move into an unknown environment. For this to happen, the leader of the group has to exhibit commitment to the move, and the team members have to convince the others to pack up their belongings. If the change were taking place in a vacuum, logic would rule the day. Instead, change occurs in social settings wedded to the security of tradition and wary of the risk of the unknown.

Tradition means giving votes to the most obscure of all classes—our ancestors. It is the democracy of the dead. Tradition refuses to submit to the small and arrogant oligarchy of those who merely happen to be walking around.

G. K. Chesterton quoted in
A Certain World by W. H. Auden

The Role of Performance Measurements

Focusing on the benchmarking process itself provides companies with major performance improvements. To keep these improvements going, and to build upon them, the measurement system has to be refocused from results to actions. If the job is done right, the desired results will be achieved. No amount of pressure for results, though, can fix a broken process. The impact on the performance measurement system, then, of adopting the new forms of management, such as the Japanese management style, is that the process, not results, is the key dimension. Linking together the activities into a value chain emphasizes the interdependence between units and individuals and changes the focus of questioning from "Who screwed up?" to "What went wrong?"

Implementation of new processes and procedures is never complete until the measurement system is brought in line. People respond to the tools and measures used to evaluate them and will do some of the most unusual things to ensure that they meet their goals. It is no accident, then, that the success of the benchmarking process is dependent on identifying, and monitoring, the right set of measurements.

The embedded nature of measurements in the benchmarking process begins with the preliminary screening of the organization's internal activities to develop a set of benchmarking criteria, and extends all the way through the implementation of the changes that the organization puts in place in response to the findings. If measures are not changed, then the implementation is doomed to failure. It is only a question of when, not if, the failure will occur.

"What gets measured gets done" has never been so powerful a truth.

Tom Peters
Thriving on Chaos

What Next?

Benchmarking is an ongoing process of change that begins with a request from a customer and ends with meeting those needs. This is not to say that the process really ends; the organization sets and pursues improvement goals on an ongoing basis. As part of the cycle of continuous improvement, each separate benchmarking project moves through a series of defined steps:

1. Identify the core issue.
2. Establish the baseline internal performance levels and information.
3. Gather external information.
4. Analyze information and benchmark results.
5. Implement changes in existing processes to reflect these results.

Benchmarking does not start when the company goes outside for information; it begins when a problem is identified by the customer, an internal task force, or some other means. Each problem is an opportunity for improvement. Benchmarking starts with this recognition, focuses on uncovering the core issues and practices that are currently in vogue, and ends with a question: "What next?"

In approaching the benchmarking process, then, the key is to understand what is expected to be gained before any significant resources are committed. Information may have value in and of itself, but it is *value-creating* when it leads to decisions and actions that improve existing practice. Change for change's sake is not the objective; change that enhances the value of the firm for all its stakeholders is.

When you have duly arrayed your "facts" in logical order, lo, it is like an oil-lamp that you have made, filled and trimmed, but which sheds no light unless first you light it.

Antoine De Saint-Exupéry
The Wisdom of the Sands

4: INTERNAL BENCHMARKING: GATHERING KNOWLEDGE ABOUT CURRENT PRACTICE

> In great affairs we ought to apply our-
> selves less to creating chances than to
> profiting from those that offer.
>
> F. la Rochefoucauld
> *Maxims*

To gain the maximum benefit from the benchmarking process, a company first has to understand and clearly document its existing practices and procedures. This exercise provides the details necessary to focus the study on key aspects of the unit's or company's performance; identify inherent, structural, and performance drivers; and establish opportunities for improvement. The improvements are from one part of an organization learning from another; the company profits as communication improves; pockets of excellence are identified; and practices are standardized to reflect best practice.

Internal benchmarking is both a free-standing exercise to improve existing performance and the critical first step in all external benchmarking projects. It is useful in any organization where two or more locations perform the same type of task. (Most decentralized companies can benefit by identifying best practice internal to the firm, then incorporating it in their ongoing operations.) It short-circuits the "not created here" argument that can often be used to delay change. The definition of internal benchmarking is as follows:

> The comparison of similar operations or functions across a company, or with associated companies, in order to identify the level of service that is best practice within this common setting.

Internal benchmarking details the common elements in similar operations, isolates those that should be standardized but aren't, and starts the first round of constructive discussions about what to change and why.

THE INTERNAL BENCHMARKING PROCESS

The physical process of performing the activities is the input, or framework, for conducting the study (see Figure 4.1). By reviewing existing activities, the company obtains needed information on who is involved in the various parts of the process, why they are involved, what they are doing, and why they are doing it. Getting answers to these questions is the objective of the initial operations review.

Who Is Involved? and Why?

The first question, "Who is involved?" places the organizational framework around the activity being studied. The information needed is not the names of the individuals but rather the number of people required to perform the activity, their respective "level" or position within the company, and how they are organized, or managed. These structural details establish the baseline of operations. Since cost reduction mandates are often the impetus for the benchmarking process, understanding current resource demands is a necessary starting point for identifying opportunities for improvement.

Just because individuals are involved in the activity does not mean they are needed. The next two stages of the initial inquiry, then, try to uncover the reasons for particular persons' involvement; specifically, what they are doing. Some people may be involved in a process because they perform a vital operation or task or have needed expertise. Others may be in the loop because they bear final responsibility for the outcomes. When individuals do not fit any of these scenarios, the reason for their involvement should be queried. They may be adding value, but then again, they may just be the remnant of an "empire-building" exercise or history (in other words, work continuing to be done when the reason for the work has disappeared).

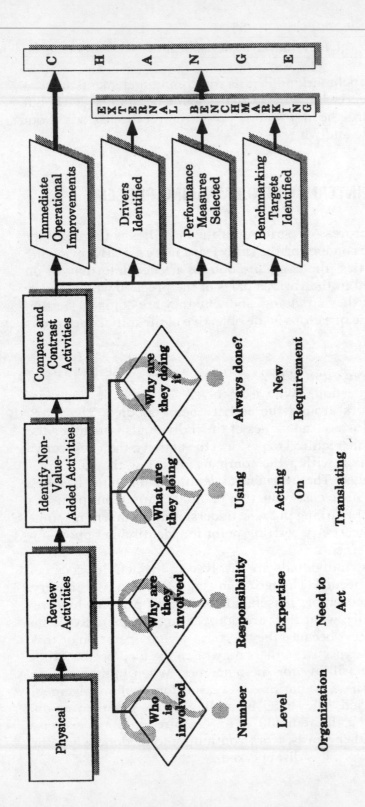

Figure 4.1   The essence of internal benchmarking.

The next step in understanding existing procedures, then, is to find out why the task is performed. If someone answers, "It's always been done this way," that is a signal that quantum leaps may need to take place. The work may be necessary, but then again, it may not be. Even if the task is fulfilling an existing requirement, it may not be adding value in the customer's eyes. Instead, it may reflect layers of unnecessary bureaucracy or established practices that are ineffective, inefficient, or redundant.

Defining what each individual does and why he or she is doing it lays the foundation for internal improvements. The objective is to sort the process steps into bundles, or groups, of value-added/non-value-added activities.

There is no position in the world more wearisome than that of a man inwardly indifferent to the amusement in which he is trying to take part.

Phillip G. Hamerton
The Intellectual Life

This assessment is exemplified in the amount of paper associated with monthly reporting to senior management in many companies. For example, in a large financial service company, a review of the monthly reporting package found that a quarter of the reports could be eliminated. Most of these reports had their genesis from a single request made by senior management for information related to specific market issues, such as special currency analysis for Mexico and Brazil.

As time passed, staff responsible for producing the reporting package continued to prepare the requested information, just in case, until it became a regular part of the monthly reporting package. "We always do it." The market issue, however, was resolved—as in the example with the company reducing its exposure in those currencies—but management never communicated that the information was no longer needed. Instead, they ignored those pages and focused on key indicators and information related to the new issue.

When a new CFO of the company was appointed, he questioned the report content. After a series of interviews with senior management the reporting package was revamped with some reports issued on a weekly basis and others on a quarterly basis. The distribution was also modified to accommodate the changing needs of the management team.

Developing Task-Resource Maps

The output of this exercise is a series of process maps. Figure 4.2 shows a *process map* that details the field sales process for a major pharmaceutical company. The major activity clusters are depicted as boxes while the inputs and outputs of the activity are noted in parentheses. Figure 4.3 shows an *input-output map* that expands on one part of the overall process, sample tracking,

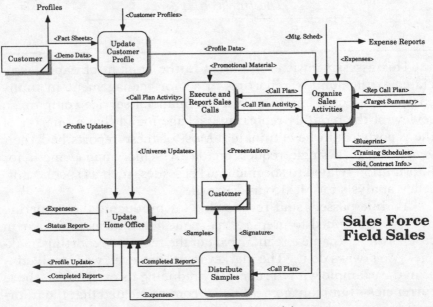

Figure 4.2   Process model.

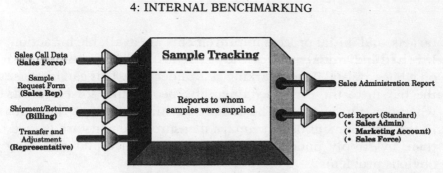

Figure 4.3   Input-output diagram.

noting the inputs to the process and the outputs that are yielded. This map can be enhanced by attaching resources, such as people and facilities, to it.

These maps are the basis for the first round of constructive analysis of existing practice, for identifying areas where change is needed (that is, excessive levels of non-value-added work being done), and also provide the information needed to assess the resource and cost implications of any proposed change. This can lead to immediate operational improvements, as unnecessary work or cumbersome workflows are eliminated. In the process of performing the operations review, then, the organization gains in-depth knowledge about existing practices, which can identify non-value-added aspects of these activities. Removing unnecessary work, and the resources it consumes, can provide immediate cost savings as well as improving the responsiveness of the organization to customer requests.

Moving Toward Action

> It seems all the average fellow needs to make him take a chance is a warning.
>
> Kin Hubbard
> *Abe Martin on Things in General*

Once the analysis is complete, existing practices, personnel requirements, the drivers of the activities, the benchmarking targets, and initial process improvements are available for action. Involved individuals will already have areas that can be worked on while external benchmarking gets under way. This can increase the buy-in to the process immensely; people like to see results when they put in effort. The completed study serves as the input to the development of benchmark measures. Benefits are gained, then, by simply understanding existing practice and removing obvious problems.

This sounds simple enough, but untangling the web of tradition that led to the current set of practices is a different matter. If a report is discontinued, a task changed, or some other such "minor" improvement made, will it trigger an entire chain of problems that were unforeseen by the change agent or internal benchmarking team? Given the high level of interdependence in the modern organization, it is very likely that removing one card from the card house may create repercussions. On the other hand, it may not. How do you find out? It has always been common knowledge that the best way to find out if anyone is using a report is to stop sending it out. If no one calls asking for it, it probably isn't used (at least in recent history).

The same logic applies to the types of changes that result from the internal benchmarking analysis. It is difficult to identify all the secondary channels of activity that flow from the main activity being analyzed. While this might lead one to leave well enough alone, in reality failing to make a change is a decision that may have greater downstream costs than attempting to improve a process. Anyone who is radically affected will speak up. That in and of itself is a hidden benefit of the internal benchmarking process— it helps identify poorly understood interrelationships within the organization. The knowledge gained can be put to use to proactively manage these interrelationships more effectively, enhancing the value creation process overall.

Much of the most useful knowledge has to be buffeted into us.

John Lancaster Spalding
Aphorisms and Reflections

GETTING THE MOST FROM INTERNAL BENCHMARKING

> If you must play, decide upon three
> things at the start: the rules of the
> game, the stakes, and the quitting
> time.
>
> *Chinese Proverb*

Benchmarking establishes performance expectations or goals for participating companies. These goals are usually based on the practices of other organizations, though, not the one performing the study. So why and when does internal benchmarking enter the picture? Because it details existing practice, internal benchmarking sets a baseline and definition of the company that has many benefits. Specifically, internal benchmarking should be done:

1. To detail existing processes and activity networks—establish baseline
2. To identify gaps in performance in similar internal processes
3. To bring all internal operations up to the highest possible level of performance given existing constraints and assumptions
4. To identify the first round of improvement efforts—cherry picking
5. To establish common practice and procedures
6. To open up communication lines within the organization
7. To create organizational commitment to benchmarking
8. To spearhead the total benchmarking process
9. To prioritize benchmarking opportunities
10. To identify and classify the key performance drivers into inherent, structural, and performance categories

Cherry-Picking Improvements

One of the most important items in this list of uses for internal benchmarking is the opportunity to "cherry pick"—to identify areas or activities that can be improved without going outside the organization. When process flows are completed, resources are mapped to the process, and task structure, sequence, and methods documented, communication around key issues is encouraged and can be focused on identifying potential areas for improvement.

The detailed process flows can be used to isolate value-added from non-value-added activities and to begin the streamlining of the customer-supplier networks that are the basis for the customer perspective that is so critical to achieving world-class performance. Resource utilization can be examined and compared with respect to a defined set of tasks, providing a rational basis for preliminary improvements and cost reductions.

Why Do We Do That?

> Reality is pretty brutal, pretty filthy, when you come to grips with it. Yet it's glorious all the same. It's so real and satisfactory.
>
> George Bernard Shaw
> *Fanny's First Play*

The detailed analysis of the existing task structures and methods can pinpoint areas that lead everyone to say, "Why do we do that?" It's not hard to get change started when everyone recognizes the problem and, more importantly, no one is seen as *owning it*, or having caused it. Solutions do not come from pointing fingers or placing blame; they evolve from objective analysis of the process and the problem, not the people who are caught up in the "activity trap."

Work processes develop over time. Unfortunately, very few tasks are ever discontinued, while many enhancements are added. The result of this incremental and random growth in work processes is unnecessary redundancy, antiquated checklists, procedures that no longer serve a purpose, and a tangled flow of procedures that can often result in the "customer" receiving materials or stacks of papers that do not only *not* meet specification, but that require *rework* (undoing what the supplier just did) before new tasks can be performed.

Internal benchmarking, then, allows a company to "clean house" before inviting other companies in (that is, external benchmarking).

We have noticed a disposition on the part of the human race always to take its logic with a chaser.

Don Marquis
The Almost Perfect State

Meeting the Person at the Desk Next Door

Opening internal communication channels is another key element in the initial stages of benchmarking. In fact, benchmarking is communication; it is about learning from one another. This learning can only take place if everyone feels free to share information and can see some benefit coming from it. Establishing a common language within the company can also help overcome unnecessary barriers to ongoing activities and potential change.

At the same time that it provides the potential for getting the benchmarking process off on the right footing, internal benchmarking, if done poorly, can also make subsequent efforts more difficult. The danger lies in how the information about internal operations is obtained and how it is used. If the information is obtained through a participative process that stays focused on the process, rather than the people element, individuals are unlikely to feel threatened. On the other hand, if corporate staff wanders into a division, demanding that management and other employees in the group "cooperate," the gates of change may slam shut before they are ever fully opened.

As part of the process of continuous improvement, benchmarking is by definition a participative exercise that starts with the people doing the work, relies on their recommendations and buy-in to the change process, and ends with their decision to implement the identified process improvements on an ongoing basis.

Internal benchmarking, then, can serve a vital role in establishing commitment and the open communication and sharing of ideas that separate successful change efforts from those that don't work as well. The primary focus has to be on developing the trust, commitment, and internal dialogues that will lead to ongoing change. Even "best practice" and "cherry-picking" opportunities should be identified by the participating managers at the individual sites; those who do the job every day are the ones who have to change. They had better believe in the change process, or it is simply an exercise in futility.

Which Way Did You Say We Were Going?

I live from one tentative conclusion to the next, thinking each one is final. The only thing I know for sure is that I am confused.

Hugh Prather
Notes to Myself

Finally, internal benchmarking highlights areas or specific parts of a function that need to be improved. A general complaint, such as "Things just take too long to get through the back office," doesn't provide enough detail on whether it is the way the workflow is organized, the required checkoff list followed in getting the order entered and credit approved, or the "batching up" of orders that is the problem.

The problems may not even center in the back office; the process may be stalled because certain forms or information are needed from the salesperson or the customer. If there are problems in the back office, is it in the order entry department, in credit approval, in scheduling, or where? By laying out the handoffs and activities required to get an order filled, internal benchmarking provides the first clues in how to improve responsiveness and reduce nonessential activities that delay the process.

Internal benchmarking, then, is really not an option; it is the critical first step in completing a benchmarking exercise, which establishes the baseline of existing performance, identifies organizational best practice, and provides the detailed operational process flow analysis that is the underpinning of the entire benchmarking and continuous improvement exercise.

BENEFITS OF INTERNAL BENCHMARKING

We rarely gain a higher or larger view except as it is forced upon us through struggles which we would have avoided if we could.

Charles Horton Cooley
Life and the Student

As this chapter has detailed, internal benchmarking provides a score of benefits above and beyond opening lines of communication and creating commitment. Among these benefits, internal benchmarking:

1. Overcomes the "not created here" syndrome early in the change process
2. Helps obtain information to trigger continuous improvement efforts
3. Provides a clear picture of what the organization's true problems are
4. Recasts the problems facing the company, helping to weed out issues that some part of the organization has already found an answer for as well as providing a baseline of acceptable performance
5. Makes the company focus the company's resources on problems that affect more than one department or division so it can improve the organization in a consistent manner
6. Ensures a bigger "bang for the buck" when external benchmarking is performed

Where Did This One Come From?

> For I kept my heart from assenting
> to anything, fearing to fall headlong;
> but by hanging in suspense I was the
> worse killed.
>
> Saint Augustine
> *Confessions*

The "not created here" syndrome is one of the most troubling roadblocks facing a change agent or benchmarking team in any organization. If the problem could be solved with internal resources, devoid of any outside influence, then the change process would be unnecessary. The reality of the fact is that companies seem to repeatedly resist externally driven change processes. This "easy out" reflects management's belief that their company is unique and that solutions that work at another company just won't fit there.

In reality, there are more similarities than differences between companies. The value of benchmarking, management education, consulting, computer programming, and a whole host of other management tools and procedures relies on the fact that common threads can be found between apparently different organizations. Claiming uniqueness is just another way to avoid the need to change.

Internal benchmarking focuses on practices that *are* currently being done *within* the company. Blunting this change-resisting tactic, it eases the change process and helps individual managers see that they can learn from benchmarking. In conversations between managers in different departments or divisions, it is quite likely that someone will suggest that external information may help as much, if not more, than the lessons learned within. Either way, the first step to change is taken with limited impact on the "security" of the participants.

Creating an Environment for Improvement

> People often complain of their environment: it is dull, colorless, or even
> hostile; and it never occurs to them

> to enliven it or rectify it rather than
> just endure it. A lamp doesn't com-
> plain because it must shine at night.
>
> Antonin G. Sertillanges
> *Rectitude*

Another benefit of getting internal people to talk is that it created a continuous improvement support group. Once best internal
practice is identified, the top-ranking group can guide other participants in setting realistic objectives for reaching their level of
performance. Each one of the milestones established in this manner reinforces the concept of continuous improvement; the logical
movement toward competitive excellence.

Continuous improvement efforts usually start in some small
part of the organization. While the people who are benefiting from
the improvements may actively promote the changes to other
parts of the company, it is difficult to seed new ideas into established environments. Future success, though, may be dependent
upon supporting these "islands of excellence."

Internal benchmarking can provide this support by highlighting the improvements the top-ranking groups have made in an
objective and nonthreatening way. It can set up a healthy internal competition that both reinforces the change process and le-
gitimizes those groups currently experimenting with new methods and materials. Internal benchmarking, then, can "support
continuous improvement" as its defined purpose, enacted by identifying best practice within the firm.

Identifying the Weak Spots

> My notion is that no man knows him-
> self or can arrive at truth concerning
> himself except by what seems like in-
> direction.
>
> Sherwood Anderson
> *Letters of Sherwood Anderson*

Just as internal benchmarking can identify the islands of excellence, it can also pinpoint, with often startling clarity, where

things are not under control. The objective in finding the weak spots or bottlenecks is not to lay blame on the manager in charge of that operation, though, but rather to focus on improving the process so the entire organization can function more effectively.

It would seem that problems should be easily spotted using existing performance measurements. Isn't that what they're for? In reality, measurement systems hide as much as they reveal. For every event that is measured, or *made visible*, another is hidden from view (*invisible*) because no numbers are placed around it. Benchmarking develops a new set of measures that can bring a new set of problems to the surface. Finding and fixing the weak links in the corporate chain is a value-creating process.

Setting a Baseline

> A true knowledge of ourselves is knowledge of our power.
>
> Mark Rutherford
> *Last Pages from a Journal*

Items 4 and 5 in the list of benefits at the beginning of this section stem from the same fact: in order to assess what path ahead is best, a company has to know where it is and what the score is. It is not unusual for different divisions or different regional offices to operate in totally unique ways. Sometimes it's difficult to believe that the two sites are part of the same company. Since the "in-charge" managers seldom talk among themselves and are often in open competition for the next promotion, they are unlikely to share the secrets they use to outperform their neighbor.

This is one of the repercussions of decentralization. When companies establish free-standing units that openly compete for scarce corporate resources, they create boundaries that block the flow of information from one group to the next. In these situations, little exchange of operating details occurs. That means the lessons learned in one part of the organization have no chance to spread. They stop at the door of the division head's office.

Companies can no longer afford to let the intellectual property developed in one part of the overall operation remain unfarmed and unfertilized. Active exchange of ideas among managers who, in reality, have a vested interest in each other's success is much more likely to provide the formula for success. And when improvement efforts are undertaken, the knowledge gained can be spread internally, benefiting multiple parts of the company rather than just one small segment.

Finally, looking inward for excellence provides the baseline or "straw man" which each division can be judged by and external benchmarking built on. There is no reason to look outside for improvements, which may or may not fit the company, when someone inside has already cracked the problem open. Internal benchmarking, then, opens the lines of communications within the organization, removing boundaries that impede continued growth.

I tell you, sir, the only safeguard of order and discipline in the modern world is a standardized worker with interchangeable parts. That would solve the entire problem of management.

Jean Giraudoux
The Madwoman of Chaillot

Getting the Most for Your Money

On a final note, internal benchmarking helps a company maximize the positive aspects of existing practice, focusing the external benchmarking process on those elements that are less well done. By coordinating the activities and objectives of several departments or divisions, internal benchmarking paves the way for change in more than one area at once. Working from a common framework and with common objectives, individual departments can band together in the analysis, and implementation, of new processes and procedures. For the company as a whole, it means far less "reinventing" of the solutions will occur. All participating groups will learn, and have the opportunity to change, within the same time period. They can work together, sharing resources and successes as well as failures, speeding the learning process, and increasing the value of the benchmarking exercise.

Internal benchmarking is a free-standing exercise that can be used both to standardize existing practice and minimize the tendency to reinvent practices that are already well understood in some part of the organization or that have failed in the past. It also provides the requisite knowledge about existing practice that is essential to the success of an external benchmarking project. Internal benchmarking may be a simple comparison of how different people perform the same task in the same department, or it may be an expanded comparison of performance across different regions or divisions of a large company.

In the process of learning more about how current work is performed, the concept of continuous improvement is brought to life and the handcuffs of tradition broken. Good people don't want to do unnecessary work. Only by understanding how their efforts tie into the larger company effort, and more importantly, how they affect the company's overall performance against customer expectations, can individuals learn to embrace change. Both the employee and the company benefit through this increased participation and motivation for improvement. Internal benchmarking, then, can trigger the cycle of continuous improvement, driving it into the very fiber of daily activities. It is a powerful tool, and one that is easily accessed by all organizations, regardless of size, structure, strategy, or environmental demands.

Man wins destiny only through ties: not through coercive ties imposed on him as an impotent creature of great forces that lie without; but by ties freely comprehended which he makes his own. Such ties hold his life together, so that it is not frittered away but becomes the actuality of his possible existence.

Karl Jaspers
Man in the Modern Age

5: AVON PRODUCTS: PUTTING INTERNAL BENCHMARKING TO WORK

Type of Benchmarking Used: Internal
Purpose for Use: Standardization before making
    changes to meet recent customer requests
Area examined: Customer service branch offices

Lessons Learned:

This study provides a detailed overview of the process of
internal benchmarking—how it can be used to generate
productive competition between units within an organization and how improvement efforts can become team-
based.

It is of interest because it serves to identify differences
in practice within an organization, and how these can be
used to benefit all affected units. It also illustrates how
the benchmarking process, through the development of
"straw man" models of excellence, objectifies the change
process, and provides every affected unit with a clear set
of goals, or targets, for improvement.

The focus in the case is not on the cosmetic industry.
Instead, it is a good example of how any company can
approach standardizing operations in several geographic
locations, picking the best practice from each as the goal
for all.

THE SETTING

One company, Avon Products, has found internal benchmarking to be a viable first step in improving its responsiveness to customer requests. Avon Products is a beauty products company with a twist. Avon does not sell its products in retail outlets; the only way its products can be obtained is through one of its national network of sales representatives. These field sales representatives are self-employed individuals who develop their own customer base by providing personal health and beauty products and services within the framework of a catalog-based distribution network.

Servicing the needs of these representatives is not a small task. There are over 450,000 representatives distributed across the United States. To meet their demands for products and services, Avon maintains five geographically dispersed customer service and distribution centers. The sites are each responsible for roughly 100,000 representatives. Each of these branches exists, then, to support the field sales representative networks in its region by responding to ongoing and ad hoc problems; order taking is not its primary function. Gary King, director of customer service of Avon, describes the branches' role:

> Customer service to us is service to our sales force. The questions
> we answer for them are in relation to their business, e.g., account
> or shipping information.

Customer service in this setting, then, is one step removed from the final consumer. It is in reality the distribution network for Avon products which accumulates and fills the small orders from individual sales representatives and handles any problems in billing and receipts between the company and the field sales representatives. Field sales representatives translate final customer needs and add to them their own requests, pushing both back to the company for resolution.

Figure 5.1 lays out the framework for the internal benchmarking process conducted by Avon in 1990. The core issue that the company was addressing was the effectiveness of the customer service operation. Avon was faced with an increasingly clear

Issue

Effectiveness of Customer Service Operations

Situation

500,000 sales representatives
Five regional branch offices
Considering implementation of "800" service
Other improvements under review including:

- Bilingual reps
- Additional hours
- Specific representative/customer service relationship

Research/ Findings

Key interviews

- Brand managers
- Senior management

Measurements

- Customer service heads
- Gross level/not aggregated
- No standard data

Changes

- Lots of numbers, but no comparison
- Standardize against "straw man"
- Identify and prioritize improvement opportunities

Figure 5.1 Avon Products, Inc.: internal benchmarking objectives.

mandate from its field sales representatives to provide more support services; the questions were what services were being provided in each of the five regional offices currently and what improvements could be made to the total system's performance level of quality. While service upgrades had occurred in the past, they had been done in a piecemeal fashion, with each branch developing its own response to service requests. Seeing itself as a national sales network, Avon management decided that it should provide a uniform front to its field sales force: a representative in Texas should receive the same support and services as a representative in Maine. The company had to learn about itself before it could embark on further change.

Understanding Customer Expectations

During the 1980s, Avon, in the search for efficiency, had been encouraging its sales representatives to use written communications as much as possible. The sales representatives, on the other hand, continued to request more responsive support from the company. In late 1989, the company decided that it would increase the number of services available over the phone. The decision to enhance services came after the company became involved with an extensive service quality study. The premise of the study was that, through a survey of the existing customer base (that is, Avon representatives), the company could define the expectations of service levels, develop measures around what it was already doing, and then measure the gap between customer expectations and current performance. Heskett *et al.* provide some insights into this process:[1]

> Customers often are much better able to articulate expectations about results to be achieved from a service than they are about the way services are delivered and the kinds of encounters they involve....(They) may be able to express expectations about some kinds of service processes more clearly than others. Even then it is often done indirectly...given that service quality is what is delivered in relation to what is expected, inadequate information about what to expect often represents a root cause of perceived poor service....This is particularly critical where customers have high perceived risks and need some degree of control over the service process.

The Avon sales representatives definitely feel an inherent level of risk, and need for control over the customer service function, since they are the ones that respond to specific inquiries and complaints from the end user of the product. Individual sales representatives are in business for themselves. These problems affect *their* personal welfare and the welfare of their families. In addition, most Avon representatives trade extensively with family and friends. This means that any problem is important to them, because it affects people they care for.

The services provided by each of the Avon branches before the standardization project was undertaken can be seen in Figure 5.2. While many services were available at each branch, some were performed only in centralized locations. The table reflects those services supported by telephone; representatives were encouraged to place orders in excess of fifteen items on written purchase orders, which were processed in another part of the company.

Creating a Self-Reinforcing Service Cycle

By recognizing the risks and uncertainty faced by the field sales representative, Avon management was following the recommendations of various service quality management programs. They were attempting to create a self-reinforcing service cycle, which would help the company leverage the value a customer

Services Offered	Pasadena	Newark	Springdale	Morton Grove	Atlanta
Add on Order System		●	●	●	
VIP 800# (Special Commun. Rep.)		●	●		
Duplicate & Partial Shipment 800#	●				
Carol Cook (Collect or Refund)			●		●
Interactive Voice					
• Rep. Line	●				
• District Manager Line (800)	●	●	●	●	
CASSIE Computers (PS-2s)	●	●			●
• (District Managers)					
Upgraded Customer Service Fac.		●	◐		
Note Pad System			●		

Figure 5.2   Avon Products, Inc.: services offered by branch.

would receive from the service being provided against the cost of providing that service. Heskett *et al.* provide the four criteria or starting points for developing service excellence:[2]

1. The value associated with the results a service provides and the quality of the way it is delivered depends on the extent to which a provider can reduce a customer's perceived risks.
2. Increased value in relation to the costs of acquiring a service leads to a higher probability that a customer will become a repeater.
3. Repeat customers, because they have established expectations, growing respect for the provider, and greater knowledge of what is expected of them in the service delivery process, are less expensive, and therefore more profitable to serve, than new customers.
4. The value of service to a repeat customer grows with the reliability of the way it is delivered and the results it achieves.

Avon faces a "customer" that has repeated contact with the service delivery system, relies on the system for satisfying the demands of friends and family for various products and the solution of various problems, and is personally at risk in the problem resolution process.

All of these factors combine to underscore the fact that Avon's field sales representatives definitely expect a certain level of support services from the company, which they may be able to, but just as likely cannot, define precisely. Given this ambiguity, Avon management felt that the joint experiences of the Avon personnel in the five branch offices might provide a good baseline for identifying existing requirements, as well as apparent expectations, of the field sales representatives. This led to the first round of analysis by the company, as described by Gary King:

> In January of 1990 we brought the five regional managers together in a two-day conference in order to lay the groundwork for what we wanted to accomplish in 1990 in terms of the management of our customer service network.

Human resources was the first area we started to drive at. The second was tracking some of the critical call statistics between regions and publishing them on a U.S. basis, so regions could compare their volume and service levels with their peers.... It wasn't to set up competition, but rather to instill loyalty, and a desire to improve in each of the regions.

The list of items to track was developed during that January meeting, so there was no problem using it on an ongoing basis. We put together the report and began to drive the human resource change process by asking each of the five centers to take the lead in one part of the call service improvement process. One focused on developing a new questionnaire to be used in the hiring process, another to develop voice response applications, and so on. Everyone was basically relying on everyone else to do some piece of the 1990 overall plan.

Figure 5.3 shows an analysis of daily call distributions, both on an hourly basis for an "average" day, and on the differences in the total number of calls per day by the day of the week. This was based on the key information presented in Figure 5.4. The analysis helped management develop staffing demand patterns that would ensure an adequate level of responsiveness throughout the day and the week without incurring excessive cost.

Closing the Performance Gap

At this stage, it became clear that although management had accumulated a lot of numbers, very few valid comparisons between branches could be made. Actual practice was quite varied across the five branches, making it quite difficult to isolate which region represented "best practice." This led them to develop a *logical straw man*, which reflected the best practice for a series of tasks, and to devise measurements that captured the essence of this "best" performer. The straw man was not based on any one branch office but rather consisted of pieces of each: each branch excelled at a different set of customer service tasks. The benefit of this approach, beyond the development of an ideal branch service unit for everyone to work toward, was that it depersonalized (or "debranched") the change process. This opened up opportunities for each branch to improve; no one location was privileged or ignored.

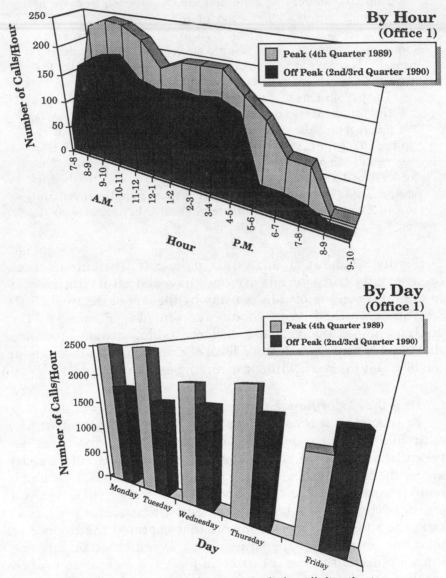

Figure 5.3   Avon Products, Inc.: daily call distribution.

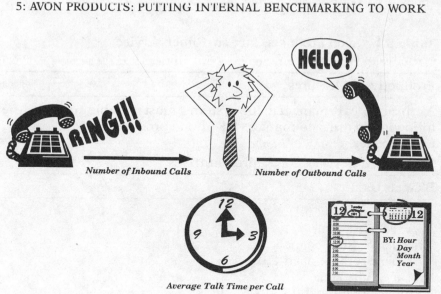

Figure 5.4   Avon Products, Inc.: individual representative data.

With the straw man in place and agreed upon by the five regional branch managers, the benchmarking exercise could begin to focus on measuring each branch against this ideal. Measurements now had a purpose: they could be used to identify performance gaps at each branch as well as to support the standardization of the service delivery system. This straw man also served as the basis from which to choose among available alternatives for enhancing the support services. Finally, in the process of developing the straw man model of the customer service group, areas where standardized telecommunications solutions could be effectively utilized were identified.

The regional management team decided to track the productivity measures listed in Table 5.1 on an ongoing basis. These measures provided the first wave of change for the organization. Measurements are powerful tools in the change process for any organization. At Avon, they clearly identified areas where each branch was meeting expectations and where improvements needed to occur. These measurements removed the ambiguity from the change process, providing each manager with the tools necessary to meet the corporate service standardization objectives.

Table 5.1 Avon Products, Inc. customer service
operations review

Productivity Measures
All branch call management systems must be able to track the following in order to manage telephone productivity goals across all branches.
Segmented Services for Representatives
Branch Data
Total Number of Calls Average Wait Time Number of Busy Signals Number of Abandoned Calls Average Talk Time Number of Outbound Calls Made

The entire process led to rapid improvements in the service delivery system at Avon. Once again, Gary King provides some insight here:

> By the end of the year, when we held our last conference to cap off what we had accomplished as a team and prepare for our key fourth quarter selling period, one of the comments was that through this process it was not clear at the end who was moving faster—the benchmarking team or the implementers at the regional offices. As recommendations were coming in, some were being implemented right away; the sites were driving full speed to implement and institutionalize the recommendations that came out of the study.
>
> The reason for this was quite clear. The service branch managers had been part of the study and had set the requirements, so they had a lot of buy-in to the internal process. This was supported by the fact that internal benchmarking was in conjunction with our culture.

The interactive nature of the benchmarking process supported its rapid implementation. This fact, combined with the fair level of expectations set up by the straw man approach, helped blunt traditional barriers to change. The internal benchmarking process presented a list of alternatives that *were created at Avon;* the "not invented here" syndrome had no place. Finally, the change process was done with extreme sensitivity to the existing culture; the way the study was conducted, the development of early commitment, and the use of regional competition to raise the level of enthusiasm for change, all reflected time-honored traditions within the company. The change process was succeeding, because a significant number of implementation barriers were removed.

Service Gaps and Opportunities for Improvement

In performing the operational review and customer service analysis, Avon management did identify service gaps and began reviewing a series of options to help close these gaps. The types of improvements the regional management "team" considered included increasing the number of field sales representatives that could use the company's "800" number to place orders and make other inquiries; providing 24-hour, seven-days-a-week coverage in the customer service area; assigning specific customer service personnel to the top selling sales representatives; and adding a bilingual representative to each branch to support Spanish-speaking sales representatives. Each of these changes would address one or more of the identified gaps; the questions were which should be done first, why, and where.

The entire range of improvement opportunities that were discovered in the course of this study are detailed in Appendix 5. While many changes could be made, immediate priorities had to be set. Figure 5.5 summarizes the list of priorities chosen by the branch management teams. At the environmental level, it was decided that modular furniture would both provide better space utilization at each of the branches and improve the general work environment for the sales service agents by increasing their privacy and providing convenient storage and access for specific customer files.

A second issue that came to light was that Avon district managers were not fully utilizing the existing status-reporting system (CASSIE) because they were unfamiliar with the available services and how to use them. This was leading to unnecessary calls to the branch, which tied up resources, decreased overall responsiveness to bona fide field sales representative problems,

- **Environment**

- **Call Management System**

- **Training**
  - Technical
  - Formal
  - Standardized Across Branches
  - Advanced (Service Plus)

- **Reduced Call Volume**
  - Use of Information Technology
  - Policy Changes

- **Human Resources Initiative**
  - Recognition Awards
  - Review of Current Salary Structure

- **Regular Meetings for Customer Service Supervisors and/or Managers**

Figure 5.5   Avon Products, Inc.: summary of immediate priorities.

and increased the required staffing levels at each of the branches. These calls were a non-value-adding part of the branch's workload; the tasks were redundant, they wasted valuable human resources at the branch, and in reality they were a slower (less responsive) way for the managers to get the desired information. The existing requests were also analyzed for efficiency.

To meet this problem, better use of existing branch information technology was instituted to sort incoming calls into specialized channels. This standardization benefited the organization right away by providing a broad-based problem resolution network. A field service representative, calling from a tone-dialing phone, could activate the service channel needed. This routing, along with the development of computer-based procedures for processing the inquiry, helped elevate service quality and ensure the consistency of ongoing operations. The telecommunication package also provided the field service representatives with a list of numbers to call to resolve various types of problems, eliminating irritating and time-consuming relay games. The first phone call made would put the field sales representative in touch with someone who could resolve the problem.

Getting everyone to use these information system options meant that training programs had to be developed and given. Training programs are a natural element of any change process; new procedures and new objectives have to be clearly documented and communicated to the affected individuals. This training, though, is never a one-time event. Ongoing training is the only way to gain and maintain consistently high levels of performance. Natural turnover, the return of habitual behaviors, and changes in existing technologies make training a way of life in the modern corporation. Education doesn't end with the taking of a job—it begins there.

Standardizing the training process helped Avon achieve its underlying objective of providing uniform service to field sales service representatives across the country. It was also important to examine the schedules kept by each branch to determine whether differences were due to customer demands or to history. Keeping its eye on service quality, Avon management placed customer expectations ahead of standardization in this area. Field sales representatives were surveyed before schedules were changed. At the same time, demands for bilingual support services were detailed.

Across the board, Avon benefited from the internal benchmarking process. In addition to meeting the original objective for standardization of its field sales support services, Avon discovered opportunities for improved utilization of existing information technologies and branch resources. Management also discovered that there were customer-defined boundaries to the standardization process; some regional branches would have to continue providing unique services (such as bilingual agents).

In the spirit of continuous improvement, the change process did not stop at the end of one year. Instead, says Gary King,

...the change process is continuing. We are refining the measurement tools used last year to do a new level of reporting, and getting further and further into classic process control, where we are attempting to ensure that the measurements we are taking are aimed at the right spot in the process of handling a telephone call.... The survey of customer expectations and the benchmarking process are helping us to narrow the gap between service provided and service expected—to meet and exceed customer expectations.

These changes are based on a sound knowledge of customer expectations, a clear understanding of current customer service activities, an agreement on the defined level of desired performance within each branch field office, and a desire to strive continuously to serve better the field sales representatives and the customers they support. The internal benchmarking process is allowing Avon to achieve these goals by employing careful use of financial resources, as existing practice is standardized and telecommunication advances used wherever they can yield benefit to the customer. Keeping an eye on the customers and their needs is shaping the change process and its effectiveness across Avon Products' entire sales and distribution network.

INTERNAL BENCHMARKING: TOOL FOR IMPROVING PERFORMANCE

Never look down to test the ground before taking your next step: only he who keeps his eye fixed on the far horizon will find his right road.

Dag Hammarskjöld
Markings

Benchmarking provides a reference point, a vision of excellence that can only be reached by understanding what the customer requires and then delivering it in the most effective and efficient way possible. While most benchmarking articles and books point toward developing external reference points, in reality much can be learned by looking first for best practice within a company. No matter what type of subsequent information is sought to confirm and develop continuous improvement objectives for the firm, a

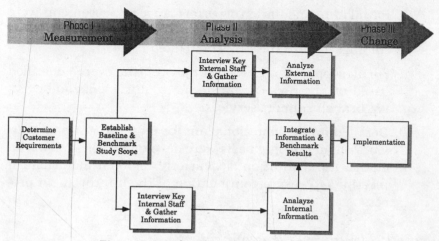

Figure 5.6   The phases of benchmarking.

clear, concise understanding of what is currently done and what is the requisite first step toward competitive advantage.

Internal benchmarking, like all benchmarking projects, moves through three primary phases, as suggested by Figure 5.6. How were these stages reflected in the benchmarking exercise completed by Avon Products? Here is a recap of the major events in Avon's analysis and implementation:

1. Customer expectations that were not being uniformly met triggered the search for improvement.

2. A support service standardization strategy was chosen.

3. Avon management chose the human resources component of the regional branch network as the key area in improving overall performance.

4. Regional branch managers were called together to begin working on the project. Initial performance requirements and measurements were chosen.

5. An operational review of each branch was performed.

6. A uniform support service profile was developed (the logical straw man).

7. Measures were chosen that could move each branch toward this desired level of performance.

8. Initial implementation of performance improvements were undertaken in tandem as each branch addressed its shortcomings against the straw man model.

9. Further opportunities for improvement were identified based on the review of customer requirements and existing branch support services.

10. Detailed implementation plans for upgrading support services on an ongoing basis were developed. These plans included the institution of quarterly regional management meetings to ensure continuation of the improvement process.

Phase I: Identifying the Requirements

Phase I of the benchmarking process encompasses the selection of the functions to be benchmarked, identification of appropriate performance measures, and, when appropriate, the choice of external benchmarking targets. Events 1 through 4 were part of the first phase of the benchmarking process at Avon. The starting point was the identification of customer requirements that were not being met on a consistent basis. This was bolstered by a corporate decision or strategy to provide standardized support services at each of the five regional branches.

Within this strategy, the company could have focused on many different functional areas of the branch in the benchmarking process. Human resources was chosen as the central area, because the support services network was intensely reliant on personal contact between field sales representatives and Avon support services employees. In addition, human resources were a major cost element in operating these branches; any changes made would have to be done with an eye toward its financial implications.

Once this basic frame was developed for the benchmarking exercise, management passed the project on to the regional branch managers. Since they were the ones who would have to implement and live with the policies and procedures that would result from the study, their buy-in was essential. In addition, this group was able to brainstorm their way to the list of logical performance measurements for use in the operational review quite rapidly; they knew what it took to make a branch run both efficiently and effectively. At the same time, corporate management was able to avoid two pitfalls in the change process: the "not invented here" syndrome and the failure to capitalize on existing knowledge (reinventing the wheel).

Phase II: Fact Finding and Focus

Armed with a set of measurements, the regional management team was able to embark on Phase II of the benchmarking process: gathering and analyzing information. There are three primary steps making up this phase: interviewing key staff, gathering information, and analyzing and comparing data. Events 5 through 7 in the list at the beginning of this section were used to complete this stage at Avon.

The key staff was actually part of the benchmarking process in this situation; there was no need to interview them when they were the source of the change process itself. This led them to the information-gathering stage, which was centered on the operational review of each branch's current performance profile. Operational reviews are the heart of internal benchmarking, whereas they are merely one part of the information gathering required in an external benchmarking project. At Avon these reviews provided the first level of detail needed to understand existing practice and develop a model that would frame the standardization process.

Working within its culture, Avon management knew that setting up the straw man was the best way to use a tradition of performance competition between the regional branch managers to drive the change process. The additional benefit of developing an objective model of "good" service was that it left each branch with a clearly defined goal; improvements could begin immediately, with the motivation for and measures of success in place.

Phase III: Putting Improvements in Motion

The final phase of the benchmarking process is where the benefits are reaped. At Avon, the implementation process itself evolved into a two-stage process, as captured by events 8 through 10 in the list at the beginning of this section. Having already adopted the philosophy of continuous improvement as defined by customer expectations, it was natural that the change process would not stop once the static goal of support service standardization was achieved. Instead, short-run improvements to move the branches toward desired ongoing levels of performance were enhanced with a long-run dynamic objective of continuous improvement, implemented through quarterly meetings of the regional management team.

The implementation phase is often the most difficult part of the benchmarking process. Avon Products was able to circumvent many of the traditional barriers to change by actively involving those individuals who would have to spearhead the change process at the branches. Participation, combined with a sensitive, intelligent use of the existing culture of competition, accelerated the change process and ensured its institutionalization. A clear recognition of the need for buy-in at the operational level, a recognition that different branches excelled at different aspects of the support service function, and the intelligent use of performance measurements all led to the rapid deployment of the knowledge and suggestions emerging from the benchmarking process.

Diligence is the mother of good luck, and God gives all things to industry. Then plough deep while sluggards sleep, and you shall have corn to sell and to keep.

Benjamin Franklin
Poor Richard's Almanac

APPENDIX 5

AVON PRODUCTS, INC. CUSTOMER SERVICE OPERATIONS REVIEW

Improvement opportunities identified as areas that should be addressed *immediately* are highlighted in boldface type in the following list.

Information Technology

- *CASSIE:* **District Managers are not fully utilizing the CASSIE system. This results in unnecessary calls to the branch.** This is in large part due to

    - Insufficient initial training

    - Need for ongoing training

    - "Fear" of the computer

    - Hard disk storage of PC equipment being used

    - Information easily provided by calling the branch

    Effort must be made to have the CASSIE system rolled out to all District Managers (Morton Grove still pending). Additional training as well as clear concise instructions regarding what information is available through CASSIE should be provided in order for Managers to make full use of the system, thereby reducing the number of calls to the branch.

- *Conversant:* **A "bulletin board" feature is needed on the Conversant system to eliminate customer service reps from having to respond to product quality problems (such as Spooky Tunes) and merchandise shorts.** These day-to-day issues can be addressed through a general message. The Conversant system should also be used to reduce incoming call volume by responding to order inquiries as follows:

Manager

Account Balance
Shipping Info
Credit Hold/Release
Add-on Order
CSR
Voice Mail
Transfer

Honor Society/Presidents Club

Campaign Info
Quality/Stock Info
Account Balance
Shipping Info
Add-on Order
Order Problems
CSR

Sales Representatives

Campaign Info
Quality/Stock Info
Account Balance
Shipping Info
Add-on Order
Order Problems

■ *Atlanta Call Management System:* **Install improved call management system at the Atlanta branch.**

■ *PC Portability:* Consider laptop computers in place of PS/2s being used by District Managers to allow for portability and increased use of the CASSI system.

Organization

■ *Support Services:* Consider maintaining a separate Customer Service support group, which would be supervised by a different individual than the telephone supervisor. The support services group would handle the following activities:

■ Instant delivery

■ Leads

■ Separate mail

■ Special projects

■ Order and shipping services for top producers including add-on orders (if not on POET)

■ Delivery clerk

■ Generalist

■ Add-on orders (over 10 items)

■ Credit check

■ Contracts

■ *Secretarial/Clerical Support:* Each branch should have a secretary/clerk supporting customer service activities with the following duties:

■ Merchandise requests

■ Literature and supplies

■ Answer supervisor's phones

■ Reports and attendance

- Time cards

- Work orders

- Typing

- Fragile reconciliation

- A secretary/clerk performing the above duties would allow more time for supervisors to manage the telephone specialists and for telephone specialists to remain on the phone assisting sales reps.

- *Regular Meetings:* **Hold regular meetings (two to four times per year) for Customer Service Supervisors and/or Managers to exchange ideas and share experiences.**

- *Managers/Assistant Managers:* Duplication of work can be occurring on the part of the Telephone Specialist as well as Managers and Assistant Managers when both Managers and Assistant Managers call in with the same question or request. The magnitude of this problem varies from branch to branch and district to district, but it needs to be addressed to reduce time wasted by two persons performing the same activity.

Work Activities

- *Outbound Calls:* Outbound calls are also made for the following reasons:

  - Voice mail calls are returned.

  - Calls are made to key District Managers to see if there's anything they need.

  - Calls are made to top producers to see if there's anything they need (proactive calling in Atlanta only).

  - Incoming calls to specific personnel who are unavailable at the time of the incoming call must be returned.

  - Calls are made to inform Managers/Reps when orders are going to be late.

  - Responding to separate mail.

In addition, much time is spent returning telephone calls. Reasons for returning phone calls include the following:

- Managers are calling in and asking customer service reps to call several sales reps back.

- Time is needed to pull invoices.

Communication is needed to promote the handling of calls at the time of the incoming call. This will reduce time spent returning calls and their associated costs.

- *Separate Mail:* During slow periods, separate mail is distributed to the telephone reps in order to respond by telephone. This promotes the use of the telephone system rather than mail and should be done across all branches.

- *Policy Changes:* **Reduce incoming call volume through policy changes.** For example:

  - Set a maximum item limit for add-on orders. All orders exceeding the maximum must be put on a purchase order. Atlanta currently has a 15-item limit.

  - Formalize policy for partial shipments—reship entire order under certain conditions (for example, more than half the order is missing).

- *Personal Telephone Calls:* Determine method of tracking personal vs. business calls. This will help establish accurate productivity statistics.

Training

- *CASSIE:* Training is needed for managers to make better use of the CASSIE system.

- *Special Training Facilities:* Consider a separate training area to better train new telephone specialists and maintain integrity of productivity statistics.

- *Telephone Specialists Training:* Formal and advanced (Service Plus) training needs to be provided on an ongoing basis to the telephone specialists to continually improve the quality of service. In addition, provide technical training as necessary.

- *Standardization:* Hold workshop/conference to bring all branches together to share training ideas and standardize training curriculum as appropriate across branches.

Service Levels

- *Hours of Operation:* Conduct a survey of reps to determine the need for Saturday support for reps and managers beyond 4th Quarter.

- *Consistency Across Branches:* Determine if it would be beneficial for the various branches to maintain similar schedules. Currently, Morton Grove closes lines for reps at 4:30 p.m. while Newark is open until 10:00 p.m.

- *Pasadena Manager Line:* Currently Pasadena's Manager line closes at 3:00 p.m., but Managers are requesting that lines remain open longer. Pasadena should determine how to adjust its hours of operation for Manager calls.

- *VIPs:* Handling of top producers varies across branches. While Newark and Atlanta give special attention to top producers, Morton Grove feels it does not have the manpower to provide this special attention. Pasadena gives special attention to its "Top 30" producers. Atlanta has shown success in "upselling" to top producers through proactive callbacks. Consideration should be given to using this sales technique across all branches.

- *Spanish Telephone Specialists:* There is a need to determine whether support for the Spanish-speaking reps is adequate at all the branches. Some branches expressed concern that they are not providing adequate support to Spanish-speaking reps and managers. If considered inadequate, this issue should be addressed as appropriate for each individual branch.

Environment

- *Work Space:* Modular furniture is needed to make better use of space at the branches. Newark has already added carpeting and partitions, which have greatly improved conditions. Other branches should follow suit.

- *Paper Management:* Consider a paper management system for the various forms and literature that telephone specialists must have on hand to perform their function. Morton Grove is currently in the process of evaluating several different systems.

Human Resources

- *Responsibilities:* **Corporate culture has dictated the differences between Manager Telephone Specialists and Sales Rep Telephone Specialists.** Often it is more difficult responding to the needs of the sales rep. An analysis needs to be done to determine if the position should encompass both types of duties, if different salaries are indeed warranted, and how this issue should be addressed.

- *Flexible Hours:* Supervisors stated that it is sometimes difficult to get employees to work flexible hours to cover the new extended hours of operation. This is especially a problem for Newark. (Atlanta and Morton Grove are not having a problem in this area.) This can be resolved through

  - Developing incentives for working flexible hours

  - Employing more part-time employees

  - Employing more agency employees.

- *Recognition and Incentive Awards:* **This area was not discussed in detail but needs to be addressed at future meetings.**

Costs

- *Salaries:* Telephone specialist salaries are somewhat higher than other firms. Evaluate the cost difference between hiring internal versus using agency employees and determine most appropriate solution.

- *Overtime:* Overtime is considered to be at a high level, especially in the fourth quarter. Overtime can be reduced through

  - Four-day schedules of 10 hours per day

  - Employing part-time personnel

  - Employing agency personnel

  - Staggered work hours to cover peak call periods

6: CONTINUOUS IMPROVEMENT: THE UNDERLYING GOAL

Planning and competition can be combined only by planning for competition, but not by planning against competition.

Friedrich August von Hayek
The Road to Serfdom

Competitive advantage is not gained through industrial espionage. Instead, it is the result of planning for competition as defined by the customer and evaluated by the marketplace. Today, effective planning means the adoption of "continuous improvement" as the ultimate goal the never-ending quest to be just a little bit better, every day, in every activity.

The alternative, maintenance of the status quo, results in a constant backsliding—a loss of competitive position that may well prove fatal. Perhaps one of the most graphic examples of this fact is found in the saga of the American steel industry. Rather than changing over to more efficient blast furnaces that would reduce the feasible size of a plant and allow for lower prices to the marketplace, top managers in this industry clung to traditional production and management approaches. In response to their competitive backsliding, they sought trade restrictions on foreign steel rather than new ways to do business. Failing to respond in a timely manner to these threats, the entire industry was devasted by the onslaught of foreign competition. While a few of these former giants have been able to cling to existence, the basic fact remains that the American steel industry is merely a shadow of its former self today.

Revitalization: A Never-Ending Objective

> Never cease to be convinced that life might be better—your own and others'.
>
> André Gide
> *The Fruits of the Earth*

To counter the organization's natural tendency to deteriorate, individuals and the teams they populate must work to revitalize operations, infuse them with the incremental changes that ensure their vitality, and constantly search for those innovations (quantum leaps) that will enable the organization to recreate itself. While this may sound great, the obvious question to ask next is "How?" For many years, the best consultants and business leaders have tried to answer this elusive question. The plethora of "fads" populating the management landscape attest to the sincerity of their efforts.

In the 1980s the "Japanese management system" became the fad of first choice, whether focused on manufacturing processes (such as just-in-time manufacturing) or the quality improvement effort. While many tag this as just another splash in the pan of consulting tools, useful now but of little long-term merit, more and more businessmen are realizing that this "fad" is different. The Japanese approach looks at the company as a system of interlocked activity networks focused on providing value-added products to the customer.

Continuous improvement, or *kaizen*, is the core of the Japanese management philosophy that has led to their rapid attainment of a global competitive advantage. It is an incremental change process that focuses on performing existing tasks more effectively: small improvements made in the status quo as a result of ongoing efforts.[1] In a continuous improvement environment, every individual, whether in management or on the shop floor, assumes responsibility for the quality, timeliness, efficiency, and effectiveness of the *productive process*.

The productive process is composed of the people, methods, machines, materials, and measurement systems used to produce a product, perform an operation, or complete some other activity. It is the dynamic flow of resources through the organization that results in a value-added product (whether physical goods or a service) that meets customer requirements. To attain world-class competitive ability, therefore, management must turn away from its focus on maintaining existing processes through the development of "fat," functionally oriented structures to embrace the fluid environment of continuous improvement and its concern with products, services, and customers.

Abandoning the "Meet Standard" World

No sooner do we take a step out of our customary routine than a strange world surges about us.

J. B. Priestley
All About Ourselves and Other Essays

In adopting continuous improvement as the underlying goal for the organization, management is abandoning the world where *individuals constituted sources of error, not assets*.[2] This is in direct contrast to the management philosophy of the early 1900s which revolved around a belief that workers should be relieved of the need to think, as management analyzed and detailed each movement, each action, that needed to occur. Omniscient management led a docile workforce, pursuing the belief that if the preset procedures were followed and output standards attained, the organization would prosper.

In a "meet standard" world, continuous improvement is neither desired nor possible. In fact, an entire measurement system called "standard costing" was built around the belief that meeting planned output levels using planned amounts of resources was the key to success. Any manager plagued today with the residuals of that measurement system—the dreaded variance reports and hours of pointless justification for "missing the target"—understands what establishing a firm, unbending standard means in an uncertain world: it means that gamesmanship will abound.

There is one overriding tenet of management: "You get what you measure and reward." In a "meet standard" world, what is measured and rewarded is compliance with the status quo; meeting, but not exceeding or falling short of, the preset goal. It is difficult enough to get people to embrace change under the best of circumstances. It is nigh well impossible to get them to change when their entire history with the organization has been characterized by rewards for mediocrity and punishment for risks taken that did not pan out. What is measured and rewarded is sameness, not innovation—meeting standard, not continuously improving.

Benchmarking for Continuous Improvement

Benchmarking is emerging as a valuable tool for initiating, guiding, and depersonalizing the path to continuous improvement. By establishing a new set of measures, it serves to unravel the "meet standard" mentality. The benchmarking activity is focused on the process and on identifying and rewarding continuous improvement. It provides a structure around the change process that emanates from the objective assessment of the competitive environment. Therefore, benchmarking lays the groundwork for breaking out of the past to establish a new culture that takes the best of the past with it but leaves unproductive baggage behind.

Alan Kantrow, in his recent book *The Constraints of Corporate Tradition*, notes:[3]

> Neither blind resistance to change nor wholesale junking of the past makes for sensible development. Gradual adaptation does. Decisions, discoveries, and innovations are not brilliant flashes of the knife, which sunder what follows from all that went before. In themselves—and especially in the institutional context through which they work—they represent processes of change, gradual unfoldings, piece-by-piece rearrangements of prior identifications and allegiances. They represent an ongoing adaptation to the ever-shifting mix of what past and present make available. Displacement goes on, in a sense, all the time.

Kantrow calls this process of gradual adaptation a form of organizational "muddling through." Muddling through can work if there is enough time, enough luck, and enough resources to enable the organization to survive its missteps and missed opportunities, but it is an inadequate basis for competing in a global marketplace where organizations are struggling for survival, not incremental profits. The game has changed drastically, it would seem. Today there's little room for attaboys—only for the question, "What's next?"

Yet the concept of gradual change described above is the key concept in a continuous improvement setting. The difference lies in the randomness of the change process. Muddling through suggests that a reactive management style will work, as long as it is unfettered from the bonds of Scientific Management and its pursuit of truth. Continuous improvement, as triggered by and defined through the benchmarking process, pursues this change in a focused manner.

The Benefits of Adopting Continuous Improvement

There are five major benefits that arise from adopting continuous improvement as the basis for managing an organization:

1. It generates process-oriented thinking.
2. It involves the whole organization in ongoing problem solving.
3. It establishes horizontal activity networks that serve to integrate the organization.
4. It creates responsive, customer-driven product delivery networks.
5. It institutionalizes the process of ongoing change and learning.

Process-oriented thinking refers to a focus on the way things are done; on the activities that are performed and their value to the ultimate customer. It is concerned with the "what," not the "who," in problem solving. This is reflected in the following comment by Imai:[4]

The process-oriented way of thinking bridges the gap between process and result, between ends and means, and between goals and measures, and helps people see the whole picture without bias....A process-oriented manager who takes a genuine concern for process criteria will be interested in: discipline, time management, skill development, participation and involvement, morale, and communication. In short, such a manager is people-oriented.

A process-oriented approach focuses on the action as well as the outcome, seeking to improve the outcome not by mandate, but by a carefully guided analysis of the process itself, with an ever-watchful eye to improvement.

A former manager of Eaton Corporation, Robert Stasey, described a situation where a process-oriented approach was embraced, but perhaps one step too late:[5]

> We kept having problems with the circuit board in one of our counters. Every tenth or so unit we tested would be bad, even though we were promised zero-defect performance by our supplier. In response to the problem, I and one of my top managers flew to the supplier's plant, ready to pin the blame there. After wading through reams of evidence about the quality of the process, and products, delivered by the vendor, the conversation turned to our testing procedures.
>
> The initial response of the vendor's engineers was graphic; the tests we were performing to "ensure" quality on our end were damaging the boards. Our testing equipment was outmoded. That wasn't the only problem, though. After we stopped the testing we still had random failures. This time, though, we looked at our own processes rather than seeking out a scapegoat. Sure enough, we found the problem. One of our machine operators liked to dress well for her job—nylons every day. Well, those nylons rubbing together as she moved created friction; which she discharged every now and again when she touched a board. The damage was unintentional, but very real. The problems were all in our processes, not those of our supplier. It was a hard way to learn, but learn we did. From then on we always looked at our own processes first, seeking improvements in our own shop first.

Management Is More Than Process Analysis

Thinking process, though, is not management. Management requires the interaction of individuals in the pursuit of a common goal. Traditionally this common goal was dictated by management; today it is emerging through the participation of every individual in the organization in problem solving and goal setting. Some would say that the organization of today employs the "whole person" rather than a strong arm and that the benefits of this enlightened view are just beginning to be felt. Decades of research suggests that a participative management style garners higher levels of loyalty and satisfaction from the workforce. But the benefits extend beyond "feeling good." An involved workforce provides a multitude of eyes and perspectives for identifying, analyzing, and solving ongoing problems and creating future opportunities. Continuous improvement is based on participation; it cannot function without it.

Continuous improvement means more than asking for input from the workforce, though. Because they focus on their part of the process itself, continuous improvement–based techniques *establish horizontal activity chains* that serve to integrate the organization around the customer's needs. This integration weds the destinies of individuals and functions, nullifying the impact of "parochialism," the us-versus-them attitude that can destroy the cohesiveness and responsiveness of a firm. Linking activities together into value chains (sequences of activities that begin with a request for service from a customer and end with the delivery of that product or service) clearly details the impact each individual has on the organization's ability to meet customer expectations and provides the basis for identifying and eliminating non-value-added activities (*activities*, not *people*).

Horizontal linking of activities and functions *serves to open communication channels*. Open communication lays the groundwork for the creation of responsive customer service networks that can rapidly and effectively react to questions and problems. By placing "boundaries" around a customer network, the performance of that network can be measured against the criteria used by the customer—does the product arrive on time, in the right quantity and quality necessary to meet my needs? The improvements in communication cannot be directly traced to the bottom line, but the benefits are clearly there in terms of higher levels of customer satisfaction and the ensurance of long-run profitability.

The final benefit of continuous improvement–based techniques is that they *institutionalize the process of change* within an organization. In eliminating the status quo as an acceptable level of performance, management is giving a clear signal: change is no longer an event, it is a way of life. Each individual is expected to pursue constant improvement—constant learning—and is being given the tools, power, and knowledge necessary to make this a reality.

A Hidden Flaw

All of this may sound like a broken record to managers who are busy implementing just-in-time (JIT) or total quality management (TQM) in their company. Adopting continuous improvement is the only way to ensure ongoing competitive success, period. Yet the concepts embodied in "continuous improvement" are not enough to structure the implementation of this new management philosophy. In pursuing improvement, a manager may ask "Why" five times to isolate the root cause of a problem, but the "How" to change, which follows, is equally important.

In fact, if any criticism can be leveled at the current wave of "continuous improvement" seminars and books, it is that they are vague. They fail to set down a clear mechanism for understanding and implementing the philosophy. Without this structure, the change process takes on the trappings of a religion, as the followers chant on and on the mantras of improvement. This religious overtone has not helped the diffusion of the continuous improvement management philosophy. It has instead given the skeptics a rallying point, as they point the finger to another instance of "management by fad."

The unstructured nature of the continuous improvement message is not the only problem beginning to surface. *Because it has been predominantly implemented through JIT/TQM approaches, continuous improvement has retained an internal focus*. While customer-oriented performance evaluation systems have been developed to ensure that the system provides some minimal level of service, there is a major gap between "customer-oriented" and "customer-driven" systems.

Customers Set the Pace

In a customer-oriented setting, the organization recognizes that the customer has specific requirements; however, those are not translated into specific measurements of the performance of the customer network but instead are reflected in a heightened focus on internal efficiency. The best example of this is the "cycle time" measures that are used by most JIT companies. Nine out of ten companies using JIT measure cycle time, but this measurement is restricted to the time it takes to physically make the product. It is a tightly defined measure of the elapsed time between the launch of an order in the shop to its movement into finished goods.

What does the customer want? The time period the customer is concerned with is from the time an order is placed, or project initiated, until the product is productively functioning in the customer's facility. A company that focuses solely on improving against its internal measures of performance may totally miss the fact that the "customer contact" cycle is the key to externally evaluated performance improvements, not the production cycle. To the customer, a day lost is a day, whether caused by order processing or machine 54. A delay is a delay.

Finally, while continuous improvement efforts focus on involving the workforce, they provide few definable tools for overcoming the natural barriers to change that exist in every organization. Since the change process is relatively unstructured and people-intensive, it can easily become derailed should the "change agent," or "explorer," leave, tire, or get distracted by other events. With its heavy reliance on the presence of a "champion," most continuous improvement efforts can get bogged down in the mire of organizational politics, as claim and counterclaim are traded in a never-ending debate without an objective means for reaching a decision.

A Champion Exits

Stanadyne Diesel Systems provides a good example of this problem and how it can be turned around. The "champion" of the JIT/TQM implementation decided to move off of center stage, leaving for a position as head of manufacturing. The void left by his decision was evident; the improvement effort bogged down as individuals, used to relying on the champion for guidance and direction, now had to rely on their own inner sense of what types of actions and results were desired.

It is quite likely the "champion" stepped offstage to actually force the learning process into the organization. Continuous improvement is not an issue of leadership. It is an embedded philosophy that guides ongoing activities. To make the final transition to a continuous improvement world, each manager had to learn how to apply the concept. Being placed on the firing line (that is, applying the concept) is the one sure way to drive this message home.

Stanadyne is a success story because, after some initial foundering and confusion, the organization did learn to apply the concepts. The champion, having moved off of center stage, still occupied an influential role and could nudge the learning process along in a less obvious way. The ultimate test of a change process is whether or not individual managers can apply and use the tools without intervention from management or the "scout" who led them to the new land. If the change agent doesn't step down, the change may end up being cosmetic—the "settlers" will stay at home.

The Basis for Establishing Continuous Improvement

To remove the change process from the political arena to a more productive level where action can occur requires more than good intentions. In fact, when an organization pursues continuous improvement, several key issues have to be recognized if success is to be achieved:

- Clear goals have to be identified.

- People have to be convinced that it is in their best interest to change.

- Organizational barriers to change must be overcome.

- Focus has to be expanded to include external, objective measures of performance that are driven by a clear understanding of customer needs.

- Management has to reinforce the change message continuously and consistently.

- The change process has to be depersonalized.

In other words, the change process itself has to be seen as objective if it is to provide the framework for the attainment of world-class competitive capability. Benchmarking is the tool that turns the fuzzy process of continuous improvement into an objective plan of action.

LEAPFROGGING CONTINUOUS IMPROVEMENT

Organizational change can occur in small steps or quantum leaps (see Figure 6.1). This chapter has gone into considerable detail about the way that benchmarking supports incremental change processes, but the story doesn't end there. By utilizing "best-in-class" benchmarking, organizations are leapfrogging the improvement process, moving the entire game to a new playing field.

Incremental changes (see Figure 6.2) can plateau off after a period of time, as the improvements gained from small changes to the existing system yield smaller and smaller benefits; the "law of diminishing returns" takes over. As long as the change process is constrained by existing assumptions and approaches, there is a limit to the amount of improvement that can be made. Most companies in the United States today have a long way to go before reaching this upper limit, but they will reach it if they faithfully pursue continuous improvement.

Best-in-class benchmarking, with its shift in perspective and assumptions about the optimum way to process or structure certain

Figure 6.1   Leaping quantum.

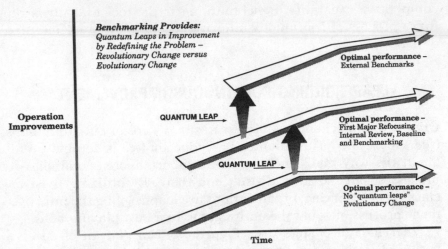

Figure 6.2 "Leapfrogging" continuous improvement.

activity networks, provides an organization with the tools necessary to leapfrog the improvement process. Figure 6.2 indicates that in doing so, best-in-class benchmarking changes the rules of the game, looking outside of accepted industry practice to recognize that each activity network has parallels in some quite unusual places. If a manufacturer wants to establish a "world-class" logistics capability, it can turn to the best in its industry or to the best in the world. "Best-in-class" may be Federal Express or United Parcel Service, depending on whether the transport is on the ground or in the air.

Redefining the Rules

> Wit is the sudden marriage of ideas which before their union were not perceived to have any relation.
>
> Mark Twain
> *Notebook*

Innovation is "a drastic improvement in the status quo as a result of a large investment in new technology or new equipment."[6] There is no doubt that innovation or drastic change can occur when new technology or equipment is involved, but it can be equally due to the use of new techniques or processes with the same set of physical resources. Just-in-time manufacturing (JIT-M) is perhaps the best example of the latter case. In most JIT-M implementations, very little money is spent on new equipment. Instead, existing machines and people are simply rearranged to match the assembly sequence followed by the product. By redefining the "best," or most effective and efficient way to organize the production process, companies are reaping large benefits from reduced work-in-process inventories, more rapid throughput (cycle time) and improved quality. Changing processes or changing the culture of an organization can have more far-reaching effects than simply tweaking its equipment and technology, because it changes the basic fiber of the social organization that uses these resources.

It is short-sighted to suggest that innovations can only come from new resources. Many a great chef has been born by simply redefining which set of "raw materials" in the kitchen belong together. Each new creation in the kitchen is in reality just the same old ingredients in a different package. Yet few would argue that a master chef will yield far different "results" from these "same old ingredients" than a five-year-old child. Same set of resources, but careful combination in the right amounts and in the right manner, separate a culinary masterpiece from an inedible porridge.

The goal is to attain greater effectiveness in the customer's eyes: using the best mix of resources possible both to maximize customer satisfaction and to provide strong economic rewards for the firm's investors and employees. Just because a certain structure or procedure has worked "well enough" for the past twenty years doesn't mean that major improvements aren't possible. But, it is doubtful that these opportunities will be seen if management looks no farther than its own borders or industry practice.

Rewarding Continuous Improvement

Continuous improvement is the result of sound teamwork, integration of the organization into activity networks, and the belief that no one is ever done learning and improving. This is a radical departure from the "meet standard" mentality that characterizes the modern organization. Throughout this chapter, benchmarking has been shown as a way to drive the message of continuous improvement home, yet one critical factor remains: "You get what you measure and reward." The measurement aspect of this has been addressed, but continuous improvement will not occur if the gains are not equally shared.

Implementing continuous improvement forces companies back against their basic belief set, starting with the central role played by individual effort and individual rewards. Continuous improvement works from an assumption of teamwork, a teamwork which is reinforced through the benchmarking process itself.

The transition to a cooperative workplace will not occur just because management wants it to or just because everyone more clearly understands the final goal. There must be an incentive for change that provides a middle point between the individual incentives that currently dominate the reward structures of organizations in the United States, Canada, and the UK and the total team-based incentive systems that can be found in Japan. Continuous improvement, as supported by a benchmarking-based measurement system, must reflect the context in which it develops.

Edward Lawler III, a well-known organizational researcher, suggests that the reward system in these "high-involvement workplaces" will be individualized along the dimension of skills and the rewards for skill improvements; performance-based, or all salary, in nature rather than piece-rate or hourly as currently practiced; egalitarian in their employment of *gain sharing*—participation of employees in the gains from continuous improvement efforts; and growth-oriented through ownership rights, flexible fringe benefits, participative appraisal, and fewer perquisites for all.[7] In other words, the *"continuously improving organization" cannot afford to grant special rights to the privileged few*. Doing so will negate any attempts to gain the active and open participation of individuals throughout the organization.

The privileges of rank, then, may well disappear in the egalitarian organization of the 1990s and beyond. Yet this should not be a trend resisted by American, Canadian, or British culture, dedicated to equality—or should it? It would be naïve to think that those individuals that have power and privilege today are going to freely and openly give them up "for the greater good." This would sound a bit too egalitarian to most. However, there will be a flattening out of the organization, as horizontal activity networks replace traditional line-and-staff organizations. There will still be chiefs and indians, but in the general meetings each will only have one vote. The JIT-M implementation at Eaton Corporation provides an example:[8]

> In putting in JIT, we had to have everyone willing to work with us. It couldn't be ordered from the top; it had to be done willingly. So we put it to a vote. The spread of JIT, and the development of new job classifications to support it, was presented to the workforce for their decision. If they had voted against it, we probably would have had to stop. They didn't. But each person voted based on their own conscience. And after the fact, those individuals who didn't want to get involved were allowed to fill the more traditional jobs that remained. You can't mandate continuous improvement; you can only suggest it. Then it's up to everyone else.

Individuals on the plant floor and in the back office are the ultimate winners in the game being undertaken. They will be assuming more responsibility, but with it will come increased control over their destiny and a larger share of the gains their efforts provide. Middle management is projected by some to be the loser, but this is not necessarily so. There is little doubt that the days of the large corporate staff are numbered, but instead of seeing the changes as a threat, middle managers in organization after organization are getting involved in value-added efforts that more fully utilize their existing skills, and are helping these individuals develop new tools and an ability to integrate that will serve their companies well in the competitive environment of the 1990s.

In fact, the company's very survival may rely on middle management's assumption of these new, challenging, and highly unstructured roles. The explorers and scouts are usually middle managers; if they disappear from the corporate frontier, the settlers will probably never venture out to the new lands. The gap between the top and the bottom of the organizational pyramid may be decreasing, but the webbing that will continue to hold the two layers together is an active, problem-solving middle management team.

BENCHMARKING

The real losers, then, are the naysayers . . . the dead-enders who will not try to change, with or without the facts so clearly provided by the benchmarking process. Benchmarking is the first step in an organizational innovation that promises to transform the organizational landscape forever. The explorers have found a new land, and the scouts are reporting back that the path ahead may be bumpy, but there is no alternative. They've begun to chart the course ahead, and are waiting for the settlers to arrive.

Neither a wise man nor a brave man lies down on the tracks of history to wait for the train of the future to run over him.

Dwight D. Eisenhower

Benchmarking Your Way to Continuous Improvement
What is benchmarking, then? It is a managerial climate comprised of three distinct elements:

1. Obsession with quality and continuous improvement.
2. Achievement of a spirit among the people that they are a vital part of a team.
3. The identification and correction of problems by means of data, not opinions, and with a focus on the process.

It is an integral part of the continuous improvement process leading to world-class competitive capability. Through its support of continuous improvement, total quality management, and total employee involvement, benchmarking leads to competitive advantage through the elimination of waste. Attaining excellence through small, incremental improvements requires constant benchmarking of where the organization is and what the best are doing. It sustains the efforts of supervisors and managers to encourage, guide, and support employees in the improvement process, all in a never-ending process where there is no "good enough," only "getting better."

> There is at bottom only one problem in the world and this is its name. How does one break through? How does one get into the open? How does one burst the cocoon and become a butterfly?
>
> Thomas Mann
> *Doctor Faustus*

7: LOOKING OUTWARD: THE BASICS OF COMPETITIVE AND INDUSTRY BENCHMARKING

> Competition means decentralized planning by many separate persons.
>
> F. August von Hayek

When most people think about benchmarking, they look to competitors or their industry for improvement ideas. In fact, many people suggest that benchmarking is not a new concept, but rather an elaboration of the competitive assessment techniques born in the 1950s. There truthfully are very few new ideas under the sun, but an existing idea applied under a different set of assumptions makes for a new set of practices and new knowledge. "Know thy enemy," then, is not the essence of modern benchmarking; instead, it focuses on the *processes* used by competitors, as well as industry trends, to identify opportunities for continuous improvement, not price cutting.

Is "catching up with the Joneses" a justifiable reason for undertaking benchmarking? Bob Camp, in a recent article, responded to this question in the following way:[1]

> You mean, "Aren't we just bringing companies up to the same level of mediocrity?"...First of all, that's a major attainment in and of itself. You don't want to overlook the benefit of doing just that. If all the companies in the U.S. pursued best practices function by function, we might have some major gains. Second, the layman's definition of benchmarking is finding and implementing best practices. You find best practices, but you innovatively implement them and that's where you get the extra mileage out of benchmarking.

Benchmarking, then, is *action-generating*, not simply scorecarding your position against your company's direct competitors. Competitive and industry benchmarking provide the details needed to catch up, and then surpass, the companies that are vying for your stakeholders and profits.

Competitive vs. Industry Benchmarking

Competitive benchmarking focuses on key production methods and characteristics that can provide a competitive advantage over a company's direct competitors. It is the most similar to traditional competitive assessment of all the benchmarking approaches, yet it is markedly different. The target isn't knowing the score but rather changing it. If Competitor A can deliver the product in two weeks while it takes us five, they have a competitive advantage. Knowing this fact is not comforting, but it is undoubtedly action-generating.

In a traditional setting this action may not be totally constructive (for example, existing manufacturing managers change jobs after receiving an exit "visa" from management that's sure it's a "people problem" solvable with new blood). Hiring the competitor's manufacturing vice president may lead to improvement, but changing people is a radical solution that can cause as many problems as it solves; it is a one-time change that may leave the underlying process as inadequate as it was before the "change" occurred.

Competitive benchmarking looks for problems in *the way the work is done*, not the people doing it. The objective is to catch up and surpass competitors' performance. The difference is in how this is accomplished. In a traditional setting, solutions are static, often people-centered, and seldom sustainable. Benchmarking transforms the change process into a continuous improvement effort focused on the process, utilizing the knowledge of existing employees to drive the change. It supports learning at the organizational level, which leads to continued innovation and change. So even though competitive benchmarking may look like its ancestors (competitive assessment), it is a far different approach with different results.

Industry benchmarking is used to establish performance standards and to detect trends in the competitive environment. While competitive benchmarking may include two or three of a firm's closest competitors, industry benchmarking looks for general trends across a much larger group of related firms. The best way to keep the two approaches separate is to remember that for each product a company may have one or two competitors, but as a company it *participates* with an entire conglomeration of firms with similar product lines or market segments. Industry benchmarking is a much more general procedure that sets a firm against companies with similar interests and similar technologies, attempting to identify product and service trends rather than current market share rankings.

The key thing to keep in mind is that competitive benchmarking is narrowly focused on the firm's performance against two or three companies that sell the same products to roughly the same markets. Industry benchmarking is broader, focuses on trends rather than existing competitive positions, and is used to examine subsystem performance (for example, delivery channel responsiveness). The line between the two approaches is vaguely traced in the sand; where does "targeted" study give way to "trending"? There is no answer to this question today, nor need there be. As long as the competitive lens is adopted, its magnification can remain a matter of taste.

HISTORICAL DEVELOPMENT OF COMPETITIVE ANALYSIS

The only things that evolve by themselves in an organization are disorder, friction, and malperformance.

Peter Drucker

Americans thrive on competition. While some social critics may decry this statement, it remains a cultural fact nonetheless. What makes competitive and industry benchmarking interesting is the multiple dilemmas or twists it creates in the competitive arena. The three major issues in this area are (1) foreign practices, (2) antitrust legislation in the United States, and (3) knowledge vs. collusion (or, leveling the playing field).

On the Inside Looking Out

It is no secret that the United States funded its own competitive troubles. Under the auspices of the Marshall Act, following World War II the industrial sectors of Germany and Japan were rebuilt using predominantly American financing and American industrial expertise. Deming was one of the many American experts who augmented the financial support. Bringing with him an entire range of quality improvement techniques and concepts, he helped establish the competitive prowess of the Japanese. The Germans, already known for precision engineering, did not need this type of support. The capital alone was an adequate boost to regaining their competitive ability.

By the early 1970s the impact of Japanese and German companies and products were being felt in the American marketplace. The American steel industry was one of their first "victims." Industry by industry the strength of these competitors began to be felt. Some companies, like Harley-Davidson, at first succumbed to the threat and then fought back to regain their original markets. Others quietly faded into competitive oblivion.

Few would undo the sequence of events that have led to the current competitive crisis in the United States. Today global competition is a fact of corporate life; it can be discussed but not changed. The only constructive questions management can ask surround the issues of strategic response to these challenges. Since "business as usual" will quite likely lead to no business at all, changing products, processes, and management techniques is not an option but a requirement for survival.

Benchmarking was developed by Xerox in response to the competitive threat it faced from the Japanese. Launched in 1979, competitive benchmarking at Xerox initially focused on unit manufacturing cost. To accomplish this, "reverse engineering" was performed on competitive products to compare operating capabilities, features, and mechanical characteristics.[2] The phrase "product quality and feature comparison" was used by Xerox to describe this process.

When the benchmarking process was formalized, Xerox had to turn to its Japanese affiliate, Fuji-Xerox, for help. Why was it necessary for Xerox to turn to its Japanese affiliate? Several reasons are given by Xerox managers, including the need to understand the difference between the costs of a Xerox product made in the United States and one made in Japan (in other words, internal benchmarking). It didn't take long to determine that manufacturing costs were higher in the United States. In fact, competitors were selling copiers for less than it cost Xerox to make them.

Armed with this knowledge, Xerox began pushing for answers. A corporation-wide effort to understand internal cost structures and performance was instituted in 1981. Prior to this date, comparisons had only been done on internal operations; after 1981 Xerox turned to its competitors for information. External benchmarking was instituted as the basis for evaluating and targeting continuous improvement. Today Xerox has regained and even surpassed its pre-1979 competitive position. It continues to promote benchmarking in the drive for continuous improvement and competitive advantage.

Antitrust and Competitive Assessment

While Xerox spokespersons suggest that reverse engineering and knowledge gained about Japanese manufacturing processes underscored its adoption of benchmarking, there is an inherent specter of antitrust litigation in any discussion of competitive or industry analysis. Antitrust legislation got its birth in the Sherman Act of 1890, which banned any trust or other business combination that interfered with interstate or foreign trade, monopolized, or attempted or conspired to create a monopoly. Most importantly, the Sherman Act was interpreted to make any fixing of prices, division of markets, or similar collusive activities among competitors illegal—even a crime. The breakup of Standard Oil into 30 separate competing firms in 1911 was one of the government's major applications of the Sherman Act.

The reach of antitrust legislation did not stop with Standard Oil. The Clayton Antitrust Law of 1914 made it illegal for corporations to group together under interlocking boards of directors. This law also prohibits several unfair business practices that tend to decrease competition in certain circumstances. For example, large firms might, to eliminate smaller rivals, buy the stock of (or, as the result of a loophole-closing amendment in 1956, merge or form joint ventures by other means with) their competitors; force their customers to sign long-term exclusive dealing agreements; or make them buy goods they did not want to get the goods they needed. The Clayton Act, as amended by the Robinson-Patman Act, outlaws price discrimination that gives favored buyers an advantage over others. In order to protect the free market, then, the government instituted a series of laws that attempted to eliminate collusion among "competing" firms.

The threat of litigation, and the associated enormous legal costs and potential damages that might result through treble damages and criminal penalties, stopped much communication between companies in the same industry in the United States. Collusion may have been curtailed, but so was industry innovation. Only recently have the United States antitrust laws been amended to recognize the legitimacy of some joint research and development (the National Cooperative Research Act of 1984), but the degree of protection afforded even for this technical and scientific cooperation is limited. The basic features of this act received wide bipartisan support because of a belief that performance of many American industries was lagging in comparison with technological developments emanating from other countries, particularly Japan and parts of Europe.[3]

Among Japanese companies, information is freely shared. In fact, the government supports and encourages the sharing of research and development breakthroughs among competing Japanese firms, and also funds industry consortia to focus on establishing competitive advantage in certain markets and technologies. High-resolution television is one outcome of these government-supported efforts in Japan. In Japan, then, sharing of market information is government-sponsored rather than discouraged.

This open attitude was also present in Europe. However, European companies no longer have the freedom or encouragement to cooperate comparable to that of the Japanese. EEC antitrust rules are beginning to approach, and in a few areas even exceed, the severity of U.S. rules. Such rules are considered more a part of an integrated, overall economic policy than those in the U.S.

Knowledge vs. Collusion

These major policy differences do not translate into a level playing field for firms competing at home and abroad. Many in the U.S. argue that antitrust legislation, developed to protect the competitive underdog in the heydey of American manufacturing, is now crippling those it set out to protect. If the United States is to compete in a global marketplace, rules and regulations born of the isolationist period may have to be overturned.

The real issue, though, is whether or not knowledge about competitive practice is the same as collusion among competitors.

The U.S. antitrust laws are concerned with exchanges of information that lead to price fixing or limitations on competition that would otherwise exist; they should not be concerned with exchanges of information that allow more vigorous competition. Knowledge is information applied to problems, and the subsequent solutions that arise. It is understanding that helps guide decision making and focus attention on critical success factors for survival and competitive advantage. It is not collusion.

Collusion suggests a victim—that individuals or companies join together to discriminate against customers or weaker counterparts in order to secure additional revenues and market share or to distort the economy by interfering with the optimal functioning of competition and reducing output. It suggests price setting, not the price-taking environment facing American companies today. Antitrust legislation, then, appears to have outlived its usefulness. American industries, for the most part, no longer have sufficient international market power to set prices and define the conditions for distribution of their products. Instead, they are frantically clinging to existing market share as foreign competitors (who are less hampered by antitrust concerns) chip away at them.

Benchmarking and Antitrust

How do the antitrust laws apply to benchmarking, then? The answer is that, if properly conducted, they don't. Unlike competitive assessment, benchmarking is focused on improving the processes by which goods are made, distributed, or serviced. The focus is not on market share or price but rather on "best practice." Benchmarking lets a company know how far away it is from "best practice" and what types of processes are used in other firms, but it doesn't delve into specific cost factors, prices, or related issues. This position is underscored by the following statement:

> At base, benchmarking is really just a formalized way of managing change....Denial is not an unusual reaction for a company stunned by the gap between its operational performance and that of a best-practice company. In fact, it is the typical first step in the rehabilitation process.[4]

Unless change, or continuous improvement, is also forbidden by antitrust legislation, it appears that benchmarking best practice is secure from government oversight for now.

In fact, if the required "rehabilitation" of American competitiveness is to occur, the government may actually have to assume a new tack, namely, supporting more "communication" between competing firms. As long as the conversations stay away from price setting, and as long as the firms are actively competing at home and abroad against foreign firms, it seems that society will benefit rather than lose from the "collusion." The key is to remain focused on the *process*, to use the information to effect *organizational change*, and to search for *best practices* across a multitude of operational and support functions.

Costs are driven by the products, processes, resources, people, and traditions that combine to create the modern corporation. Understanding how other companies have solved this organizational design problem can help reduce the total cost package faced by a firm, enabling it to compete more effectively in the global marketplace. Without the ability to compete on a level playing ground, with the same types of information and informational resources as their foreign counterparts, American companies remain behind the eight ball, waiting for the fatal blow to occur. While that phrase is perhaps a bit melodramatic, there have been enough corporate fatalities of late to suggest that something has to change. The United States competes as a nation against other nations, all searching for the profits and increased standard of living that competitive success provides. That is the playing field and game that is being played today with ever-heightening vigor by companies scattered across the globe.

Before leaving the area of benchmarking and antitrust, then, what is the verdict? Although this area hasn't been specifically addressed by the government, what most experts are saying is that as long as benchmarking firms aren't asking for price information or data on the future plans (that is, strategic objectives) of their competitors, they are safe from antitrust worries. As long as the company remains focused on the *processes used* rather than the prices of its competitors, antitrust legislation does not apply. If this line is crossed, then benchmarking isn't at issue; monopolistic practice is. Benchmarking is focused on *initiating changes in processes and procedures* to support continuous improvement as judged against best practice in an industry or function. When properly conducted, it is far removed from the concerns of the Sherman and Clayton Acts.

Because of the severity of antitrust penalties and the complexity of some antitrust theories, legal counsel should ordinarily be sought in connection with any competitive or industry benchmarking initiatives. But it should not be assumed that the antitrust laws will make the project a complete non-starter.

JUMPING BARRIERS TO BENCHMARKING INFORMATION

> In the country of the blind the one-eyed king can still goof up.
>
> Laurence J. Peter

> As life is action and passion, it is required of man that he should share the passion and action of his time, at peril of being judged not to have lived.
>
> Oliver Wendell Holmes, Jr.

It's comforting to know that carefully structured benchmarking is unlikely to end in a trip to the federal courthouse, but that fact alone is unlikely to make one's competitors willing to cooperate. Getting competitors to cooperate with a benchmarking study is one of the great challenges facing any organization. That is why companies often turn to outside help when they embark on this type of project. Buying expertise, legitimacy, and third-party help to collect the data and interface with competitors, a company can shave months of effort off of the benchmarking cycle of learning.

Industry benchmarking can be achieved using an industry association. This decreases the cost of the benchmarking exercise to the participating firms, but it can rarely be directed to the specific issues and concerns of one company. Association-based studies, then, can provide a reference point for a company but cannot replace the targeted efforts of one firm or a consortium of firms.

One such study was sponsored by the Association for Services Management International. The objectives of the study, entitled "Service Operation Strategies of the 90s," were as follows:

■ To identify operating practices and philosophies employed by some of today's leading service organizations in both North America and Europe

■ To highlight best demonstrated practices from the diagnostic organizational appraisals

■ To understand the effects of future market trends on the application of service strategy

The diagnostic was designed to ensure that the benchmarking elements were measured on an equal basis across all participants. The study covered performance reporting, quality improvement, product design, logistics, and dispatch and scheduling.

In some situations, then, industry associations are being asked to serve as clearinghouses for benchmarking information and studies performed by its members and others. As a clearinghouse the industry association has to establish guidelines for benchmarking to ensure that members can understand the drivers affecting the process and establish the requisite level of comparability or "apples-to-apples" analysis in each situation. These guidelines are necessary, as industry associations don't have the manpower to research the details about each benchmarking study that is being performed by its members.

Where does that leave the company wishing to undertake any type of benchmarking project? First, management can put together its own benchmarking task force or team to coordinate benchmarking efforts and to visit companies that have successfully implemented benchmarking in the past. This knowledge, combined with the support of the industry association, can help break down the barriers to competitive and industry benchmarking. Often the key factor is the sensitivity of the benchmarking information to the strategic position of the firm, as suggested by the following comments:[5]

While some companies have had good experiences benchmarking within their own industry, it is usually in staff, not line, functions. Bentzel (of Alcoa) says he was surprised by the easy access he had to competitors. But the functions he was benchmarking should be taken into consideration. "In the nonmanufacturing areas, direct competitors have very little problem talking about such topics as closing the books, order entry, or any other processes or subprocesses."

By the same token, Dallas-based Oryx Energy got a surprisingly favorable response when it decided to benchmark its competition in the Gulf of Mexico, but only on routine operations. ... Thirteen of the 15 companies Oryx approached participated in the project, which benchmarked everything from the staffing of offshore platforms to automation to catering. Note, however, that Oryx was focusing on operating practices at existing wells and not on top-secret information.

Oryx obtained critical information from its competitors, which it used to reorganize its Gulf of Mexico operations. It is quite likely they offered to share the results of the study with these same firms, providing them with information at little or no cost that could help shave significant dollars from the cost structure of their firms.

Sometimes the request for such information can fall on deaf ears, though. Most benchmarking experts suggest in these cases turning to some type of consulting firm for help, at least for the first study. Whether this will work for every company is also a question, but after the initial study is done, the company may be able to launch a consortium that will make future access more reliable. In the next chapter, Janssen Corporation's success in taking this route is described in detail. The vital factor is that access to competitive information about processes is possible; it simply has to be clearly focused on nonstrategic issues and concern itself with the processes used to obtain results, not the results themselves.

A Learning Process

Competitive and industry benchmarking represent potential profits for participating firms. Conducting them requires patience, a willingness to learn, and an open mind about the source and definition of best practice. While competitive and industry benchmarking may seem the most obvious way to begin, it inevitably leads to best-in-class benchmarking. Learning about benchmarking comes from doing it: application and elaboration of the concept within your own organization.

Becoming the "best of the best" requires gradual exploration of the terrain, a willingness to accept the not-so-pleasant realities of how your organization stacks up against other, best-practice firms, and the use of that information to refocus existing efforts and plan for continuous improvement. Gaining this knowledge is a learning process that begins with the analysis of existing practices (internal benchmarking), moves on through a comparison of your company's performance against its competitors (competitive and industry benchmarking), and comes full circle as individual "value chain" performance (for example, customer service and support) is evaluated against best practice for that role or process (best-in-class). Each link in the benchmarking chain accelerates the improvement cycle that underlies value creation. Without these external "shoves," it is easy to settle into complacency, bureaucracy, and organizational decline.

Knowledge is the only instrument of production that is not subject to diminishing returns.

J. M. Clark

APPLYING COMPETITIVE AND INDUSTRY BENCHMARKING

There are situations where competitive and industry benchmarking makes sense, and times when it is not the approach to use. These two "sister" benchmarking concepts should be used whenever

1. Products or customer segments are the focal point of current questioning.
2. The process is related to an inherent feature, such as a rule or regulation, of the industry.
3. Competitive problems are preventing the firm from reaching its performance goals.

Competitive stress is the trigger for most initial benchmarking projects. Although some are drawn to it through a love for fads, this love can turn into a nightmare as the harsh realities of a company's true competitive status are revealed in the course of the project. While benchmarking can be undertaken "casually," it cannot be used effectively in this mode. Unless management is willing to take the tough first steps to address the weaknesses that benchmarking reveals, there is little value to be gained from it. It's hard to ignore the facts, though, once they're presented.

The benefits of benchmarking stem from its objectivity and the undeniably strong influence of facts and figures in American business culture. Managers who live and die by the numbers are more likely to be convinced of the need to change by benchmarking results than by any other means. Often grabbed as a lifeline by a company facing rapid competitive decline, benchmarking triggers the cycle of continuous improvement required to survive in a global economy.

Complacency is the root cause of competitive decline. When funds are plentiful, individual managers seem to lose track of the fact that customer satisfaction is the only thing keeping them in business. Struggles over budgets dominate the corporate landscape, escalating the internal focus, or myopia, that cuts the company off from its stakeholders. Successful companies, like successful people, can become arrogant, losing sight of the people and values that led to their good fortune. As with individuals, companies are also brought up short by adverse events that shatter the illusions of invulnerability and bring reality back into focus. Success is a temporary event unless it is pursued as a goal never to be reached. Undertaking a benchmarking project can be a humbling experience, but humility, or a belief that one can always do things a little bit better, separates the winners from the "also-rans."

Benchmarking is a self-improvement and management process that must be continuous to be effective. It cannot be performed once and disregarded thereafter on the belief that the task is done. It must be a continuous process, because industry practices constantly change. Industry leaders constantly get stronger....In an environment of constant change, complacency is fatal.

Robert C. Camp
Benchmarking: 10

8: JANSSEN PHARMACEUTICA: FOCUSING THROUGH COMPETITIVE ANALYSIS

Type of Benchmarking Used: External, competitive
Purpose for use: Analysis of relative cost structures
  and productivity for administrative staff; Gain understanding of relative value of centralized versus
  decentralized organization of administrative areas
Area examined: Administrative overhead

Lessons Learned:

Participation in a benchmarking study can provide a valuable sanity check for internal benchmarking procedures
as well as targeting areas where improvement needs to
occur.

Administrative overhead is not confined to those functional units traditionally viewed as overhead. Administrative costs are spread throughout the organization.

Value added can be measured, and applied, in the administrative overhead area. The goal is to eliminate non–
value-added overhead throughout the organization.

Benchmarking is just the beginning. There is a need
to refine the analysis, establish industry forums, and expand the study to include best-in-class analysis to identify
bottleneck, or less competitive, areas. Competitive benchmarking, then, helps to identify and prioritize opportunities for improvement.

Competitive benchmarking is the first step in securing
an understanding of the relative performance of an organization. In this case, the focus on administrative overhead
provides a backdrop or area of concern that is common to
all companies in all industries.

THE SETTING

Janssen Pharmaceutica (Janssen) is a wholly owned subsidiary of Johnson & Johnson, which develops and manufactures over-the-counter drugs, prescription drugs, and biologics. With sales in excess of $325 million per year, it is a company known for its focus on research and development as the basis for competitive advantage. Significant resources are dedicated to ongoing research and development projects, making Janssen one of the most aggressive pharmaceutical research companies in the world.

Over the past few years, Johnson & Johnson has supported internal benchmarking and analysis of its administrative overhead area, identified as its "Achilles heel" by various Wall Street analysts. The company, as a whole, understands that this area is a top candidate for performance improvement. Coming from a tradition of decentralization, Johnson & Johnson management has undertaken an analysis of the feasibility of selective centralization of critical administrative functions in order to reduce the level of duplication (of both costs and efforts) inherent in a decentralized strategy (see Figure 8.1).

Round 1: Participating in a Benchmarking Study

Late in 1989, Janssen management was asked to participate in a competitive benchmarking study of administrative overhead in the pharmaceutical industry sponsored by one of its competitors. Having been assured by the benchmarking "facilitator" (an independent consulting firm) that all companies would remain anonymous, David Sheffield, Vice President of Finance for Janssen's United States operations, agreed to participate.

The rationale behind the heightened concern over administrative overhead in the pharmaceutical industry is captured in Figure 8.2. Industry pressures in the areas of intensified government regulation; loss of patents; spiraling marketing costs; increased emphasis on product differentiation; escalating research and development costs; and pricing pressures from government, health agencies, and organized procurement groups, as well as the impact of generic drugs on product profitabilies were all pushing toward an increased focus on trimming administrative overhead. It was increasingly obvious that to remain competitive, pharmaceutical firms would have to focus their spending, enhance the

Issue

Ongoing recalibration of administrative benchmarks including research and development

Situation

Participated in a competitive administrative benchmark study in 1989
Continued benchmarking efforts and analysis within Johnson & Johnson
Identified additional issues, specifically research & development
Wanted to establish ongoing external dialog and promote additional benchmarking efforts

Research/Findings

Key Interviews
- Financial Directions
- CFOs

Measurements
- Administrative costs as percent of revenue
- Cost per employee
- Employee cost to total cost
- Administrative productivity
- Allocation practices

Changes
- Conducted forum to present findings and meet counterparts
- Identified areas to analyze further internally
- Identified potential future benchmarking studies

Figure 8.1   Janssen Pharmaceutica: competitive benchmarking objectives.

BENCHMARKING

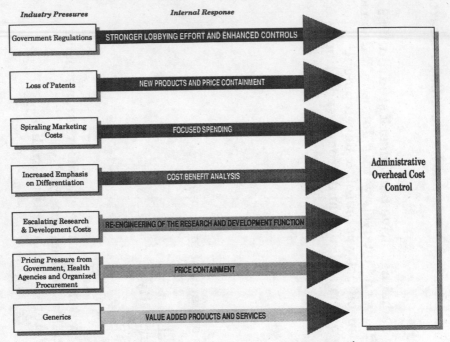

Figure 8.2   Janssen Pharmaceutica: rationale.

value-added component of overhead deployment, and push toward increasing the research and development "yield" in terms of new products, price containment, and time to market.

The study was seen as an opportunity to gain outside benchmarks, and information, to help Janssen tackle the tangled web of administrative overhead and identify opportunities for improvement. The impetus for the decision to start looking for external benchmarking information was described by Sheffield in the following way:

In a word, the impetus was competition. We've always fared well when dealing with competition, but we recognize that doing business the way we've always done it is no guarantee of success. To remain competitive today you have to have an external perspective; you need to identify those world-class companies that are handling their business differently than you are. From having access to that kind of information you learn things, pick up new ways of doing business, and can use that and other information to become more competitive.

Janssen, then, was unwilling to rest on its laurels. It knew that it was currently in a strong competitive position, but it was also wise enough to know that in a competitive global marketplace standing still would put it at the back of the pack very rapidly. The only way to stay ahead in the competitive game was to be constantly looking for ways to change and improve. If that meant emulating best practice in competitive firms, then that would be the path chosen. The key was getting an action plan in place that would lead to improvement, given that Janssen had already learned as much as possible from its internal benchmarking partners at Johnson & Johnson.

In the initial study, Janssen was a "taker" of the information. It could not tailor the questions or the approach to its own needs. However, management knew that this was a quick and efficient way to begin focusing their own efforts in the administrative overhead area.

The areas of administration covered in the first study were finance, general production, information technology, corporate services and site management, general marketing, and corporate administration. Obviously, Janssen also considered research and development to be a critical administrative cost, but it had to accept the fact that the information on its relative performance in this area would not be obtained from this study. The information that would be provided by the study included the following:

- 1988 head count in administrative areas
- 1988 employee costs
- 1988 gross operating costs, before charge-outs
- Background company information
- Internal "customers" of administrative services
- Types of administrative services provided
- Methods used to allocate administrative costs

This information would give Janssen a good understanding of its relative position in thcsc kcy areas of performance measurement for administrative overhead.

The first study was based predominantly on questionnaires. Out of an initial "hit list" of 20 pharmaceutical firms, 10 companies eventually participated. Approximate sales dollars and head counts were used to anchor the benchmarking study and results (see Figure 8.3). Janssen proved to be one of the midsize compa-

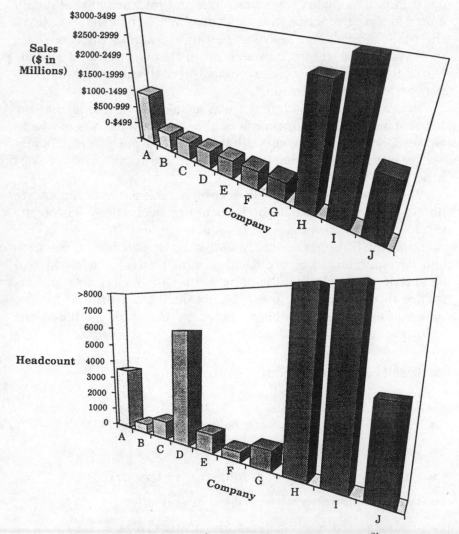

Figure 8.3   Janssen Pharmaceutica: company profiles.

nies in the study in terms of total sales, with a fairly low head count level. The final sample, then, appeared to break into two halves: midsize and very large pharmaceutical firms.

The 10 pharmaceutical firms responding in this study were evenly split between domestic United States and foreign ownership. Relatedly, 50 percent maintained decentralized management structures, while 20 percent were centralized and 30 percent used hybrid structures (i.e., a mix of centralized and decentralized functions). Of those participating, 50 percent reported that their dominant industry affiliation was "ethical [that is, requiring a prescription] and over-the-counter pharmaceuticals." 20 percent of the remaining dollarized sales were in biologics, 10 percent in health care supplies, and 20 percent in miscellaneous categories.

The first interesting information provided by the study was the relative distribution of "full-scope" versus "limited-scope" service profiles. In line with the decentralized management structures, 60 percent of the firms responded that administrative services were focused on "full-scope" breadth of services defined at the strategic business unit level. In other words, each business unit, as a customer, was receiving a full range of support services.

In order to ensure that an "apples to apples" comparison could be made across the participating firms, the study also detailed the way the various major support areas mapped to specific functions or activities (see Figure 8.4). No matter how the target firms

Finance	Information Technology	General Marketing	General Production	Service & Site Managment	Corporate Administration
Controller's Office Acquisitions & Financial Analysis Treasurer's Office	Information Technology	ProductMarketing Physical Distribution Distribution/ Customer Affairs Marketing Administration New Product Management Promotions	Technical Operation Administration Technology Production Engineering Import/Export Plant Site Administration	Purchasing Engineering Administrative Services	Corporate Administration External Affairs Corporate Law Human Resources Office of the Chief Operating Officer

Figure 8.4   Function-to-component mapping.

"classified" their own operations, the study consistently placed the noted functions inside of the support service area. This allowed the study sponsors to compare cost per function performed, rather than take a risk that different companies would use unique terminology or function clustering that would make comparisons impossible.

Initial Results

In reviewing the initial results, Janssen management were encouraged. Their informal assessment of their competitive management of administrative overhead was confirmed. Among its peer companies, Janssen was delivering the same services with fewer people and fewer dollars than average. The distribution of and allocation methods for these costs varied, as suggested by Figure 8.5 and Figure 8.6.

Across the board, Janssen was faring well against its competitors. Yet its managers didn't feel as though the study was giving them the information they really wanted, as Dave Sheffield commented:

> When we got the report back, we obviously reviewed it to see how we fared, to look for the best companies, and related issues, area by area. In some areas we were encouraged; others became opportunity areas. We seemed to be doing all right in the administrative overhead area in general but weren't as good in the marketing area.
>
> What was interesting, though, was that the results could make you either comfortable or uncomfortable, but they didn't really give you much more than that. The report was like a scorecard: you end up knowing the score and how you rank, but it didn't tell you what you could do to improve. We didn't really know how the others were doing business. So the first study was "Let's get some data and see how we look"–focused, like a snapshot.

Even the snapshot was blurred for Janssen, though. Since a significant portion of their administrative costs were driven by research and development, they wanted a bit more information before they embarked on the next stage of the benchmarking path: developing programs for continuous improvement.

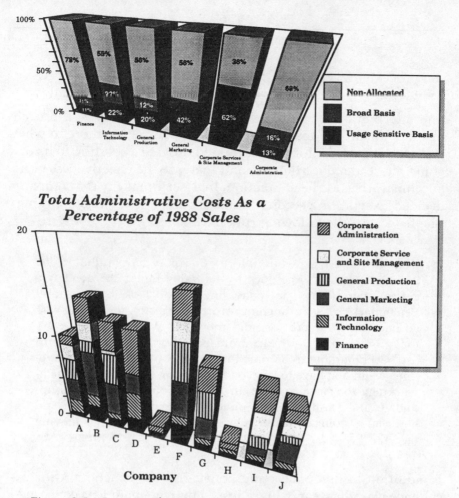

Total Administrative Costs As a Percentage of 1988 Sales

Figure 8.5   Janssen Pharamceutica: analysis of administration cost.

COMPONENT	ALLOCATION METHODS	USAGE SENSITIVE	FREQUENCY	TYPE OF DATA
FINANCE	• Gross Operating Expense	–	Monthly	Budget
	• Percentage Of Transactions	Yes	Monthly	Budget
INFORMATION TECHNOLOGY	• Actual Hours, CPU Seconds	Yes	Monthly	Actual
	• Gross Operating Expense	–	Monthly	Actual Budget
GENERAL MARKETING	• Product Cost	Yes	Monthly	Actual
	• Units Shipped	Yes	Monthly	Actual
	• Number Of Orders	Yes	Monthly	Actual
	• Gross Operating Expenses	–	Monthly	Actual
GENERAL PRODUCTION	• Square Footage	–	Semi-annually	Actual
	• Actual Hours	Yes	Monthly	Actual
	• Estimated Usage	Yes	Monthly	Budget
CORPORATE SERVICE & SITE MANAGEMENT	• Actual Hours	Yes	Monthly	Actual Budget
	• Number Of Employees	–	Monthly	Budget
CORPORATE ADMINISTRATION	• Actual Hours (estimated)	Yes	Semi-annually	Budget
	• Gross Operating Expense	–	Monthly	Budget

Figure 8.6   Allocation methods.

STAGE TWO: REFINING THE DATA

The information from the first benchmarking study had proven of value to Janssen management, but it had served more to whet their appetites for information than to provide a solution to its ongoing quest to reduce the cost and increase the effectiveness of its administrative overhead function. In describing why the company decided to sponsor a second round of competitive benchmarking, Sheffield gave the following rationale:

> Keep in mind that, while information may have value at one point in time, as time goes by its value fades. We don't target to where things are today, but instead look to the future. Benchmarking is an ongoing process; it's not something you do once, fix your process, and move on. What is best-in-class today is not best 3–5 years from now. So, if you are going to use benchmarking to become more competitive, it is not a one-time event. You have to keep on monitoring, and keep on benchmarking. You have to have an information source that is up-to-date and valid in terms of identifying where you are and how you're doing, because you're always shooting at a moving target.

In addition to this underlying belief that the benchmark for excellence was always moving, Janssen management was concerned that leaving research and development out of the picture was illogical in an industry that lived and died by the effectiveness of its research laboratories. On average, pharmaceutical companies were spending 7 to 10 percent of their sales dollars on the administration of their research and development efforts. That was too big a piece of the puzzle to leave unexplored.

In the second study, 15 of 50 contacted companies participated. The results once again supported Janssen's competitive position in the administrative overhead area. Its total administrative costs as a percent of sales was 19.5 percent versus 28.6 percent for its peer group and 24 percent for the more general sample of firms studied. Conversely, Janssen dedicated 9.8 percent of its sales dollars to research and development administrative costs, compared to 10.5 percent for its peer group and 7 percent for the more general industry sample. While the total dollars in this area were significant, strong research capability was a defined critical success factor for Janssen. It would not be an area targeted for cost/performance improvement.

On the other hand, the second study confirmed the evidence gathered in the first study: Janssen appeared to have opportunities for cost reduction in the corporate administration and general marketing areas. In both of these, Janssen's relative expenditures exceeded those of its peers. Sheffield knew the problem went even deeper than the study suggested, though:

> We wanted other companies in Johnson & Johnson to also begin looking at overhead in a broader context. We wanted to try and educate our senior management about the fact that administrative costs exist everywhere—if they aren't doing research and development, don't directly sell the goods, or don't make it, the costs are overhead.

Just categorizing overhead by function, then, did not seem adequate. Sheffield and his management team knew that overhead is spread around "direct cost" areas, that everyone is involved in administration to some degree, and that these are the hidden costs that have to be examined for their value-added component, trimmed, or eliminated.

Returning to the results of the second study, Janssen was able to get a fuller rating of its performance against competitors when it was in the driver's seat as study sponsor (see Figures 8.7 and 8.8). In fact, being able to pick out "peers," or direct competitors, provided Janssen with significantly better data to analyze its position. As suggested by Figure 8.7, then, Janssen had three "peer" firms in the study: companies G, M, and O. In looking into the detailed breakdown of administrative cost distribution [Figure 8.8], Janssen was spending a smaller percentage of its sales dollar on the finance and corporate services and site management than its peers, and in the mid-to low-range on corporate administration, information technology, and the office of the Chief Operating Officer. Finally, Janssen placed on the high end for research and development, as well as general marketing costs.

Obviously, their performance in the research and development area was good news to Janssen. Given that this area was a defined

BENCHMARKING

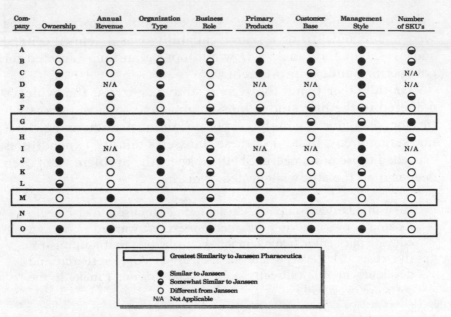

Company	Ownership	Annual Revenue	Organization Type	Business Role	Primary Products	Customer Base	Management Style	Number of SKU's
A	●	◕	◕	◕	○	●	●	◕
B	○	○	◕	◕	●	●	●	◕
C	◕	○	●	○	◕	◕	●	N/A
D	●	N/A	◕	○	N/A	N/A	●	N/A
E	●	◕	◕	◕	○	○	◕	◕
F	●	○	○	◕	◕	○	◕	○
G	●	●	●	◕	●	◕	●	●
H	●	○	●	◕	●	○	●	◕
I	●	N/A	●	◕	N/A	N/A	●	N/A
J	●	○	●	◕	●	○	●	○
K	●	○	●	◕	○	○	◕	○
L	◕	○	○	○	○	○	●	○
M	○	●	●	●	●	●	○	○
N	○	○	○	○	○	○	○	○
O	●	●	○	●	○	●	●	○

☐ Greatest Similarity to Janssen Pharaceutica

● Similar to Janssen
◕ Somewhat Similar to Janssen
○ Different from Janssen
N/A Not Applicable

Figure 8.7   Janssen Pharmaceutica: *company comparisons.*

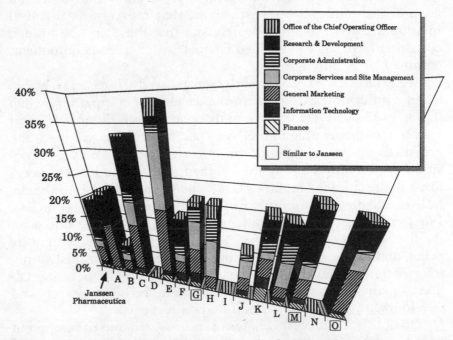

Office of the Chief Operating Officer
Research & Development
Corporate Administration
Corporate Services and Site Management
General Marketing
Information Technology
Finance
Similar to Janssen

Figure 8.8   Janssen Pharmaceutica: *total administrative costs as a percentage of 1990 sales.*

"critical success factor" for their current strategy, it wasn't targeted as a high priority for reduction efforts. On the other hand, there was general agreement that Janssen's general marketing costs needed attention.

Putting the Information to Work

Competitive benchmarking helped Janssen prioritize its improvement efforts but could provide little guidance on how it was going to trim costs from this area. It was also clear that the dollars recorded as marketing costs were understated: marketing support costs were known to be scattered throughout the administrative overhead area. What was needed, then, was a clearer understanding of the *process* used to manage marketing efforts in other companies. This finding led Janssen to take a unique tack with its benchmarking efforts: firms that participated in the second study were invited to attend an industry forum to discuss overhead issues.

The motivation behind the forum concept was described by Sheffield in the following way:

> The initial idea came out of the need to take some action to get behind the data in the study. Having the information was fine as a scorecard and to get a fix by functional area where you stood against your competitors, but it didn't tell us where to go from there. So we'll be using the forum to present the results, to bring the participating parties together, and to give them an opportunity to network and talk to others about how they're doing business, and to learn from that.
>
> I've found that having this data doesn't automatically lead to doing anything with it; it can make you happy or sad, but not much smarter. You can't immediately go after the areas where you need to improve, because you don't know how the other companies work. If you are going to go through the benchmarking effort, you have to remember that it's only a starting point. You need to do something with the information once you get it. The forum is one approach for taking and turning data into action. Networking with the forum participants will help us do the same thing.

Obviously, one of the first questions raised, as the forum idea was explored, was the antitrust implications. After looking into the issue, it became clear that antitrust wasn't applicable. As noted by Sheffield, "In the administrative overhead area you're not swapping trade secrets, you're simply trading information about how you do work." Since the forum would focus on overhead administration practices and avoid all discussions of strategy, pricing, and product costs, Janssen's management felt relatively secure in sponsoring the industry meeting.

That doesn't mean that Janssen hasn't already encountered barriers to its "information sharing" approach. But they are pushing forward, using their external benchmarking facilitator to ensure that the correct signals are given to their competitors, the government, and other outside sources about the focus and intent of the industry forum.

Moving Toward Best-in-Class Performance

Embraced as a tool for continuous improvement, competitive benchmarking is helping Janssen focus its attention on those parts of its administrative function where it appears to be using outdated processes and procedures to complete its work. The value of the study has come from a better understanding of where they need to improve, not from where Janssen is doing well. Competitive benchmarking is being used as a tool for action, not for avoidance:

> Some people take the benchmarking information and put it in a file if it doesn't look good. You can do that, but it's not going to make you competitive, and it will catch up with you in the end. You want to surface the critical information, not to make people look good or bad, but rather to learn how to get better. If people aren't willing to share here, then they won't be adding value to the process. You need to understand what you are doing and how, looking for ideas on what you are doing, and need to do, within your organization to get more competitive. Benchmarking has to focus on making the organization better; even if you score well, and are rated a star in every area, it's not a flag to wave in front of your boss. It's a trigger for constructive change—that's where the value can be gained.

Benchmarking, whether done internally, externally against competitors, or in light of best-in-class practice, costs money. Unless resources expended are parlayed into performance improvements, the dollars are wasted. The objective, then, is to learn how to do things better. Every company can make improvements in the way it conducts its business; there are no exceptions to this fact. A company that is rated "best in class" on one criterion may be performing very poorly on another.

Competitive benchmarking, then, is a tool for identifying and prioritizing improvement efforts. It is a continuous process, because the competition is unlikely to be standing still, with the performance measure constantly being raised.

ADMINISTRATIVE OVERHEAD: ISSUES TO REMEMBER

Janssen's administrative overhead analysis provides a point of departure for almost any modern corporation. It is a fact of life that creeping layers of bureaucracy have added to the "rigid" cost structures of American companies, trimming profits from the bottom line and placing increasing pressure on manufacturing and marketing to enlarge the pool of dollars available for overhead consumption.

Measured as one large "glob," administrative overhead is practically impossible to control. In contrast to the tight controls placed on manufacturing cost, effectiveness, and productivity, overhead areas remain a veritable sinkhole for corporate profits. No one doubts that every white-collar employee is working, but what they're doing is another issue. In looking into corporate overhead, then, companies are beginning to tackle the difficult area of white-collar productivity. (Appendix 8 provides further detail on the concept of white-collar productivity.)

How do you measure the output and value of administrative work? In some areas, such as purchasing, countable outputs can be identified (such as number of purchase orders cut and number of vendor contracts established) and performance measurements noted (such as purchase price variance and quality of incoming materials). In others, such as information technology, it's much more difficult to define the outputs created or to measure their effectiveness.

It should come as no surprise, then, that while some allocation bases were identified for each of the studied areas (for the second study these bases are summarized in Figure 8.9), in reality

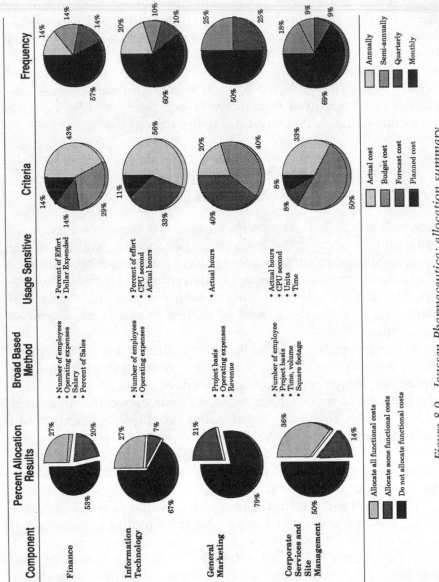

Figure 8.9   Janssen Pharmaceutica: allocation summary.

less than half of the administrative overhead in participating firms was allocated. Performance measurements in these areas was even less defined; as noted in Janssen's final report from its facilitator, "few companies use performance measures to assess administrative overhead." The study revealed what was probably already known to all: administrative overhead is a burgeoning problem that is difficult to analyze and control.

Janssen, as sponsor of the second study, gained much more information than it had received as a participant in the first study. It received a detailed analysis of the results, an assessment of where the company could benefit most from improvement efforts, and an initial action plan for generating improvement in these areas.

Yet even Janssen recognizes that the competitive benchmarking process is only a starting point. Understanding where it needs to improve provides very little information about how to tackle the change process. This has led Janssen management to sponsor the forum and to entertain the idea of pursuing a "best-in-class" benchmarking study to better understand how to gain improvements in its corporate marketing group.

Competitive benchmarking, then, is a valid scorecard for assessing current performance, identifies opportunities for improvement, and supports the analysis necessary to develop action plans to gain on the competition. It does not, however, provide the detailed process knowledge required to actually get better. Competitive benchmarking is, instead, a logical first step in an overall strategy to implement process improvements across the organization. It is never an ending, but rather a beginning, to gaining a competitive advantage.

APPENDIX 8

CONTROLLING ADMINISTRATIVE OVERHEAD

■ Escalating R&D and product development costs—a recent university study found the cost of developing a new drug averages $125 million and takes approximately 10 years.

■ Volatile regulatory environment—the prospect of price controls represents a serious threat to industry prosperity.

■ Shift from ethical to over-the-counter products—cost pressures are introduced with the need for additional manufacturing, distribution and marketing resources.

Elements of White-Collar Productivity

White-collar productivity can be assessed, measured and improved by reviewing the elements which together generate productivity and by identifying improvement opportunities and implementing recommendations for improvement. The four elements of white-collar productivity are

■ Effectiveness

■ Organization

■ Motivation

■ Process

Each is discussed in greater detail as follows:

Effectiveness is defined as the relationship between strategy and work activities. If the relationship is weak or questionable, the employees' time should be shifted to more productive tasks that directly support the strategy. For example, if customer service has been designated as a strategic initiative, but the customer service function is understaffed and poorly trained and no improvement programs have been funded, positive management attention is indicated.

Organization is the structure of business functions, work activities, operations and reporting relationships. The following characteristics of nonproductive organizations should be identified with a view towards eliminating or improving them:

- Overlap/duplication

- Fragmentation

- Inappropriate groupings or functions or alignment of functions

- Inefficient reporting relationships

- Excessive management layers

- Clarity of mission

- Appropriateness of job design

Motivation is defined as the extent to which employees demonstrate commitment to achieving business objectives. Turnover should be low; offer element should be strong or effective. If not, the reasons should be determined, analyzed, and resolved:

- Turnover

- Performance feedback

- Contribution visibility and recognition

- Autonomy

- Group identity

- Teamwork

- Management style

- Career planning and development

- Training

- Communication

Process refers to the flow of work, work methods, and technologies. These areas are reviewed to assess productivity:

- Value-added activities, operations, and steps

- Bottlenecks

- Scheduling and backlog control

- Degree of automation

- Control and transfer points

Measurements of White-Collar Productivity

Achieving productivity improvements in white-collar environments is difficult if not impossible, unless appropriate performance measures are developed and installed. We provide examples of effective measurements of white-collar productivity:

Goals: Continuous improvement and elimination of waste.

Productivity

- Units of output/Number of employees

- Units of output/Cost to produce

- Value-added work operations/Non-value-added operations

- Costs to manage/Number of subordinates

Throughput Time

- Time required to process work or complete work products

Quality

- Number of errors/Unit of time
- Error-Free work product transactions/Work product transactions with errors

Others

- Deadline accomplishments percentage
- Customer satisfaction index
- Degree of employee commitment/Involvement (organizational climate)

Allocation Methods

Administrative productivity can also be measured by employing usage-sensitive allocation methods to drive costs to users. In addition to the objectives of fully allocating costs and measuring product profitability, usage-sensitive methods enable

- Measurement of organizational profitability
- Influencing of management actions—on both the service provider and user sides

Features of a usage-sensitive allocation method include

- Use of internal "products"
- Holding users accountable for costs and products
- Holding providers accountable for actual versus budget performance

Note that allocating costs based on usage statistics requires more effort than allocating based on broad-based indicators, primarily due to the need for usage data collection systems.

9: VALUE FROM THE CUSTOMER'S PERSPECTIVE

> As in other things, so in men, not the seller but the buyer determines the price. For let a man (as most men do) rate themselves at the highest value they can; yet their true value is not more than it is esteemed by others.
>
> Thomas Hobbes
> *Leviathan*

Companies have traditionally managed their operations in terms of resources, input-output chains, and prespecified control points to monitor individual and group conformance to the required processes and procedures. With the focus on maintaining the status quo, the primary concern has been with making changes to the detailed tasks and the underlying resources consumed whenever a demand for improved performance is heard from the marketplace. This myopic focus on internal efficiency has given everyone the feeling that the company is responding to customer requests, but the response has been unfocused. If the customer complained about price, then prices were cut. To support the cut in revenues per unit, a cost reduction mandate would be issued: "Everyone is to trim 5 percent from their budgets."

The flaw in this logic is the simple fact that companies often forget to go back to the true customer to ensure that the value-added services are still being provided to the level and extent necessary. Setting arbitrary cost reduction targets across the board does not take into account the fact that some services or activities may be valued by the customer and should actually be increased, while others are non-value-adding and should be eliminated completely, not streamlined. In fact, obtaining complete information on what the customer values and how these needs are being met through existing processes and activities is a difficult and constantly shifting effort. The key to customer responsiveness is asking the customer for input on what services and products are valuable and which should be eliminated.

In order to be an effective management tool, benchmarking has to start from a concern with the customer. Richard Schonberger describes this as a "customer-in" organization:[1]

> The customer is *in* the world-class organization, not outside of it. The reasons are sound: If left on the outside, the customer gets treated with indifference (at best) and offers the same in return. That spells temporary relationships: customers are poised to fly, like a nervous flock of geese in a grain field.

Companies are beginning to realize this fact. Caterpillar, Inc. knows that its customers expect a high-quality, trouble-free product. The total package or product purchased by the customer extends beyond the physical product to include one of the best service and repair part delivery systems in the world in any industry. While the customer would prefer a product that never needs repairs, the types of stresses and strains Caterpillar's products are subjected to in the field means that breakdowns are going to occur. Each hour lost in a major construction project due to equipment problems results in unrecoupable losses for the construction company. They need the problem fixed, and fast. What Caterpillar's customers buy, then, is the bundling of a high-quality product with the supporting service capabilities. The key factor is remembering that the product itself and the value placed on it are defined by the marketplace.

Identifying the Disconnects

While fulfilling a customer request has always entailed the linking of various tasks into an activity chain flowing horizontally across the organization, the design and management structures used by most companies have emphasized the vertical chain of command. Focused on control above all else, traditional management models have encouraged clear separation of duties and a functionally oriented structure to combat the complexity of organizational work. While this separation may have appeared to increase management's control over the company, in reality it created false barriers that blocked the smooth flow of the activities needed to meet customer requirements. Many a "ball" has dropped into the crack between departments or functions, with little or no way for management to figure out how, and why, the problem occurred.

Understanding "value" from the customer's perspective means addressing the disconnects, whether the gap is due to cost, delivery, or any of a broad range of issues—not by cutting or changing what management believes to be non-value-adding services but rather by asking the customer what types of services are valued. While customers may not understand how their needs are being met by the company (in other words, the actual physical structure of the customer service delivery system), they do know whether or not their needs are being met by that system. Kammlade *et al.* reflect the problems a company faces here:[2]

> Traditional approaches to overhead reduction are based on the view that organizations are collections of individual activities taking place in various departments. Activities are considered for elimination or reduction based on their importance to department objectives. In most instances, however, departmental objectives are viewed very narrowly. As a result, the eliminated activities and tasks may have to be reinstated because the underlying causes, which may be the needs of another department, have not been addressed. Getting at these underlying causes requires viewing an organization as a network of linked business processes. Each process is a series of related activities, and several departments may have shared responsibility for the entire process.

By doing benchmarking, the company is looking outward for clues on how to improve its performance. Benchmarking forces the company to go back to the customer and to talk in terms of the services provided. Once the company has a clear idea of what the customer needs, it can generate internal dialogs among employees at all levels in terms of the existing level of service being provided and how best to respond to customer-defined opportunities for improvement. The goal is always clear: to increase the level of value-added service to the customer.

Identifying the primary disconnects between what the customer values and what services and products are being delivered usually begins with the recognition that a problem exists. Before any action can be taken to address the problem, it has to be clearly identified and defined. Often the real problem will be signaled by some breakdown in the process, by recurring budget overruns, in connection with the development of a new product or process, or by some other crisis. What the breakdown or disconnect means is that there is a difference between what is perceived as value-added by the customer (internal or external) and what is being provided by the supplier.

During the budget process the product-testing laboratory of a computer company requested an increase in resources to meet an increase in demand for its services. In a traditional setting, the request would have been granted or denied with little analysis of the underlying work being performed. In reality, the increased workload was due to the fact that the usual range of tests being performed was not catching ongoing problems with the product. Marketing, coming across a consistent pattern of errors, had begun to request a duplicate set of tests for every product sold, to cut down on these problems. In reality, what was needed was not the duplication of the entire battery of tests, but rather increased attention (in other words, *new* tests) focused specifically on the problem area. Changing the testing procedures was what was needed, not performing the same tests twice.

Once the symptoms were recognized, management could turn its attention to determining the "root cause" of the ongoing failures. Design changes were set in motion to eliminate the problem. Getting to the core problem required open communication between the customer (marketing) and the supplier (the test laboratory). Fixing the problem required pushing even further back into the value chain, linking with the design engineers to obtain a long-term solution.

DEVELOPING A
CUSTOMER-DRIVEN COMPANY

Inevitably, the culture within which we live shapes and limits our imaginations and, by permitting us to do and think and feel in certain ways, makes it increasingly unlikely or impossible that we should do or think or feel in ways that are contradictory or tangential to it.

Margaret Mead
Male and Female

Understanding the core issue is the first step in addressing the disconnects between the services a company is providing and those that the customer requires. Given this core issue, the next step is relating the problem to the ongoing operating policies and procedures within the organization. The objective is to develop an understanding of how the services are currently supported and what types of changes to people and resources will need to take place to meet *true* customer requirements. Those activities that do not add value or support delivery of a value-added service component become targets for elimination, freeing up the resources needed to improve areas that are more critically tied to value in the customer's eyes. Meeting customer requirements, then, does not simply mean throwing more resources at the problem; it means making better use of existing resources by eliminating sources of error and reducing the number of non-value-added activities performed on an ongoing basis.

Management usually believes that it knows what the customer wants and that checking with the customer to verify the facts is both unnecessary and dangerous. It's unnecessary because marketing is paid to keep close to the customer; the danger lies in possibly raising expectations, revealing potential weaknesses, or identifying problems that might have gone unnoticed before.

The problem is much more difficult than this (see Figure 9.1). The relationship between a customer and a company is initiated by a customer request for some form of product or service. Look-

9: VALUE FROM THE CUSTOMER'S PERSPECTIVE

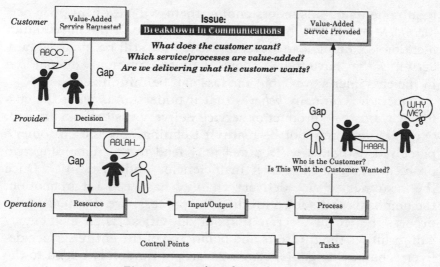

Figure 9.1   Identifying the gaps.

ing at Figure 9.1, you can see that the term "value-added" is used. Value is what the customer is willing to pay for; it is all reasonable effort and expense caused by the desire to meet customer expectations. Any activity or cost that does not add value in the customer's eye is waste. If a company is lucky or has enough market power, it can pass this waste on. Otherwise, the waste eats into profits and impairs the long-run competitiveness of the firm.

Translating the customer's request into an action plan at the organizational level requires a clear understanding of what is wanted and the communication of this need throughout the organization. This is the first place that a gap between customer expectations and the actual product or service provided by the company can occur. In discussing this type of problem, Kammlade *et al.*[3] identify four categories of concern:

Gaps: customer requirements that are not met
Waste: activities that add no value as defined by the customer
Inefficiencies: complex methods that cause long lead times
Instability: output that is erratic or unpredictable

In defining the company's response to a customer request, gaps are the most damaging, because misspecifying the customer's requirements or misunderstanding them will result in poor performance overall no matter what else is done. If the miscommunication is caught, some level of waste may still be incurred (any activities that have to be undone or redone are non-value-adding in the customer's eyes), but the loss can be minimized.

Once the company *believes* that it understands what the customer wants, the product or service delivery system is activated. (Note: beliefs may not be reality!) Defining how the customer's perceived demands will be met may lead to the remaining two problems identified above: inefficiencies and instability. Once the customer service delivery channel has been set in motion, the emphasis shifts to controlling the process. Are the steps in the process treated as discrete units or activities? Then inefficiency can result, as the tradeoffs and balancing of the entire service delivery channel is ignored. Are new orders randomly added to the existing schedule based on the "squeaky wheel" criterion? Then production will be completed in a haphazard way. Instability in the production process ripples backward into the organization, creating friction, overtime, and stress, as well as forward into missed deliveries and unhappy customers.

Smooth execution of the tasks within the customer service delivery channel is a prerequisite to even beginning to meet customer expectations; it is a necessary, but not necessarily sufficient, level of operation. This is the area where many of the new management and manufacturing approaches such as total quality management (TQM) and just-in-time manufacturing (JIT-M) are focused. These approaches begin from a definition of what the product or service delivery system is designed to provide. They seek to eliminate any waste, inefficiency, or instability that impedes the effectiveness of the delivery system. This means that if any breakdown or error in actually identifying what the customer requires is unaddressed, the company may end up delivering the wrong service in a very efficient manner.

Quality: Foundation for Value Added

In order to consistently provide a high-quality product or service, a company has to identify and eliminate the causes of nonconformance or error. One of the major causes of ongoing problems are the artificial boundaries (such as departments or functions) erected across the activity chain. These boundaries impede the smooth flow of work, create more problems than they solve, and can prevent the company from reaching its goals. Tackling these problems requires adopting a focus on the process first and the traditional responsibility, or control points, last. Management's job is not to control; it is to provide leadership and facilitate coordinated action across the organization. In this setting, quality is defined as

> giving the customer or the next person in the process, a product or service that meets requirements, and doing this in a way to ensure that each task is done right the first time, every time.

Achieving a consistently high level of product and service quality is based on detailed knowledge of the process itself. Good processes are what make things work well; quality can be improved *only* through improvement in the process, *not* by inspection.

Pursuing quality first seems to be good business practice or simple common sense. In reality, though, companies often do not completely understand their processes very well; the focus is usually on the results, not the steps needed to get them. When companies come up against a major crisis, some unmet expectation that the customer *is willing to bring* to their attention, then the impetus for understanding the process is created. World-class performance, and the benchmarking procedures needed to get there, require that the company come to grips with the fact that though they may be working hard, it's doubtful that all that effort is seen as equally value-adding in the customer's eyes.

Battling the Grasp of History

> Tradition does not mean that the living are dead, but that the dead are living.
>
> Gilbert K. Chesterton

Having good people do the wrong things well does not seem likely to lead to long-term competitive success. Instead, management needs to identify the *critical success factors* the company needs to address in order to meet or exceed true customer requirements. This understanding cannot be generated from within. When the customer is left out of the strategic analysis process, history and gutfact rule the day. Set within the existing power structures of the company, the planning process takes on the trappings of a political convention—lobbying for resources, making deals, and selecting "candidates" for the upcoming year. Change in this setting is difficult; incremental shifts and new "directives" may take place, but it's hard to shake the feeling that it is just more of the same in a shinier package.

In this traditional world, the gap between customer needs and a company's products and services widens over time. While the founders of the company may have had a good handle on the customer and the customer's needs, deeply entrenched layers of bureaucracy probably do not. The gap between what the customer wants and what is provided can widen to the point that market share begins to erode and a state of emergency (crisis) is declared. Falling sales and profits lead to drastic cost reduction efforts, triggering a downward spiral of performance. The radical changes needed to recover competitiveness may come too late or be turned aside by an entrenched culture that is now operating from a "fight or flight" basis. Middle managers, seeking to spearhead required changes, are rebuffed, are given inadequate resources, or worse yet, terminated in the latest round of head count reductions.

Middle managers are the cannon fodder in this downward spiral. Not surprisingly, they are also the most common source of innovative concepts and programs in companies. While the trend in today's corporation is toward flatter management structures accomplished by reducing the middle management ranks, there is a growing concern that companies are getting rid of the very people who can facilitate change in an entrenched culture resistant to any idea not invented internally. The scene painted is purposively bleak; short-sighted management is usually internally focused management. If the market and the customer are setting the definitions of excellence and value-added service overall, the role of each individual and each project can be objectively evaluated on whether or not it contributes to meeting customer needs in the short and the long run.

Starting at the Source: The Customer as Driver

This one thing I do, forgetting those things which are behind, and reaching forth unto those things which are before.

Philippians 3:13

A more encouraging scenario arises when the customer is the driver of product, process, and service efforts. Going to the customer first provides the company with an objective set of expectations and service requirements, which can help focus attention on real problems. Viable solutions are defined, not by their cost or the political clout of their advocates, but rather in terms of maximizing value in the customer's eyes. In the search for innovative ways to improve performance, management encourages the development of new programs and procedures. The result? At the least, these externally driven changes will lead to continuous improvement in the company's products and services. If talking with the customer opens up new avenues for products and services, the company can leapfrog the competition and establish a competitive advantage.

The key difference? In a traditional setting, management is *reacting* to ongoing changes, trying to scramble fast enough to stay in the game. If the other contenders have already rounded the halfway marker, it's unlikely the company can win the race. Placing high enough in the competitive standings (that is, market share) to stay in the market becomes a very real concern. When the customer serves as the primary force behind change, management can *proactively* shape the competitive market, setting the pace for the competition. In the former case, corporate life is one long firefighting exercise; in the latter, managers have the time to plan for growth, train the workforce to meet need demands, and establish critical skills and competencies to ensure long-run success. Which team would you prefer to play on?

Many companies now provide "vendor scorecards" to indicate their level of satisfaction with the services being provided

BENCHMARKING

(see Figure 9.2). As can be seen from this evaluation, the customer is basically satisfied with Bradford Soap Works' performance. The problem spot appears to be on-time delivery. If the measures are correct, the product never arrives when wanted (or almost never).

While this is definitely an opportunity for improvement, the scorecard also puzzled the management of this firm. Placing a call to their contact in the customer's staff, they found that their measured performance reflected an informal arrangement between the two companies. To save freight charges, the customer would

June 1, 1990 to May 31, 1991

I. QUANTITATIVE CRITERIA

A. QUALITY PERFORMANCE

Points
95*

$\dfrac{\text{Total shipments rejected}}{\text{Total shipments received}}$ $(6.587/219,995) * 100 = \underline{2.99}\%$

B. ON TIME DELIVERY PERFORMANCE

$\dfrac{\text{Shipments received within evaluation arrival time period}}{\text{Total shipments due}}$ $(4/31) * 100 = \underline{13}$

II. QUALITATIVE CRITERIA

A. DELIVERY

1. Responsiveness to emergency requirements: __4__

2. Adherence to shipping and packaging instructions: __4__

3. Production lead times: __3__

$(11/15) * 100 = \underline{73}$

* 0 - 0.5% Rejections = 100 Points	4.6 - 5.5% Rejections = 80 Points	** 5 = Excellent
0.6 - 1.5% Rejections = 99 Points	5.6 - 8.5% Rejections = 60 Points	4 = Good
1.6 - 2.5% Rejections = 98 Points	8.6 - 12.5% Rejections = 40 Points	3 = Average
2.6 - 3.5% Rejections = 95 Points	+ 12.6% Rejections = 0 Points	2 = Poor
		1 = Unacceptable

Figure 9.2   Vendor scorecard.

9: VALUE FROM THE CUSTOMER'S PERSPECTIVE

II. *QUALITATIVE CRITERIA (continued)*

Subtotal   Points

   B. **QUALITY**

      1. Effectiveness of internal Q.A.   <u>4</u>
procedures:

      2. Responsiveness to quality problems: <u>4</u>

      3. Cooperative in resolving rejections: <u>4</u>

      4. Suggests ways to improve products and   <u>4</u>
processes:

      5. Availability of test and performance   <u>4</u>
data:

      6. Adherence to specifications, test   <u>4</u>
procedures, and conformance
checklists:

      7. Returns policy: <u>4</u>

                      Quality subtotal: $(28/35) * 100 =$ <u>80</u>

   C. **PRICING**

      1. Competitive: <u>5</u>
      2. Adequate notice of price changes: <u>5</u>
      3. Offers price protection: <u>5</u>
      4. Substantiates price increases: <u>5</u>
      5. Suggests ways to reduce costs: <u>5</u>
      6. Willingness to negotiate: <u>5</u>
      7. Control of costs: <u>5</u>

                            $(35/35) * 100 =$ <u>100</u>

Figure 9.2 *(continued)*

"backhaul" goods from this supplier whenever possible. Several problems were identified in this approach: first, partial orders were often required due to space constraints in the customer's trucks; second, if the truck arrived early or late (as defined by the customer's desired ship date), it affected the measured delivery performance of this supplier; finally, partial shipments to meet emergency needs by the customer would once again be counted against the supplier on this measure. Removing these problems did not eliminate the need to improve, but it helped the supplier identify factors it could control and those it could not. When these factors were taken into account, Bradford's on-time delivery shot up from (4/31) 13 points to (27/31) 87 points. The recalculations

II. QUALITATIVE CRITERIA (continued)

Subtotal   Points

D. SALES, SERVICE, AND SUPPORT

1. Ability to provide technical and engineering assistance: 5

2. Support of R&D needs, requirements: 5

3. Keeps up to date on new technologies, trends, materials and methods: 5

4. Calibre, availability and effectiveness of key personnel: 4

5. Follow-up procedures: 5
6. Responsive to requests for information: 5

7. Communications - advises of pending changes, delays and problems: 5

8. Ability to provide marketplace information/data on a timely basis: 5

9. Responsive to emergency requirements: 5

10. Suggests ways to better serve Amway: 5   (49/50) * 100 =   98

CATEGORY	SUBTOTAL POINTS	X % =	TOTAL POINTS
I. Quantitative Performance			
A. Quality	95	X .25 =	23.75
B. On Time Delivery	13	X .25 =	3.25
II. Qualitative Performance			
A. Delivery	73	X .15 =	10.95
B. Quality	80	X .15 =	12.00
C. Pricing	100	X .10 =	10.00
D. Sales, Service and Support	98	X .10 =	9.80
		Total:	69.75

100 = Excellent/80 = Good/60 = Average/40 = Poor/20 = Unacceptable

Figure 9.2   (continued)

changed Bradford's overall rating to 89, showing it to be one of the customer's best vendors.

Identifying and addressing the disconnects between customer expectations and what the company actually does precedes the identification of the benchmarking targets or strategy. If the customer is concerned with the level of on-time delivery, then the best benchmark is quite likely a "best-in-class" firm like L.L. Bean. If, instead, management's concern is the standardization of customer service prior to implementing company-wide improvements, the best tool will be internal benchmarking. What does the customer really expect? This is a question that can't be answered with internal information; it requires looking at the world through the customer's eyes.

Managing the Handoffs

> Good communication is as stimulating as black coffee, and just as hard to sleep after.
>
> Anne Morrow Lindbergh

In order to begin down the path to continuous improvement, management has to revisualize the organization, focusing on the flow of activities across the functional areas rather than on the performance of any one department or person. Refocusing attention in this manner does not necessarily mean that the company has to physically reorganize its functions, but rather that the focus becomes management of the handoffs—the interrelationships and how they can be modified to improve the overall performance of the customer service delivery system. Once management has defined the goal of this delivery system by querying the customer, the objective becomes finding the most efficient and effective way to deliver the services and products the customer values.

Dissecting the activity grid cannot be done in isolation; all individuals involved in the process have to be included in the improvement program. Participation increases the validity of the information gathered and smooths the implementation path once needed changes are identified. One way to get the settlers to move into a new territory is to encourage them to visit it and to lay claim to their piece of the new terrain. Ownership of the problem and its solution by those who affect the process on an ongoing basis is the only secure path to continuous improvement.

Cost Isn't a Good Master

> First payments is what made us think we were prosperous, and the other nineteen is what showed us we were broke.
>
> Will Rogers

In a competitive market that values cost, quality, and respon-siveness concurrently, management cannot afford to focus on only one criterion in decision making. Cost is not the only thing to con-sider. While most businessmen will vigorously nod in agreement to the statement, "We have to look beyond the numbers," doing so seems to be a hobby to be pursued when times are good and abandoned when the wolves are at the door. A continuing dialog surrounds the "numbers mania" that seems to monopolize the at-tention of American managers, yet little is really being done to stem the tide. Business students still eagerly learn every statisti-cal and financial model they're fed and groan as the topic turns to "the soft stuff." Their behavior, though, is not learned in busi-ness school; it is a cultural side effect of being raised in a country where "being the best" is defined in some measurable term. "Best" athletes complete the distance in milliseconds less than their com-petition; "best" corporations yield high returns on investment for investors.

Measurements are a valuable tool for evaluating the progress of an individual or company toward some goal, but many critical factors of success cannot be measured. Time after time a business guru will conclude a hard-hitting discussion of the best practice in corporations, and how to gain a competitive edge, by noting that an "open culture" or "vision" or some equally fuzzy con-cept is critical. Businesses are first and foremost social systems; when people share a common set of objectives and an agreed-upon view of the world, coordinated and focused action is much easier to accomplish. If an organization is constantly plagued by political maneuvering in order to gain advantage (in other words, parochialism), there is far less energy and time available to work toward goals. And if agreeing on what constitutes a viable goal is an ongoing problem, very little "coordinated" action can be ex-pected.

Cooperation begins with open communication and the volun-tary observation of the ethical limits on self-interested behavior. The objective is to develop a strong social system, a shared set of beliefs, that can knit the diverse parts of the organization together. A customer-driven company finds it easier to eliminate alterna-tives that don't add value to the organization as a whole, because it provides a set of objective measures and criteria to use as the basis for evaluation. Customers, though, often talk in terms of "responsiveness," "reliability" and "reputation for quality service," which aren't easily measured. One thing is certain, though; if the company is torn by infighting or territorialism, it is quite unlikely that it will excel on these performance dimensions. The internal problems translate to wasted resources, redundancy, and unnecessary cost—quite the opposite of value added.

Final Notes

> The toughest thing about success is that you've got to keep on being a success.
>
> Irving Berlin
> *Theatre Arts*, 1958

Satisfying the customer is the key to competitive success. This well-known fact is the basis for developing a customer perspective; if what the individual, or company, is doing does not add value in the customer's eyes, it is worse than doing nothing at all. Developing a customer perspective, though, does not simply mean conducting satisfaction surveys; it requires the creation of linked value chains and internal customer-supplier relations to ensure that the delivery of a product or service can be effectively performed.

Benchmarking is based on the belief that performance against customer expectations is the only viable way to evaluate an organization or to establish action plans to improve that performance. If the change process is divorced from the customer, the communication gap will quite likely grow; tradition is a very poor basis for the future unless the customer is kept in mind. The only way to know if customers are getting what is required is to directly ask them. This query, though, must begin with an open communication of what the customer *really* expects rather than how to improve existing products and services. Benchmarking sets up the feedback channel that reconnects a company with its market and provides the basis for improving its competitive position. Throughout, the customer is an ever-present force and judge of success.

Chief executives repeatedly fail to recognize that for communication to be effective, it must be two-way: there has to be feedback to ascertain the extent to which the message has actually been understood, believed, assimilated, and accepted. This is a step few companies ever take, perhaps because they fear to learn how little of the message has actually been transmitted.

Robert N. McMurry
Harvard Business Review, 1965

10: QUALITATIVE VS. QUANTITATIVE BENCHMARKS

Why, a four-year-old child could understand this report. Run out and find me a four-year-old child. I can't make head or tail out of it.

Groucho Marx
Duck Soup

B enchmarking starts from the assumption that, even if your company should prove to be the "best in class," there's no reason to rest on your laurels. In fact, "best practice" firms have to work the hardest at improving, because they are the leaders and others analyzing their current abilities are striving to meet and exceed them. As an ongoing exercise, benchmarking focuses on quantitative and qualitative measures of performance throughout the various levels of the firm.

Sound measurements are hardly a new area of interest in the business world; they have long been the cornerstone of business education and the hallmark of a well-managed organization. Traditional approaches to measurement, though, are fraught with problems. In most countries traditional measurements are based on external financial requirements (see Figure 10.1). These requirements are then used for planning purposes to facilitate comparisons. The problem with these measures is that they are based on derived information, and as presented they have no clear relationship or linkage to the operational data. On the other hand, operations develop their own measures, again unrelated to financial results, to identify customer satisfaction and market

BENCHMARKING

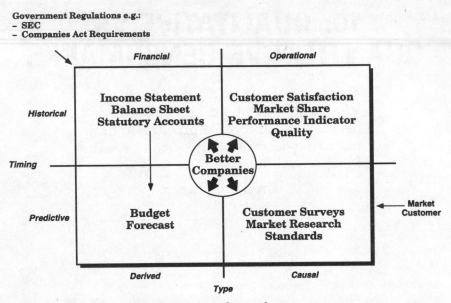

Figure 10.1   *Traditional measures.*

needs. This division contributes to conflict in evaluation of performance. These separate internal focuses miss the drivers and the critical external perspective that put measures into context.

Measuring performance requires the adoption of a critical eye, an understanding of the relationship of various parts of the organization to the desired level of performance of the whole, and a recognition that numbers do not capture the essence of competitive advantage. The latter point is the most critical to keep in mind. While quantitative measurements are a vital part of the benchmarking process, they are not the only factors to consider. In fact, in order to do an adequate assessment of the comparability of various benchmarking target firms, the benchmarking team has to evaluate the qualitative characteristics of those organizations, such as their management structure (centralized vs. decentralized) and their level of available services.

Much of the key information that adds meaning to the benchmarking process consists of descriptions of the underlying *process* used to accomplish a task, qualitative characteristics and measurements of the benchmarking subjects, and anecdotal evidence. Numbers may make the benchmarking results look "harder," but they are open to manipulation and tell only half of the story.

10: QUALITATIVE VS. QUANTITATIVE BENCHMARKS

Measuring Performance Along a Continuum

Statistics is the art of lying by means
of figures.

Dr. Wilhelm Stekhel
Marriage at the Crossroads

Measurements can be either quantitative (numbers) or qualitative (words). Quantitative and qualitative benchmarks are not isolated categories, though. Measurements can be spread along a continuum from the highly quantitative and easily gauged characteristics of a product, such as the thickness of a piece of steel, to the fuzzy, qualitative, but vital measure of customer satisfaction. At each point along this continuum, information is gleaned, but its nature and implications change.

There are numerous tools for converting or approximating qualitative characteristics with numbers, but these proxies will never have the precision of a micrometer to back them up. As part of the spectrum of measurements or benchmarks available to a company, they are a midpoint in the "hardness" scale. Hard measures (precise numbers) make the user *feel* as though they're real; facts with numbers attached seem to take on a life of their own. With each gain in precision, though, relevance or accuracy can be sacrificed. Hence, in developing benchmark measurements the goal is to get a metric that's as "hard" as it can get without losing vital insights provided by the qualitative indices.

Developing and Using Quantitative Benchmarks

Quantitative benchmarks should be both financial and non-financial in nature. They may be easily measured by an existing scale or counting system, or they may have to be collected as a separate set of measures. Obviously, cost per good unit produced, return on investment, and a series of other financial measurements are developed from an established counting system: double-entry accounting. Conversely, number of calls made to customer service, or the types of complaints received, may need to be collected on a periodic basis if records aren't already maintained.

Financial measures have a long history of usage. The most elaborate benchmarking system developed to date is the DuPont

Return on Investment (ROI) model. This model decomposes the financial performance of an organization from a global measure of return on investment down through accounts receivable turns, cash cycles, and capital intensity measures. The DuPont system is still in use today as a comprehensive model for financial control.

On the other hand, anyone who is familiar with the flexibility this counting system provides understands that the precise-looking accounting figures are, in reality, no more than estimates given a specific set of assumptions. This flexibility actually limits the usefulness of financial performance benchmarks; before one of these metrics can be used, the analyst must know how discretionary items were handled, what inventory methods were used, any major mergers or acquisitions that might have distorted performance, and a broad range of other factors. Understanding and accurately using financial data is not a simple task. It requires time, patience, and more than a casual understanding of the rules and regulations accountants follow.

Quantitative benchmarks can capture operating or product characteristics, and can reflect internally or externally focused performance. Examples include the following:

Productivity measures

- Total product output divided by total headcount

- Cost per good unit produced

- Total output of product divided by total resource inputs

- Orders processed/shipped per employee hour

- Value added per employee

- Inventory turnover ratios

- Non-value-added costs/total costs

- Value-added/total costs

Quality measures

- Yield rates

- Scrap rates

- Percent of products reworked

- Percent of total labor performing rework

- Incoming vendor defects in parts per million (ppm)
- Outgoing product defects in ppm
- Number of customer complaints
- Warranty claims
- Returns and allowances percentages
- Good units produced/planned output
- Parts availability/on-time deliveries
- Forecast accuracy
- Availability and accuracy of information
- Number of engineering change notices

Delivery/timeliness measures

- On-time delivery percentage
- Lead time to engineer (design) a finished product
- Start-up time from design to production
- Component lead times—purchased and manufactured
- Transportation lead time
- Number/percentage of late deliveries
- Number of back orders
- Number of late orders
- Manufacturing lead time (queue, move, cycle)
- Set-up number and time
- Inspection number and time
- Value-added/total time
- Waste time
- Average level of order fulfillment
- Order processing cycle time
- Average engineering change notice execution time
- Preorder cycle time

Figure 10.2   Management by the numbers.

The number of quantitative measures available is endless. Each measurement reflects a clearly identifiable characteristic of the organization and its performance that can be compared against competitors, industry average, and, to some extent, measurements obtained from best-in-class analysis.

Management by Numbers

The very ease and apparent objectivity of quantitative benchmarks is in reality their greatest danger (see Figure 10.2). "Management by the numbers" is not management; it is a game played out on the corporate stage where those most skilled at massaging their reported results succeed. Donald Curtis, in his book *Management Rediscovered*, suggests that[1]

> The modern management system can be characterized as a system of concepts and tools intended to maximize the ability of the top management group to understand, direct, and control the business. At the heart of this system are two fundamental premises:
>
> - The important characteristics of a business can be quantified.
> - This ability to quantify can be used to directly support all the management activities (i.e., understanding, directing, and controlling the enterprise).

10: QUALITATIVE VS. QUANTITATIVE BENCHMARKS

These two premises, as they are used in the American management system, are false and lead to a management style I call
"Analogue Management" or managing through representations
of reality. In my view, this management style is at the heart of
our competitiveness problem.

In many companies, days sales outstanding and inventory
turns are key performance measures with established "acceptable
levels." But as companies shift and expand their sales from a single country or region dominance to the global marketplace, these
established "acceptable levels" change. For example, in Italy days
sales outstanding are between 101 and 136 days, whereas in Korea
payment is due upon receipt. However, management reports—and
related reward systems—do not always recognize or reflect these
differences properly.

A major U.S. manufacturing company with plans to expand
internationally by three or four times over the next ten years faced
this issue. As international sales increased, days sales outstanding began to increase and inventory levels began to rise. The first
issue was identifying which geographic area was causing the increase. Management reports always reflected these measures as
domestic or international. The next question was why. Specific
customer and contract terms and conditions to achieve growth in
the new market attributed to some of the results, with the impact of cultural norms accounting for the rest. Then the question
moved to how the company was going to manage this, and how it
would recognize the impact on asset management and cash flow,
and, finally, was there a better way?

In benchmarking, the CFO found the company results were
comparable to the experience of best-in-class companies. He also
found that there was no blanket approach but that there were
opportunities to improve these measures by using creative terms
and conditions and incentives for the sales force.

Quantitative benchmarks, then, have value but are also
fraught with danger. They seem naturally to trigger goal displace-
ment, a phenomenon where the individuals focus on doing *whatever* is necessary to meet their goals rather than on understanding,

or questioning, why the task is being done at all. The task and the process of performing it are ignored by the measurement system and so are ignored by managers in the company.

Other dysfunctional consequences of an excessive reliance on quantitative measurements include "means-ends inversion" (in which people focus on following the rules and ignore the underlying reason or objective of the job), overquantification, data manipulation, and gamesmanship (such as the politics of the budgeting process). As Peter Drucker notes, "The more we can quantify the truly measurable areas, the greater the temptation to put all-out on those—the greater, therefore, the danger that what looks like better 'controls' will actually mean less 'control' if not a business out of control altogether."[2]

The value of quantitative measures and benchmarked performance targets is not to be dismissed, but it is always important to remember that the apparent objectivity and precision of a measurement is just that—appearance. As long as any influence can be brought to bear on the underlying data, the mode of calculation, or the type of presentation format in which the numbers appear, they are suspect. And as Drucker would argue, a company can look great on paper and be rapidly losing the competitive battle.

Productivity: More Than Outputs over Inputs

In their worship of the machine, many Americans have settled for something less than a full life, something that is hardly even a tenth of life, or a hundredth of a life. They have confused progress with mechanization.

Lewis Mumford

Before turning to qualitative measurements in the benchmarking process, the nature of productivity measurement in a continuous improvement environment needs to be addressed. The underlying premise is that a manufacturing decision is productive if, and only if,[3]

■ It increases throughput (the rate at which money is generated through sales).

■ It decreases inventory (things we buy that we intend to sell).

■ It decreases operating expense (money spent to convert inventory into throughput).

Productivity means more than getting more output per direct labor input. It means getting more value per dollar expended everywhere in the organization. As the lines between direct and indirect labor, line and staff, continue to be blurred by changing organizational forms, the single-minded focus on direct labor-to-output measures is inapplicable and dangerous.

A dollar saved in the back office is as important as one saved on the plant floor; both reduce society's cost to obtain the goods and services provided by the firm. Measures such as total factor productivity or "total output per total head count" provide a systemic view of performance that supports ongoing improvements throughout the organization.

Capturing Qualitative Benchmarks

By definition, qualitative benchmarks are not easily measured using existing systems or analysis. Yet they are critical factors affecting the ultimate viability of the organization and its ability to respond to competitive challenges. Some "qualitative" benchmarks that can be loosely measured and evaluated include the following:

1. The complexity of the product

   ■ Number of material moves
   ■ Number of total parts
   ■ Average number of options
   ■ Number of products produced per line, machine, or plant

2. Existing capacity

  ■ Number and location of bottlenecks

  ■ Part/component bottlenecks

  ■ Number of process changes

  ■ Preventive maintenance and repair levels

  ■ Statistical quality control capabilities

  ■ Material velocity

  ■ Average lot size

  ■ Number of material-handling control points

  ■ Demand fluctuation

  ■ Number of quality control/inspection points

3. Customer satisfaction

  ■ Intention to repurchase

  ■ Satisfaction index (summary of product characteristics)

  ■ Actual performance against expectations

  ■ Recommendation to others to buy

  ■ Perceived quality

  ■ Perceived functionality

  ■ Ease of use

4. Marketing/distribution channel

  ■ Number and location of warehouses

  ■ Number of stockouts

  ■ Total lead time

  ■ Market areas covered/penetration

  ■ Channels used versus available

  ■ Support provided/responsiveness

- Scope of coverage

- Flexibility

- Number of new products

- Product success rates

5. Paperwork

  - Number of days to process an order

  - Number of steps/hurdles faced by customer

  - Average number of contacts per order filled

  - Number of errors/rework

  - Number of exceptions generated

  - Days to close general ledger/accounts

  - Days lag in producting/distributing reports

Obviously this list could be expanded, but the message has hopefully been delivered—proxies can be developed to capture the essence of some qualitative factors, although many remain unmeasurable.

It's difficult to imagine a measurement system that could be developed to capture the impact of public policies on the organization. Perhaps a count could be made of the number of forms completed, individuals employed to fulfill reporting requirements, or days lost in completing the work, yet each of these is a resource consumption measurement, not a strategic benchmark. To become benchmarks, these measurements would need to be compared to, or more directly derived from, the analysis of a competitor, the industry, or a best-in-class firm. With these external goals defined, the organization's performance could then be evaluated relative to best practice.

Comparability Does Not End with Measures

Comparisons between different organizations have to be made carefully. Take a simple example: the performance of a credit function within an organization. While inherent, structural, and performance drivers can be identified, their interpretation requires insight and care. Why are the numbers what they are? If there are twenty people employed in your organization and five in the benchmarked firm's credit area, what does that really mean?

The first issue that has to be addressed is the relationship between the company and its customers—is it a sole supplier or one of many? Functionality then follows—do both groups perform the same tasks? What about relative volumes of transactions? Are all credit transactions equal, or do some require more time than others? If there are different "intensities" of credit transactions, what is the relative mix of difficult vs. easy transactions in your firm as compared to the benchmarked organization? Could the approach used to process these transactions be modified to make it less complex?

Not until these and a large number of other questions are addressed can the benchmark-based information be effectively used. Five may be an unrealistic number of people for the credit function in this organization, given the current structure, process, and demand characteristics it faces. That doesn't mean that a staffing level of five may not be attainable downstream, but the drivers or causes for the additional staffing must be clearly understood before any reductions or reassessment of the activity network can occur.

A STRATEGIC PERSPECTIVE

No man that does not see visions will ever realize any high hope or undertake any high enterprise.

Woodrow Wilson

To succeed today, companies must perform well on four primary dimensions: cost, quality (effectiveness), productivity (efficiency), and delivery (time). Yet traditional corporate scorecards often focus solely on the financial measures or results. There appears to be little recognition that financial results cannot be directly managed, but instead *are caused by* the level of performance on the quality, productivity, and delivery dimensions.

Measuring performance against cost, quality, productivity, and delivery criteria is the first step in achieving a strategic advantage. These measurements provide a clear picture of the here and now, of the current operational characteristics of the organization. Benchmarking moves beyond the here and now to incorporate the future, providing direction on how to overtake the competition. Measurements, then, are operational and historical in nature; benchmarking is strategic.

Developing a strategy starts from a vision of a desired endpoint: some higher objective or goal that will benefit the organization and its stakeholders. While there can be many starting points for a strategy, it is becoming increasingly clear that the only sure road to success begins by looking at the world through the customer's eyes. The best buggy whip in the world won't be a hot seller today, because it doesn't fill a need for the customer. It is an undeniable fact that the only valuable product is one the customer wants or needs.

While service and retail companies have always known that a satisfied customer is the key to success, many manufacturing companies appeared to forget this fact in the face of massive backlogs that create the feeling that the customer will take whatever they can get out the door. The increasing competitive pressures of a global marketplace have stripped away these blinders; meeting the needs of internal and external customers is the only path to long-run success. Breaking away from an internal orientation takes more than a good slogan, though; it takes focused measurements that counteract a long history of internally developed practices and processes that make it difficult to identify value-added work, let alone understand how to stop the burgeoning growth of overhead. To get a handle on controlling costs, a company has to look beyond its walls in the search for new ideas and new measures.

The Dangers of Looking Inward

> Reason may fail you. If you are going to do anything with life, you have sometimes to move away from it, beyond all measurements. You must follow sometimes visions and dreams.
>
> Bede Jarrett
> *The House of Gold*

In the past, measurements have predominantly focused on internal operations and their level of efficiency. Existing operations were analyzed by industrial engineers, allowances made for "normal" levels of downtime, waste, and idle capacity, and standards set. There were several major flaws embedded in this approach:

- Defined levels of waste were built into the system.

- Disproportionate amounts of time were spent analyzing direct labor costs and efficiencies.

- Inventory was used to absorb mistakes.

- Cost reductions were pursued at the expense of quality.

- Parochialism was encouraged and rewarded.

- Preventive activities were underemphasized.

- Non-value-added overhead was allowed to grow unchecked.

In other words, traditional measurement systems, such as standard cost-based control systems, emphasized cost control and de-emphasized planning.

Looking more closely at the list, the fact that engineered standards contain predefined levels of waste is perhaps the most crucial issue to be addressed by companies adopting continuous improvement concepts. Why? Because the two systems are in direct contradiction. In a world devoted to continuous improvement, there is no "good enough"—no level of acceptable waste. Perfection may never be reached, but it certainly will not be if imperfection is hidden from view. Any factor or level of waste built into a standard *is no longer visible* and hence is never questioned.

Undoing years of engineering and accounting tradition is not an easy endeavor, as anyone who has worked with developing measures for continuous improvement environments knows. The nagging question remains, "Do you really expect perfection?" The answer is "No," but the objective is to encourage the individual, or organization, to strive for the best possible performance it can provide. Building waste or an expectation of failure into the measurement system makes the search for the "best" impossible: everyone is working on a game plan that establishes a ceiling on performance, a point where effort is "good enough."

In fact, the entire list of problems with traditional measurement systems suggests that the game that was being played was "Hide the Information." Inventory was the great forgiver, the shock absorber that would make a bad year look good and hide inefficiency in the plant. Orders were inventoried as well as materials and finished goods. Many a plant manager could be seen wringing his or her hands as the "backlog" disappeared. The solution? Build more inventory.

The games that have been played with inventory levels and valuation are too numerous to cite here. The most flagrant abuses revolve around overhead absorption. Faced with a fixed pool of costs that "has" to be attached to product, management makes more product, "absorbing" these costs into them, and in so doing transforms expenses into assets. Inventory is then placed on the balance sheet, improving the bottom line. It is accepted practice. To question whether the additional inventory will ever be sold is sacrilege.

On the plant floor, inventory buffers one operation from the next, creating small islands of effort. Lulled into the belief that everyone is working as hard as they can, whether or not what is being done is needed or right, management has tended to focus its attention on efficiency variances, with an ever-watchful eye toward keeping each worker and machine busy. These buffers hide mistakes, creating excessive levels of scrap and work to be redone, but the numbers look good. The numbers can also be improved by not doing some things—like preventive maintenance. Just keep the product rolling across the machines, and success is ensured. In a setting such as this, more is hidden than is known.

This is especially true in the overhead area. Overhead, reported as a lump sum, is really not controlled. Budgeted spending levels may be established, but they simply grow from year to year—the baseline expense and the actual value of the activities being performed are seldom questioned. The game that emerges is simple: spend everything you ask for so next year you can get more.

This means that the budget game becomes the arena for politics and power. The best negotiators win; their more conservative counterparts lose. The game itself divides the organization, creating armed camps that can only improve their own performance by pursuing self-interest. Teamwork may be a great idea when

resources are ample, but in tight times it's every office or department for itself.

One major service company in the United States has instituted
benchmarking as part of the budget process to change the game
and foster more teamwork within the organization. In this company the cost budget for most overhead functions or centralized
services, such as treasury, finance, MIS, and building services, is
negotiated between the provider and the business unit—the internal customer.

As part of these negotiations, operations are analyzed to identify services provided; then benchmarks are established related
to the cost and service level. This information, rather than the
prior year's budget, serves as the baseline for the negotiations.
Discussions then focus on customer service requirements and improvement opportunities.

As a result of this process, the centralized cash management
department found that its systems were best-in-class, but that
their staffing costs were significantly higher than other companies
(see Figure 10.3). (The analysis revealed that the systems that had

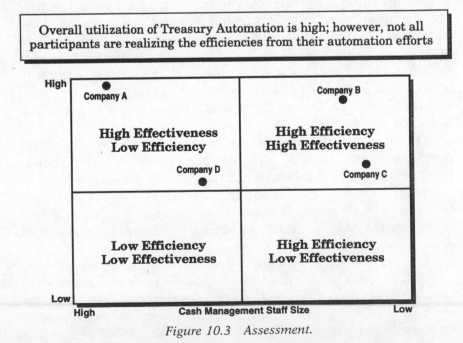

Figure 10.3 Assessment.

been developed over time had never been referenced back to the original plan in terms of work elimination—hence related staff reductions were never made.) The department reduced its staff expenses by 50 percent and instituted other operational improvements.

Expanding the Focus

> To remain unaware of what we pro-
> pose to do, never helps us to live.
>
> Josiah Royce
> *The Problem of Christianity*

Those embracing continuous improvement, are expanding their focus to include externally defined measures of efficiency and effectiveness in the areas of quality, productivity, delivery, and cost, as described in the previous section. Overproduction is not rewarded—only doing the right thing at the right time is. A backlog means some customer is waiting for goods they'd rather have—delivery measures reflect the poor performance. Output is increased but quality deteriorates? It shows up on the quality metrics.

World-class performance measurement starts from this balanced perspective, a clear recognition that improvement means moving forward, or at least holding ground, on all four measures. Visualizing these criteria as the four legs of a stool, it's clear that the goal is to balance the improvements to keep the stool level. Optimum performance is gained by keeping all four criteria clearly in mind and righting any temporary imbalances to ensure continued growth.

Motorola Corporation has instituted a balanced "scorecard" for its manufacturing group. Each JIT-M cell is evaluated on cycle time improvements, cost (in other words, productivity), quality, and on-time delivery. A bonus system is used to increase the motivational impact of the measurement system. In the spirit of continuous improvement, bonses are only given for gains on any of these dimensions. There is a catch, though. The bonus is earned if at least one aspect of performance is improved, as long as *performance on the remaining measures does not deteriorate.* This puts a series of checks and balances on the bonus system, which encourages employees to keep one eye on maintaining the status quo and the other on opportunities for improvement.

The value of the benchmarking process lies in its ability to ask the right questions, to provide a framework for understanding the nuances that make your organization different from the benchmark's performance or structure, and to identify processes that can be adapted to your organization to achieve continuous improvement.

In the fight for survival, a tie or a split decision simply will not do.

Merle L. Meacham

11: LOOKING FOR TRENDS: INDUSTRY BENCHMARKING AT EXXON CHEMICAL

Type of Benchmarking Used: External, Competitive
Purpose for Use: Identification of industry best practice in managing information system (IS) applications.
Area examined: All information system costs, applications, and structures across all user groups within the corporation/industry.

Lessons Learned:

There are a multitude of ways to gather industry data on existing practices, technologies, and management structures.

Management information systems are increasingly being used as a strategic weapon in the competitive chemicals industry.

Information technologies are transforming the activities and objectives of the modern corporation.

The effective generation, transmission, and reporting of information are the lifeblood of the organization. Being able to get this information, and act on it, faster than the competition provides a competitive advantage.

Industry benchmarking provides trends rather than static reference points about existing performance/processes.

THE SETTING

> Because both the activities of information processing and communication are inseparable components of the control function, a society's ability to maintain control—at all levels from interpersonal to international relations—will be directly proportional to the development of its information technologies.
>
> James Beniger
> *The Control Revolution*

Exxon Chemical is a multibillion dollar division of Exxon Corporation. Its sales to other Exxon affliates are done on an arm-length basis. Exxon Chemical participates in the highly competitive chemical industry with companies such as Dow, Du Pont, and Union Carbide.

Information systems are used in every function of the business, starting with the sales force and following through to customer service and support. In fact, most activities performed at Exxon Chemical are highly dependent on information systems. This trend, though, is not unique to the chemical industry. Consumer companies, such as Frito-Lay, are using information technology to provide a competitive advantage. In Exxon Chemical's case, though, it is not alone in its intensive use of information technologies; instead it is competing head-to-head with other sophisticated users.

Knowing this, and understanding the critical strategic role played by the IS (information systems), Exxon Chemical's management wanted to get a sanity check, or benchmark, of the relative degree, effectiveness, and efficiency of usage of information system technologies as compared against those of its competitors and the rest of industry. An article in *Chemical Week*

(October 17, 1990) underscores the importance of IS in the chemical industry:

> No matter how you slice it, the chemical industry spends a huge chunk of money on computers and automation. Experts peg worldwide expenditures for commercial information systems, including computers and software, at about $2 billion/year. In 1989, the U.S. process industries spent $910 million on plant-level machines and another $361.5 million on plant-floor computers.... Chemical producers also spend about $1 billion/year worldwide on distributed control systems.... Those dollars are buying an enormous amount of information. And faced with mounting environmental and safety reporting requirements— as well as increasing business pressures—chemical producers are desperately seeking ways to better handle the data.

What Exxon Chemical wanted to learn from its benchmarking study was the underlying trends in information system technology within their industry. In contrast to competitive benchmarking, then, this industry benchmarking study would focus on the way information system technologies were being used by the various players in the chemical industry, not in terms of percent of sales dollars dedicated to IS, but rather, the relative diffusion, and reliance upon, integrated information systems in conducting the ongoing operations of Exxon Chemical.

A MULTITUDE OF DATA COLLECTION APPROACHES

Due to the number of IS applications, the Exxon Chemical benchmarking study was a broad-based look at IS usage within its industry. The breadth of the analysis led to the use of multiple data sources, including published articles, presentations at trade associations, information system vendor-based inputs, customer-

supplied information, discussions with technical personnel at both competitors and outside of the industry, and direct conversations with employees of the benchmarking targets (see Figure 11.1). In all cases the request for information was accompanied by an offer to share survey results and to maintain confidentiality of proprietary information.

The industry benchmarking study at Exxon Chemical began with a discussion with Daniel Marie, worldwide manager of IS, of the types of information that the study should include, legal and ethical boundaries, management concerns about the acquisition and use of the information, and finally, an overall framework for organizing the data collection and analysis. The specific questions which he wanted answered were:

- In what direction is the industry going?
- Is there anything that our competitors are doing that we could learn from?
- What types of applications have they developed for managing various parts of their business?
- How sophisticated are their applications?
- How do they organize their IS function?

In other words, how does Exxon Chemical's management of IS compare to primary competitors and the industry, including how priorities were set and where decisions were leading?

Using Published Data Sources

Most companies do a limited amount of public discussion of their practices. For example, it is quite common for technical people to present corporate breakthroughs at association or trade meetings. In addition, there are general trends in the development and application of IS that apply across all industries. Therefore, the first place industry information should be sought is in published literature. The benefits of the initial literature search included:

1. Identifying leading-edge IS applications available.

2. Detailing which industry participants were openly discussing their use of these technologies.

3. Identifying areas that would require more intense analysis (for both direct competitors and the industry as a whole).

4. Raising issues related to the strategic, management, and operational analysis.

5. Providing an organizational structure for the benchmarking study.

The published data sources in this study provided enough information to build a "straw man" model. This model provides a reference point to later understand where everyone was, where they were heading, and why. It also identified industry experts both in academics and practice and provided Exxon Chemical with a clear picture of the areas where information was going to be relatively easy to obtain and where it would not. In other words, the literature search focused and set the scope of the remaining data collection and analysis procedures for the study. The initial model of the chemical industry's information system architecture was a key output of this preliminary analysis (see Figure 11.2).

Narrowing In on the Critical Issues

The literature review suggested that the benchmarking information would be broken into two broad categories: strategic issues and technology (see Figure 11.3). Within each of these categories, key functions were identified. The benchmarking questionnaire was developed with questions geared to highlight which companies were actively applying information technologies in these areas, how they were being used, the benefits being achieved, and how the "leaders" in each area were approaching the application of the technology.

Once the questionnaire was defined and agreed upon, the real work began. Information had to be gathered from multiple

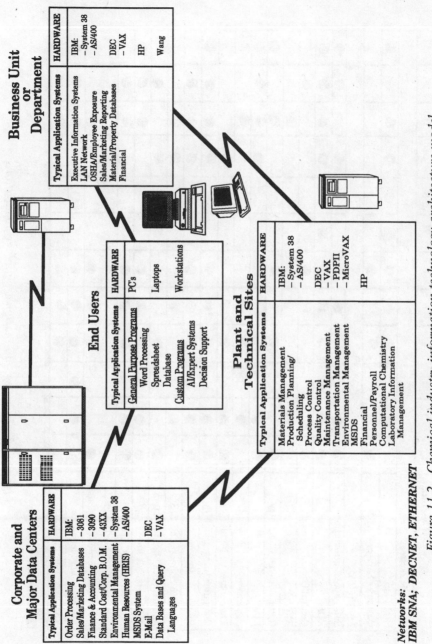

Corporate and Major Data Centers

Typical Application Systems	HARDWARE
Order Processing	IBM:
Sales/Marketing Databases	– 3081
Finance & Accounting	– 3090
Standard Cost/Corp. B.O.M.	– 43XX
Environmental Management	– System 38
Human Resources (HRIS)	– AS/400
MSDS System	DEC
E-Mail	– VAX
Data Bases and Query	
Languages	

End Users

Typical Application Systems	HARDWARE
General Purpose Programs	PC's
Word Processing	
Spreadsheet	Laptops
Database	
Custom Programs	Workstations
AI/Expert Systems	
Decision Support	

Business Unit or Department

Typical Application Systems	HARDWARE
Executive Information Systems	IBM:
LAN Network	– System 38
OSHA/Employee Exposure	– AS/400
Sales/Marketing Reporting	DEC
Material/Property Databases	– VAX
Financial	HP
	Wang

Plant and Technical Sites

Typical Application Systems	HARDWARE
Materials Management	IBM:
Production Planning/	– System 38
Scheduling	– AS/400
Process Control	DEC
Quality Control	– VAX
Maintenance Management	– PDPII
Transportation Management	– MicroVAX
Environmental Management	
MSDS	HP
Financial	
Personnel/Payroll	
Computational Chemistry	
Laboratory Information	
Management	

Networks:
IBM SNA; DECNET, ETHERNET

Figure 11.2   Chemical industry information technology architecture model.

Company	1	2	3	4	5	6	7	8	9	10	11	12
Strategic Issues												
CIM Plan		●		●	●	●		●	●	●		●
Customer Service	●			●		●						
Technology												
Sales Force Automation	●	●		●	●	●			●	●	●	●
EDI	●	●	●	●	●	●	●		●		●	●
Central Order Processing	●				●	●					●	
EIS		●										
Computational Chemistry				●		●				●		●
LIMS	●	●							●	●	●	●
Supercomputers		●			●					●		●
Environmental Mgmt Systems	●	●		●	●				●	●		
Computer Integrated Mfg.	●	●		●	●	●			●	●		●
Process Control	●	●		●	●			●	●			
Decision Support and EIS					●				●	●		
Maintenance Mgmt. System	●			●		●	●			●	●	
AI/Expert Systems	●	●	●	●		●				●	●	●
Process Design CAD/CAM	●	●		●		●				●	●	
Computer Systems Design & Development In-House	●											
E-Mail and/or Networks	●	●	●			●		●		●	●	●
Eng. and Materials Databases	●					●				●	●	

● = Identified activity

Figure 11.3   Industry information technology applications.

sources in tandem. A three-prong approach was used to get the information: supplier/vendor discussions, personal and phone interviews directly with the technical staff of the benchmark firms, and customer contacts.

Supplier/vendors are always a good place to get information. While they actively protected the confidentiality of their customers, they freely described what their systems and various software applications are capable of doing.

Benchmarking companies provided the next level of data. In the Exxon Chemical benchmarking study, most competitors were hesitant to provide technical details about their IS operations, as expected, but gladly shared management and structural information. However, not all companies could be enticed by the data-sharing process (even with anonymity).

A key question addressed during these interviews was the relationship between the IS function and the user groups. The IS departments were quite willing to discuss what *types* of services they were providing (free of technical details of how). On the other hand, user groups were more hesitant to cooperate and used the interviews as a "gripe session." When queried about the services being provided by the IS group, their first reaction was that their IS is nonresponsive. These comments had to be analyzed carefully to see what was really going on. In the end, the user-based information was less useful than originally planned.

To facilitate the information gathering and highlight similarities and differences, a "straw man" of possible management/service structures was also developed at the conclusion of the public data review. This approach placed a definitive structure around the benchmarking analysis. Two industry models emerged from the analysis: (1) a decentralized IS structure and (2) a centralized corporate IS structure with established business system staffs in user organizations that focused on improving communications and service to user groups.

Industry benchmarking, then, looks for trends in the practices and structures of competitive firms around some central theme, such as information system technology. Because of the nature of many of the inquiries, multiple data sources have to be culled. Published information is the fastest basis for much of the needed analysis. Organizing this data provides the basis for developing alternative models of the underlying process. Armed with these models, the benchmarking team can pursue more directed lines of inquiry with competitors/industry companies, suppliers/vendors, and customers. The final benchmarking product results from the careful combination of all these data sources.

THE COMPETITIVE ASSESSMENT

The benchmarking study sponsored by Exxon Chemical did yield valuable information on trends and issues in the use of information system technology in the chemical industry. Summarizing these findings (a company-based analysis is detailed in Figure 11.4):

1. The management of IS tends to be decentralized to meet diversified business needs and to get it closer to the user. Most of the companies surveyed have decentralized IS organizations. Those that are centralized disperse consultation staff to user groups.

2. The functions of corporate IS organizations are changing, to focus on providing strategic guidance and direction and supporting the development of strategically important systems. These include telecommunications and networking, customer service, and manufacturing management.

3. Companies are developing common systems that can be used globally to leverage their proprietary knowledge and technology.

4. Technology is being focused to support specific business needs. The major application areas are: sales force automation, expert systems, centralized order processing, and electronic data interchange on the customer service dimension; computer research support to reduce the time

STRATEGIC AREAS	USE THESE TECHNOLOGIES	TO ACHIEVE THESE BENEFITS	TYPICAL LEADERS
Sales and Customer Service	• Sales Force Automation • EDI		**Dow** • Central order processing and
Plant Management Systems	• Material Resource Planning (MRP) • Pro... • Co... • Ma... • Ma... • Sy...	• Improve production control • Reduce inventories	**Monsanto** • Plant of the 90's
Decision Support	• Decision Support Systems • Executive Information Systems • Database Technology	• Quicker access to data • Reduce time for analysis • Better decisions	**Hoechst Celanese** • Using IFPS and FASTAR to improve financial analysis **Company A** • EIS tracks oil prices and production
Communications	• Telecommunications • LAN Networks • E-Mail	• Improve employee communications • Better, faster information • Reduce overhead costs • Improve productivity	**Shell** • E-Mail System for 23,000 users • Standardized telecommunications reduced costs by $2.3 million **Eastern Kodak** • Global network standards and outsourcing to reduce costs 34%
Systems Support	• Shared Data Centers • Data Resource Management (DRM) • Data Center Consolidation • Outsourcing	• Reduce costs • Improve productivity • Systems reliability • Improve information & communications • Improve systems design	**Company A** • Shared data center facility **Eastern Kodak** • Outsourcing • Data center consolidation (3-1)
Human Resources	• Human Resource Information Systems • Recruiting Systems	• Improve employee productivity • Improve morale	**Company B** • Europewide HRIS tracks employee assignments

Other strategic areas shown: Order Processing and Customer Service; Maintenance Management; Computer Research Support; Process and Product Design; Sales; Marketing; Manufacturing; Distribution.

Figure 11.4 Industry information-technology applications and benefits.

and cost of new product and process development; computer-integrated manufacturing planning and implementation, and other manufacturing systems such as maintenance management to improve plant productivity; and the use of decision support and executive information systems to assist in business analysis and planning.

5. Technical applications, including computer support of R&D, process engineering design, and process control systems, have been developed by the user community independent of the IS organizations. The need for support in communications, networking, and database management now and in the future will lead to more involvement by IS in these areas.

6. There is increasing need for, and emphasis on, data resource management to coordinate the development, use, and transfer of data between corporate databases and application systems.

Exxon's Lessons Learned and Response to the Study

The real value of the industry benchmarking project for Exxon Chemical was that it provided them with actual organization models that could be compared, analyzed, and critiqued. For example, finding out that other companies with "far-flung" manufacturing facilities were using committees and team advisory councils to help set a unified direction and strategy for the IS function was a technique that could be adapted. Specific changes that were supported by the benchmark study included:

- The 1989 reorganization of the IS function. Exxon Chemical began to move away from its predominantly centralized IS structure to the decentralized model used by its peer group. This entailed a tighter integration of IS and the business, as well as increased IS "ownership" at the business unit level. At the corporate level, the focus was placed on the strategic use of integrated information from data already in service.

■ Establishment of a steering committee to set overall direction and corporate resource levels.

A second major benefit of the study was that it identified current applications of IS technology in the chemical industry. The collected data detailed the entire range of technology available. Exxon Chemical was able to compare its current IS strategies and utilization with industry trends and was able to see how other companies were benefiting from the various technologies available. Gaining such a detailed overview of the pros and cons of the available technologies helped Exxon Chemical's management to prioritize the opportunities for improvement identified in the benchmarking study, and to prevent costly mistakes and false starts.

ISSUES AND ANSWERS IN
INDUSTRY/COMPETITIVE BENCHMARKING

Industry and competitive benchmarking are related techniques for exploring existing practices and trends among peer companies. Both are focused on providing information to help an organization focus its improvement efforts and prioritize competing projects.

The Ethics of Benchmarking

In industries or competitive benchmarking studies, the ethical "boundaries" are both fuzzier and more important to keep an eye on than in internal or best-in-class benchmark studies. Why? Because industry and competitive benchmarking studies, by definition, are focusing on ongoing practices of current or potential competitors. Therefore, honesty of intent has to be always present, and never violated.

Understanding these concerns, Exxon Chemical and Janssen did bring in an outside facilitator to increase the objectivity and breadth of the study. The facilitator served valuable roles: (1) provided the requisite objectivity and confidentiality necessary to gain support from benchmark firms; and (2) because of related-industry experience, the facilitator was able to provide substantial background for, and qualitative interpretations of, the benchmarking data. Facilitators, then, can play a vital role in industry and competitive benchmarking.

A final note on industry and competitive benchmarking ethics that bears repeating: Because of the severity of antitrust penalties and the complexity of some antitrust laws, legal counsel should ordinarily be sought in connection with these initiatives.

Choosing a Benchmarking Approach

Benchmarking has been discussed as a means to compare and standardize internal operations and as a first step in diagnosing and identifying current practice within a company (internal benchmarking), as a static measurement of a company's performance in financial and nonfinancial areas as compared to its peers (competitive analysis), and as a general analysis of trends for one specific function or component of an industry (industry benchmarking). In each case, a "straw man" model has been developed that was an amalgamation of best practice within a narrowly defined industry or corporate setting.

Internal benchmarking can be both a tool for continuous improvement and the first step in a comprehensive external benchmarking project. Competitive benchmarking, on the other hand, helps identify and prioritize what aspects of the company require intense examination and improvement efforts. Industry benchmarking identifies trends and provides insight into how those trends are being set. In each of these cases, the lens has remained constantly focused on choosing a group of benchmarking targets that would traditionally be viewed as complementary, or comparable, to the firm performing the study. Even in industry benchmarking, where the strategic deployment of a specific part of the business is being examined, the benchmarking targets remain narrowly defined within companies that make the same basic line of goods.

While significant improvements can occur by adopting best industry practice, it also leads to the adoption of a set of blinders. Internally focused studies, whether within the corporation or industry, are limited by tradition. Existing practices that emerged over time have been standardized and have become the norm while the underlying assumptions of the organizing principles used by the company or industry have probably remained unquestioned and unexamined.

The focus now turns toward "best-in-class" benchmarking. Underlying this approach is a belief that improving performance in a functional area is best based on "best practice" broadly defined. In this setting, the assumption that industry peers provide the optimal match and basis for learning is dropped. Instead, the characteristics of the function, or value chain, being examined are juxtaposed against companies in other industries and other settings. The objective is to match the *processes* performed, not the structure of the companies themselves. Best-in-class benchmarking, then, provides the greatest potential for quantum improvements in performance.

It is better to obey the mysterious direction, without any fuss, when it points to a new road, however strange that road may be. There is probably as much reason for it, if the truth were known, as for anything else.

H.M. Tomlinson
The Face of the Earth

12: THE BASICS OF BEST-IN-CLASS BENCHMARKING

The great thing in this world is not so much where we are, but in what direction we are moving.

Oliver Wendell Holmes

People and companies are both enthused and limited by their visions. An individual who always says "But I can't" probably never will. A company that looks internally for its solutions, clinging to the belief that any idea not created in-house is useless, will myopically see less and less of the real world in which it competes. Conversely, people who see only opportunities in every problem and twist of fate usually find a way to turn bad times to good with remarkable speed. And companies that are constantly looking for ways to improve, and are open to the thought that other companies just might have a leg or two up on them in some areas, will thrive and grow as they pursue best practice, whatever its source.

Best-in-class (BIC) benchmarking is based on the belief that the value creation process has similar characteristics across a variety of institutional settings. The impact this has on a corporation hopelessly mired in its own traditions is suggested by the following statement:[1]

> Benchmarking, which is nothing more than admitting that someone else is capable of doing something better than you, ... helps the company set targets and determine exactly how to reach them.

Internal, competitive, and industry benchmarking can all serve as ways to break down the myopic barriers that prevent a company from identifying, adopting, and mastering best practices. If these barriers remain in place, it is quite likely that best-in-class benchmarking will never take place; by definition, it requires a clear recognition that someone, somewhere, does the job at least a little better.

Key Factors of Best-in-Class Benchmarking

> What exactly is *dantotsu?* There are several possible translations: unchallenged, absolutely brilliant, undoubtedly the best, leadership, better than best. In many ways, the best definition is the same as the goal of benchmarking, best of the best.
>
> Gary Jacobson and John Hilkirk
> *Xerox: American Samurai*

Best-in-class benchmarking is based in the same set of beliefs as the Japanese concept of *dantotsu*. Both seek to identify the best of the best practices, using them to innovatively change existing processes within an organization. In pursuing BIC projects, a company is "opening its kimono" with the understanding that improvement is needed; the study helps focus exactly what changes should be pursued and why.

As a free-standing benchmarking approach, BIC has clearly defined characteristics that set it apart from its sister techniques:

1. Target participants are identified through careful research.
2. Industry alignment is no longer a key issue in the selection of target participants. While there is a need to ensure that the basic structural characteristics (drivers) of the target firm's environment are comparable to the sponsoring organization, the concept of "matching" is much more loosely defined.

BENCHMARKING

3. It can be used to generate innovative approaches or solutions to current problems.
4. It is free from concerns with antitrust or similar regulatory issues.
5. It is intricately tied to continuous improvement objectives.

Defining success against external criteria established by the *entire* competitive environment means much more than simply beating the nearest competitor; it means setting a vision of excellence that pulls the company onto a new plane of performance. BIC benchmarking is the basis for gaining quantum leaps in competitive performance, because it redefines what excellence is. The key characteristics of world-class performance that represent "best practice" firms are reflected in Figure 12.1.

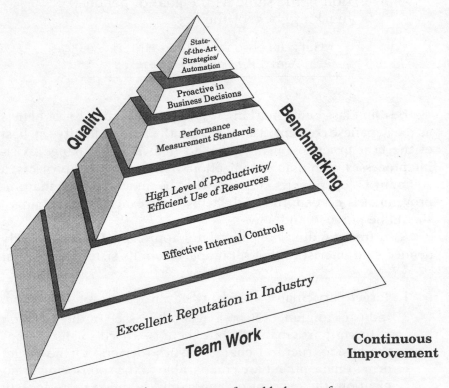

Figure 12.1   Characteristics of world-class performance.

12: THE BASICS OF BEST-IN-CLASS BENCHMARKING

The Search for Best Practice

> We have unquestionably a great cloud-bank of ancestral blindness weighing down upon us, only transiently riven here and there by fitful revelations of the truth.
>
> William James
> *Talks to Teachers*

Most companies can quickly develop a list of target companies for an industry or competitive benchmarking analysis, but they stall out when asked to identify best-in-class firms. Having never looked at their organization as a series of value chains across functional silos, let alone attempted to identify externally defined measures of their performance, it is very difficult for them to move forward without performing a literature review, analysis of the issue with identified experts in the area, and related "research" aimed at identifying participants for their study.

The choice of candidate "best-in-class" firms is further muddied by the fact that a company (perhaps the one under study?) that is best in one part of its business may perform abysmally in another. A reputation for overall excellence does not immediately track to best practice in every aspect of business operations. Similarly, companies noted to be "best" in literature reviews may not be continuing to work toward innovation; people and organizations tend to relax (that is, rest on their laurels) when they feel they're at the front of the pack. If their practices are already known, it may be more fruitful to continue the search and find a company that *learned* from the "best-practice" organization. There you may uncover amazing new twists on the concepts perfected by the BIC firm.

Research to identify BIC candidates, then, may begin with the reading of a benchmarking article that lists top performers by process, but should never end there. In the search for innovative practice, the goal is to look a little farther, a little harder, than everyone else to find that company or group that has redefined the problem and gained a competitive advantage from it.

Getting an "Apples-to-Apples" Comparison

While BIC benchmarking is indifferent to industry boundaries and virtually immune to antitrust concerns, it is vitally concerned with the structures and constraints of its benchmarking target firms. BIC approaches are much more loosely defined with respect to the source and physical comparability of two functions, processes, or roles, but the "looseness" ends there. The usefulness of benchmarking information is based on comparability: similarity in the core work flows, contextual and environmental constraints, and marketing characteristics of the target firms to those of the sponsoring organization.

What does this really mean? A BIC study attempts to identify optimal structures and practices for dealing with a specified type of work in the organization. That means that, when examining the performance of the distribution system of a company against BIC targets, the objective is to be able to match up enough of the core features of the two settings to ensure that the solutions used by the BIC firms *can be* adopted by the BIC sponsor. If a company's distribution system is centralized in one warehouse, filling orders from customers directly, or from salespeople scattered across the country, it is well advised to include L.L. Bean in its list of target firms. Their effectiveness in this type of distribution channel is world-renowned.

On the other hand, if the company has a dispersed logistics channel that merely serves as a clearinghouse for a continuous flow of standardized products to a few regular customers, the L.L. Bean distribution system will be far too elaborate and costly to consider; the *structures* of the two operations are so different that meaningful comparisons are impossible. Only if the BIC sponsor is willing to consider radically overhauling the structure of its distribution channel to provide a centralized service to a broad-based customer group can it employ L.L. Bean's approach. That does not mean, of course, that it can't pick up a few pointers at L.L. Bean (as well as a few items of clothing); it is simply that it cannot adopt many of the practices that L.L. Bean uses, due to structural or practical constraints.

In performing a BIC benchmarking study, then, a clear eye has to be kept on the *constraints and drivers* the sponsoring firm operates under. Constraints and drivers can be quite difficult to overcome. For instance, a company that manufactures jewelry is going to be unable to adopt the manufacturing procedures used by a utility. The environmental constraints make it impossible to match up the practices of the two firms.

The point of this discussion is quite simple: BIC benchmarking is confined, not by industry or product, but by the drivers that constrain the processes and procedures in one company *unique*. Structural and contextual factors (such as the regulatory environment, competitive environment, or general economic conditions) define the basic nature and tential design of work flows within organizations. Not every "constraint" is etched in stone, but some are. In undertaking a BIC benchmarking study, it's important to know which is which and why.

Focused Innovation

BIC benchmarking targets innovative practices for adoption by the sponsoring company. As these "best practices" are identified, they create the impetus for change and continuous improvement. It's hard to ignore the facts uncovered in a benchmarking study. In fact, accepting the harsh realities of existing performance is the first step in changing it for the better.

BIC benchmarking isolates the *gap* between existing practice in the sponsor company and those used by best-practice firms. Best practice, of course, may come from an amalgamation of existing approaches taken in a series of firms, but the use of the benchmarks remains clear. BIC benchmarks, juxtaposed against existing practice, let a company know, in no uncertain terms, how well it is performing. For instance, a corporate accounting group may feel as though it is really doing well when it trims the number of days it takes it to close the books from 10 days to eight. They know that more improvement will have to occur, but they're getting close to perfection, right? Wrong.

After doing a BIC benchmarking study, this same group becomes quite despondent. When compared to the target firms, they discover that the eight days currently used in closing the books is at least double what the BIC firms use. In fact, one company is identified as being able to close the books in under two days (and is targeting getting it under one). Eight days may look good compared to historical performance inside the company, but it doesn't fare as well when stacked up against best practice.

When a company identifies such a major gap, what alternatives does it have? Obviously, they can always put the results in a drawer, lock it, and throw away the key; shred them; or make paper airplanes out of them. At least in the latter case some "value" will be obtained. Having spent the funds on benchmarking, some companies have actually rejected the findings. As with death, though, bad news cannot be ignored; it can only be dealt with more or less productively.

THE FIVE STAGES OF MOURNING

> Why do we live? Most of us need the very thing we never ask for. We talk about revolution as if it were peanuts. What we need is some frank thinking and a few revolutions in our own guts; to hell with most of the sons of bitches that I know and myself along with them if I don't take hold of myself and turn about when I need to – or go ahead further if that's the game.
>
> William Carlos Williams
> *Selected Letters of William Carlos Williams*

When faced with a difficult event, such as the death of the belief in one's superiority, "mourning" for lost innocence and the securities of the past is often triggered. Like a death, the harsh realities revealed in a benchmarking study can create denial, anger, and rejection. That is why this section is so "cheerily" tagged the five stages of mourning. In accepting the facts (the performance gap) detailed in the benchmarking study, individuals are likely to go through the following stages: (1) denial, (2) anger,

Figure 12.2   Five stages of mourning—reaction to benchmark report.

(3) bargaining, (4) depression, and (5) acceptance (see Figure 12.2). These five stages of mourning are encountered whenever a person or a long-held "belief" dies.[2]

Denial: When Reality Isn't Acceptable

> One sprinkles the most sugar where the tart is burnt.
>
> Dutch proverb

Seldom do the results of a benchmarking study proclaim the sponsoring company "best-in-class" across the board. If such an event occurs, it is, like the birth of a new child, met with the requisite joy. If instead the news is less uplifting, and perhaps even discouraging, it triggers an almost automatic response from management: "This can't be true."

Unfortunately, it probably is. Swallowing the bitter pill of reality is the worst part of benchmarking. No matter how noble a person may be, finding out that you're badly behind in a game you've been playing to win is disheartening. What is stolen at this moment is the company's self-respect, in a way. Having continuously worked to beat the competition and gain a competitive advantage, having spent countless thousands and millions of dollars on state-of-the-art equipment and management training, having seeded the management ranks with highly trained MBAs, the only initial response management can have to the benchmarking results is denial. Anything else would be an admittance of failure and self-deception.

Anger: Stage Two Unfolds

> Anger is not only inevitable, it is necessary. Its absence means indifference, the most disastrous of all human failings.
>
> Arthur Posonby
> *Casual Observations*

The one danger in spearheading a benchmarking effort is the fact that most generals shoot the messenger who bears bad tidings from the field of battle. In anger, management can often refuse to accept the data, perhaps even suggesting that the study was poorly done. Not feeling any better about the results than his or her boss, the messenger simply stands by, waiting for the execution.

When benchmarking data is presented, denial very rapidly turns to anger at whatever animate or inanimate object appears to be stating the unpleasant facts. Anger and denial can result in disappearing reports, heavy use of the office paper shredder, and extensive vacations for the benchmarking team. In reality, the anger that management feels at the realization that the benchmarking report is not giving the company an A, but rather an E for effort, is natural.

The anger is really not focused on the person providing the data but rather at the story being told. Most top managers have worked hard and long to make their companies "better." To find out that the efforts have been misspent creates anger at the wasted hours and the realization of how many more hours of effort may be required to achieve world-class performance (a goal that seemed so close at hand only days before). It is not a happy event to move several mountains to get to the top, only to find that there are mountains yet ahead and little time to catch your breath. Anger is an understandable emotion when reality turns your world upside down. What is done after the anger passes spells the difference between growth and decline.

Bargaining: Let's Make a Deal with the Devil

Personally I am always ready to learn, although I do not always like being taught.

Sir Winston Churchill

Bargaining is the process of rationalizing what has occurred, of setting boundaries around a problem in order to fit it into one's existing world view. In terms of benchmarking, bargaining takes place as the measures are examined and reexamined, questions are raised about the costing method used to arrive at the reported figures, and so on. When persons move to bargaining to soften the blow of the benchmarking information, they are really trying to make the data fit their view of the world rather than actually absorbing and learning the lesson being taught.

Rationalization of a problem is usually done after reports are issued and results known. In rationalizing the problems identified in the benchmarking study, management is trying to find an error, definition, or measure that will put the picture "back in focus." If an error can be uncovered, then business can continue on as usual. If not, bargaining (trying to change the information) and rationalization (reinterpreting it to fit the desired model) gives way to depression.

Depression: We're as Bad as the Report Says...

> Nothing strong, nothing new, nothing urgent penetrates a man's mind without crossing resistance.
>
> Henri de Lubac
> *Paradoxes*

Depression is the crossroads in the learning process that is embedded in benchmarking. It starts with management's plaintive cry, "Oh my God, we're terrible." It continues through a period of intense self-reflection as the gap that needs to be crossed to gain world-class performance appears to widen, alternatives seem to fade into ungraspable mists, and a general feeling of inadequacy overwhelms the managers charged with searching for solutions.

A depression can be an extended event that permanently derails the actions and destroys the motivations of an individual "explorer" or organization. Simple tasks take on monumental size; they become unsolvable mazes of impossible complexity. So why do benchmarking? Isn't no action better than defeat? Not in a marketplace that shows no mercy to those who falter; business is not a gentleman's sport. While finding out that real performance is far below that needed to be deemed best-in-class may be disheartening, attempting to ignore it can only lead to corporate decline. As unpleasant as the truth may be, it can only be faced, not avoided.

Acceptance: Turning Defeat into Victory

> The man who gives up accomplishes nothing and is only a hindrance. The

> man who does *not* give up can move
> mountains.
>
> Ernest Hello
> *Life, Science and Art*

Learning comes from accepting reality and taking actions to change it. It starts with asking the right questions; with accepting that the benchmarking results are probably correct and that lessons can be learned from the competition. How exactly does the benchmarked firm manage the process? Do competitors use centralized or decentralized structures? What role did measurements play in changing their view of the world? Are they using a team-oriented approach for problem solving, or do individuals strike out on their own and make needed changes? Were process changes made that helped them get rid of non-value-added activities and costs? If so, what insights can we gain from their experiences?

With acceptance of the benchmarking results, analysis of how the benchmarked firms organize and manage their processes plus anecdotal evidence and comments, will bring about the realization that the performance gap can be closed. As workable alternatives are developed, enthusiasm is rekindled. The final objective, continuous improvement, is identified and pursued; perseverence ensures that it is reached.

To Create the Learning Organization

> The juxtaposition of vision (what we want) and a clear picture of current reality (where we are relative to what we want) generates what we call "creative tension": a force to bring them together, caused by the natural tendency of tension to seek resolution....
>
> "Learning" in this context does not mean acquiring more information but

> expanding the ability to produce the
> results we truly want in life. It is life-
> long generative learning. And learn-
> ing organizations are not possible un-
> less they have people at every level
> who practice it.
>
> Peter M. Senge
> *The Fifth Discipline*

The objective of benchmarking procedures is not to understand where the company stands versus other firms, file the report, and return to the status quo. It is a tool for organizational
learning. In fact, as Peter Senge suggests above, benchmarking is
one way to instill the "creative tension" that is a prerequisite to
improvement. Interestingly, Senge suggests that the creative tension required to generate organizational learning can also lead to
the feelings or emotions associated with anxiety, "such as sadness,
discouragement, hopelessness, or worry."[3] A very similar concept,
it would seem, to the stages of mourning.

Creative tension arises whenever we acknowledge a "vision"
that is at odds with current reality. What Senge suggests is that
creative tension has to be kept separate from the emotional tension that sometimes accompanies it, or it results in a lowering
of our vision. Accepting defeat may relieve the emotional tension
created by "missing the mark," but it cannot support continued
growth and organizational learning.

In a Canadian manufacturer/distributor, the board of directors
initiated a strategic review of the company in order to provide
clear guidance on issues affecting competitiveness, strategic alternatives, and a possible corporate reorganization. Over the past
decade, the company's market share had declined by 50 percent
and competition was increasing because:

■ Small suppliers were increasing their share of the market
through price discounts and aggressive sales strategies.

- The overall petroleum market had been stagnant during the last five years and forecasts indicated that the market would continue to decline. Therefore, market share would be aggressively sought/protected.

- Manufacturing overcapacity existed in both Canada and the United States.

- Little, if any, difference existed between competitive products and the Company's products.

Based on the benchmark review, if became clear the company had a "product" focus rather than a dedication to sales and service. To measure this gap the company then conducted a major customer survey to do the following:

- Identify specific causes of the decline in market share

- Understand the relative position of the company vis à vis the customer perception of best-in-class performance

- Indicate strategies necessary to implement a company turnaround

- Prioritize actions

What is interesting in all of these discussions is their similarity. Across the board, management books are preaching the need for a corporate "vision," a stretch goal that keeps everyone moving forward, looking for ways to improve reality. Benchmarking provides the impetus or tension needed to start the momentum of change, but to do its job it has to be accepted, believed, and acted upon.

Competitive success comes from constantly redefining the playing field, from learning from those who do things better, in whatever walk of life they're encountered. It takes courage, because constantly facing one's weaknesses can be a humbling experience. But from humility comes an enthusiasm to grow and learn and to overcome the hurdles ahead. Benchmarking gives the first shove needed to set the organization in motion; the resulting actions come from within the learning organization.

BEST-IN-CLASS: KEEPING THE TARGET IN SIGHT

> Before you begin a thing remind yourself that difficulties and delays quite impossible to foresee are ahead. If you could see them clearly, naturally you could do a great deal to get rid of them but you can't. You can only see one thing clearly and that is your goal. Form a mental vision of that and cling to it through thick and thin.
>
> Kathleen Norris
> *Hands Full of Living*

BIC benchmarking helps a company leapfrog the competition, providing the basis for quantum improvements in existing performance. Because it looks outside of the ordinary group of "peers" to those who perform a certain type of process or role the best, it supports innovative practice and organizational learning. Yet, BIC benchmarking is not a panacea, nor is it necessarily easy to do.

As suggested earlier, the hardest part about doing a best-in-class study is identifying comparable companies, or groups, that will support the learning process. If a chosen benchmarking target has radically different drivers, structures and constraints from your company, it is unlikely that their methods can be adapted successfully by you. Ignoring this fact is like trying to put a square peg into a round hole. The pieces simply will not fit together, and the frustration created may end up being insurmountable because of structural flaws, not in the sponsoring company or the target firm but rather in the design of the benchmarking study itself. A poorly planned BIC study can easily result in a "garbage in, garbage out" phenomenon.

Yet not being able to fit every piece of the information gleaned from the BIC study into your setting doesn't mean that the study was flawed. Benchmarking is an adaptive process; it is not a "copycat" exercise where each and every practice identified within the best-practice firms is adopted, no questions asked, at the sponsoring company. The only sure result of this approach is that the implementation of the changes will creak to a grinding halt somewhere downstream, as the "misfits" between the benchmarked firm's strategy, structure and environmental constraints, and those faced by the sponsoring company, begin to narrow, and then clog, the path ahead. The key to using BIC benchmarking effectively is to keep a healthy skepticism about the process, to use the results wisely, and constantly review the assumptions, and procedures, used to apply the benchmarking results to existing practices.

BIC benchmarking is a powerful tool for organizational learning that requires finesse in its design, application, and usage. To overcome the reality that BICs are undoubtedly scattered among the chosen target firms, a "straw man" model can be developed for BIC studies. This straw man can help the sponsoring company avoid the copycat phenomenon; instead, each suggested change can be carefully analyzed against the constraints and realities of daily life. Change for change's sake is not the objective of the benchmarking study; directed change to achieve competitive advantage in order to increase the value of the firm for all of its stakeholders is.

It is a very rare matter when any of us at any time in life sees things as they are at the moment. This happens at times...that we become aware of what is going on about us and of the infinite great worlds of force, of feeling and of idea in which we live, and in the midst of which we have always been living. These worlds are really in progress all the time; and the difference between one man and another,

BENCHMARKING

or the difference in the same man at different times, is the difference in his awareness of what is happening.

John Jay Chapman
Memories and Milestones

13: IDENTIFYING PERFORMANCE DRIVERS

The causes I am inclined to think are there all along, and the events which we see, and which look like freaks of chance, are only the last steps in long lines of causation.

Alfred North Whitehead
Dialogues of Alfred North Whitehead

Traditionally, measurement has been identified with the historical development of a scorecard that lets everyone review prior performance. Benchmarking, though, is more concerned with the future. Focused on establishing performance targets, it sets the stage for strategic planning and the realization of those plans.

An integral part of the benchmarking process is the identification of the constraints and drivers of performance for the organization. This will identify the invisible fences or existing assumptions for management. These fences may be taken down during the benchmarking process, but that can't be done if no one knows what or where they are.

A *performance driver* is a causal factor, an underlying characteristic of the organization or its environment, that dictates the amount and type of activities that are performed to meet customer demands and ensure organizational survival. These drivers can be *inherent* to the environment, and as such are not immediately changeable by the firm's actions; *structural* (that is, embedded in the current design of the organization, its location, and its history); or *performance-related* (that is, the result of the productive activity itself). A driver, then, is the answer given to the question "Why?" in the benchmarking process. When you analyze your organization in preparation for benchmarking, the unique characteristics that exist because of management preferences, geographic constraints, or any other nonnegotiable issue have to be identified and addressed. If this isn't done, an "apples-to-apples" comparison is impossible.

Performance drivers impact the entire organization, from the development of its strategy through the monitoring and controlling of ongoing operations (see Figure 13.1). Embedded in this process are a series of feedback loops that provide the means to measure, assess, and direct the development and implementation of the organization's mission: to meet customer requirements.

A series of performance drivers can be identified that reflect the environment, or the organization's response to it. The strategies, structures, and processes chosen by the firm reflect tradition

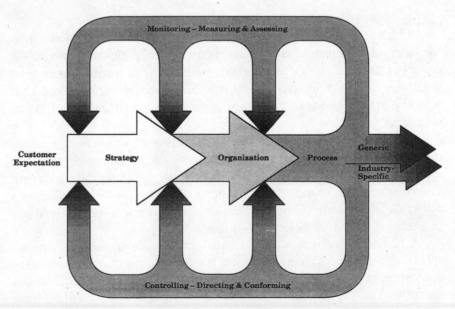

Figure 13.1   Drivers impact.

within the industry, as well as more generic responses that have been adopted over time and that work in many different settings.

These are important differences, because they underlie the benchmarking process. Industry-specific performance expectations and measurements, such as the capital intensity ratio, are best evaluated within the industry itself using internal, competitive, or industry benchmarking procedures. Conversely, should certain activity networks prove to be generic across many industries, "best-in-class" benchmarking will provide the greatest benefit. The benchmarking process, then, begins with a clear understanding of the environment, the competition, and the current structures, strategies and processes used by the organization.

Internal assessment is often the part of benchmarking that is most resisted by the companies employing it. Why? Because management *believes* it knows everything there is to know about its company; it has questions about what others are doing, not what they are. When asked to identify the most important aspect of benchmarking, Bob Camp suggested that it is

> Preparation. The prerequisite for effective benchmarking is to identify and document the work process. Then you have to prioritize which ones to go after.[1]

In all honesty, if management really knew the details of its processes, it would be unlikely that it would assume it was already the "best of the best." Internal assessment of existing work practices more often leads to an "Oh no, we don't do that, do we?".

PUTTING DRIVERS IN CONTEXT

> Learning preserves the errors of the past, as well as its wisdom. For this reason, dictionaries are public dangers, although they are necessities.
>
> Alfred North Whitehead

> A little learning is a dangerous thing, but a lot of ignorance is just as bad.
>
> Bob Edwards

Identifying performance drivers begins with understanding the internal strategies, structures, work practices, and constraints that have defined the way processes are performed within the organization. These evolve over time and persist long after the reasons for them have faded into history. This evolution is not random; it is guided by the exigencies of the moment and the need to respond to a changing marketplace. Prior practices, though, serve as both an anchor and constraint on the types of changes that can be made. Corporate momentum, once set in motion, is difficult to halt. Relatedly, some decisions affect the structure and processes of a company for a decade or more; others can be reversed rapidly with little or no "hangover" or residual effects.

Internal assessment, the first step in any benchmarking project, identifies the major business processes currently in place as well as the *reason* for them. Charting these work processes is like mapping a river; there will be a main channel or flow through the system; a series of "detours" that can be taken along the way; and whirlpools where all activity stops and an order, product, or piece of vital correspondence can be drawn into a whirling maelstrom of tasks and countertasks, never to see the light of day again. As with a river, the underlying flow through the organization is difficult to alter. Dredging new river beds and diverting the existing flows through them is a possibility; the city of Providence, Rhode Island, is witness to this fact; but it takes tremendous time, energy, and resources to accomplish it.

Setting the Stage: Driver Examples

Concepts can be difficult to grasp when painted in unfamiliar words and ways. The performance driver concept is no exception. Several applications of the approach may help solidify the ideas (see Figure 13.2). For example, a prerequisite for competitive benchmarking is the internal assessment of the entire organization. In doing this analysis, a series of environmental (that is, inherent) constraints comes into view. These constraints *cannot be changed*. The company has to work within the framework set by the environment.

The environmental context or constraints faced by most companies include the public policies regulating the practices, products, and services performed by the firm; market forces (such as a highly competitive industry with large, international players who are eating away at domestic and international market shares

13: IDENTIFYING PERFORMANCE DRIVERS

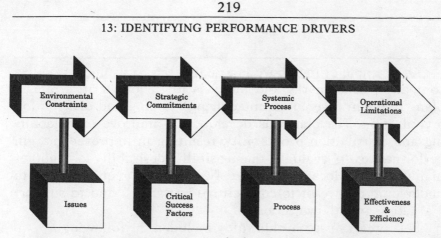

Figure 13.2   Drivers in the benchmarking process.

for your firm); product characteristics (such as shortening product life cycles); and available technologies. These factors may be influenceable to some extent by the company, but they can't be directly changed. Only if a company redefines the playing field, seizing a competitive advantage by innovatively changing the way that this constraint is responded to or managed, can progress be made in this area.

The next set of performance drivers, or defining characteristics of the organization, are actually shaped by long-run strategic initiatives and management decisions. This group can actually be split into two classes: strategic commitments and systemic processes. *Strategic commitments* are the basis for defining what products, services, and markets the company will serve; the location and number of facilities it will maintain; its cultures and values; the presence of, and relationship with, employee labor unions, and so on. Set in stone for the long run (more than 5 years), these commitments are the anchors for the ongoing management of the company. If they are changed too rapidly, the company may enter the throes of chaos or anarchy.

Removing or radically changing strategic commitments redefines what the organization is about, why it exists, and what everyone's role and objectives should be. Strategic commitments have to be reviewed, and changed, when it is clear they are impeding the company; but, management can't pursue a "strategy of the day" approach. The resources required to implement and stabilize corporate practices around a strategic commitment are simply too great; radical and frequent shifts in this area can result in organizational schizophrenia.

An example of the above is a major U.S. consumer products company's benchmarks and analysis for a long-term strategic plan. The plan covered manufacturing/sourcing and distribution organization. The plan was developed to improve manufacturing and distribution profitability, resulting in improved margin performance; to evaluate the feasibility/desirabilty of another manufacturing location; to satisfy customer requirements; to understand and react to competitive initiatives; and to support marketing growth projections.

Benchmarks used in this study included the following:

- Service levels

- Total order cycle time

- Inventory requirements

- Utilization of recent technological developments

- Transportation requirements

- Staff skills

The results included a reduction in the number of distribution centers from 18 to 5, technology enhancements, and different customer service levels.

Changing Existing Systems

The decent moderation of today will be the least human of things tomorrow. At the time of the Spanish Inquisition, the opinion of good sense and of the good medium was certainly that people ought not to burn too large a number of heretics; extreme and unreasonable opinion obviously demanded that they should burn none at all.

Maurice Maeterlinck

Current practices can be changed, but many of their systematic features require at least two to five years to modify or discard. These structural drivers include the degree of vertical and horizontal integration, the relative degree of centralization or decentralization, specific programs (for example, pay plans) and policies (for example, component sourcing), and work rules and practices can be directly affected by management decisions. But the subsequent change process won't take place overnight. Redeploying resources, redefining work practices, and convincing the rest of the organization to come along for the ride all require time. In fact, most of the time spent in the implementation of a new program or policy is not spent designing it, but rather convincing key individuals to support it.

These systems or processes are often the focal point in benchmarking. Best-in-class benchmarking, for example, is defined by its concern with changing existing processes. In these settings, the "constraints" of tradition are more easily shattered. Yet constant change in this arena can lead to a charge of "management by fad." Middle management, on the firing line for most of these change initiatives, can only handle one or two major program changes in any year. Each not only requires intensive meetings and discussions as "reality" is redefined and new visions are set for operating personnel, but they also create the inevitable flood of maintenance procedures, paperwork, and control routines that take time away from other work.

One example of changing processes is the outcome of a benchmark exercise to improve the overall effectiveness of a *Fortune* 500 company's procurement operations and ensure adherence to established norms of purchasing excellence in the United States. Various aspects of procurement practices were modeled in the exercise:

- Form and control of written policies and procedures

- Organizational structure, including reporting relationship and degree of centralization

- Formal and informal control mechanisms

- Management techniques that encourage professionalism among purchasing employees

- Approaches to communicating expected norms of purchasing behavior

- Information system applications

Based on the model, the procurement function was centralized and procedures were streamlined; user-friendly policies were developed; and a career program was instituted. In addition, new applications of information systems for monitoring purchasing activities were identified.

Systemic change is possible, but it cannot be done in every part of the organization at once. This "cold bath" approach has been taken by companies faced with intense crisis; the cost in management psyche and organizational stability and productivity is difficult to gauge. Redefining the organization to this extent is one way to change a strategic commitment. Changing a strategic commitment, though, cannot be done in a piecemeal fashion; the changes have to be focused on achieving a new vision of the organization that will replace existing practices and traditions.

Implementing the requisite programs associated with moving to a "continuous improvement" mindset is one example of how a series of apparently unrelated programs (such as total quality management and employee involvement) can be knitted together to achieve a new vision or strategic focus for a company. As long as someone is actually steering the change process, the organization will survive. If instead, the changes reflect an unfocused grasp for any solution, whether or not it fits the problems faced by the company, "management by fad" can rob the organization of the critical resources needed for survival. All change is not equal.

Short Cycle Change

> What we call "progress" is the exchange of one nuisance for another nuisance.
>
> Havelock Ellis

13: IDENTIFYING PERFORMANCE DRIVERS

Operational limitations are the basic constraints that affect the efficiency and effectiveness of daily activities. One clear example of this concept is bottleneck resources. A bottleneck restricts the flow of material through a process; it is the slowest or least effective part. This operational limitation can usually be addressed with any number of short-run decisions and actions. For instance, a bottleneck machine can be replaced with a more efficient model, or perhaps a second path or machine center can be used to double the effective capacity in the area. In either case, the operational limit can be remedied with only minor ramifications on ongoing organizational practices.

Another example of an operational limitation is the overlapping of responsibility for a certain task or outcome. In the process of analyzing the workflows to support a benchmarking initiative, management may uncover areas where conflicting responsibilities or the lack of individual responsibility is causing an excessive number of "fumbles." When the handoffs from one individual or group to another are poorly defined, fumbles occur: they are difficult to prevent. Isolating and fixing these "zones of exposure" is one of the outcomes of the internal benchmarking process.

As you move through the various layers of performance drivers or constraints, the degree of *interdependence* is reduced. Smaller and smaller areas of the organization are affected by the decisions, which means that they can be put in place in more rapid succession. The constraints faced by an organization, then, differ along several dimensions:

- The degree to which the constraint can be changed by management directive

- The period of time required to enact desired changes

- The relative impact on daily activities and operational processes

- The extensiveness of change (such as number of groups affected)

- The number of such changes that can be absorbed by the organization

- The degree to which the changes affect the social system of the company

The closer a performance driver (constraint) is to the task level or individual unit of the organization, the easier it is to change. The more mechanical or physical the change, the more rapidly it can be implemented. As the focal point of the constraint moves up into higher and higher levels of the organization, it becomes much more difficult to enact change in it. And if the change process requires a recalibration of everyone's "vision" or world view of the organization, it will be an even slower and more fragile event.

Undertaking an internal assessment, then, helps define the corporate landscape, details where the terrain can be easily adapted and where nature cannot be moved to change its shape without extreme effort. The view from a mountain ledge may be breathtakingly beautiful, but building a house to capture it may be infeasible. Not all alternatives are available for a company to pursue. By detailing existing practices and constraints, management can assimilate the information from the benchmarking study much more rapidly and prioritize improvement efforts to reflect the "stickiness" of the constraints on that process.

Finally, a working knowledge of the existing performance drivers is needed before target benchmarking firms can be chosen. Why? Because benchmarking always comes back to an "apples-to-apples" comparison. If a company doesn't know what type of fruit it grows, it's hard to imagine that it can identify the right methods and targets for improving its quality. In benchmarking, then, forewarned is forearmed; racing to the field to gather data when you're unclear what it is you want to know or how the information will fit within your context not only is costly—it can derail any future efforts before they get off the ground. History can serve as a teacher or a prison.

DRIVERS IN THE BENCHMARKING PROCESS

Man blames fate for other accidents,
but feels personally responsible when
he makes a hole in one.

Horizons magazine

Organization	Environmental Constraints	Strategic Commitments	Systemic Process	Operational Limitations
	• Skills	• Structure	• Work Force Factors	• Cost factors
	• Public Policy	− Location/Number of	− Turnover	− Value shared
	• Market	Facilities	− Selection Success	− Transfer Processing
	• Product	− Vertical/Horizontal	• Structural Factors	effects
	• Technology	Integration	− Span of Control	− Information Quality
		− Interdependencies	− Layers of Management	• • Error Type
		− Central/Local Control	− Overlap of Responsibility	• • Error Frequency
		− Roles	− Value/Skill Congruence	• • Timing
		− Missions/Characters	− Priority/Resource Match	• • Reliability
		• Culture/Values	− Points of Resolution	
		• Programs	− Skill/Life Cycle	
		− Evaluation	Congruence	
		− Compensation	− Decision-Cycle	
		− Rewards	• Cultural Factors	
		− Benefits/Perquisites	− Ownership	
		− Development	− Risk/Reward Costs	
		− Recruiting		

Figure 13.3   Examples of drivers.

Performance drivers define the boundaries of the benchmarking process, the choice of benchmarking target firms, the interpretation of the results, and the development of action plans once the results are in. This is the message conveyed by Figure 13.3. The focus of the measures and procedures used in a benchmarking study are constrained by the drivers that affect the area under examination and their relative openness to change.

Drivers and Benchmarking Measures

The definition of the benchmarking process begins with the internal assessment of existing practices and constraints. The output of this process is the targeted list of issues, questions, and measures that are used to frame the benchmarking study. If the analysis is focused on the performance of the total organization (competitive benchmarking), then key environmental constraints and strategic commitments must be clearly delineated. On the other hand, if the benchmarking study is focused on a systemic process (such as the distribution network), the environmental constraints and strategic commitments of the organization are accepted as "givens"; the focal point in the development of measures is on the process itself.

When a study is done at the operational level, the only constraints that can be affected are systemic process–oriented. Upper level constraints surround and define the tasks performed at the operational level, but they cannot be changed by decisions made this low in the organization. In this situation, the focal point of the benchmarking project is on clearly defined effectiveness and efficiency measures within a tightly defined setting.

Most benchmarking studies target changes at the systemic process level and above. While operational limitations need to be taken into consideration, they can be easily changed once the key issues in the underlying process are understood and action plans for improving them identified.

The driver hierarchy detailed in Figure 13.3 reflects a basic fact: changing upper level constraints totally redefines the game played at lower levels of the organization. Likewise, changes made lower in the hierarchy are constrained by upper level initiatives and boundaries. While their cumulative effect may be to change or eliminate a higher level constraint, it is not a foregone conclusion that changes made to systemic processes will result in a redirection at the strategic level. Systemic process changes may provide the basis for significant improvement on a defined critical success factor, or they may even create a new target for the entire industry, but they cannot eliminate a critical success factor without triggering a sequence of events much larger than a simple redesign of existing workflows.

Drivers and Choosing Benchmarking Target Sites

> I think that our power of conscious origination is where free will comes in.... We are continually choosing between the good and the less good, whether aware of it or not.
>
> Alfred North Whitehead

Nowhere does the issue of performance drivers have a greater impact than in the choice of benchmarking targets. The information and knowledge available are set by the comparative organizations chosen. If a benchmarking target site is poorly selected and ends up being incongruous to existing practices and constraints within the benchmarking sponsor site, the information gathered from it will be useless to everyone concerned. Lining up key performance drivers is the baseline for developing a group of comparative sites; the general conditions faced by the group must be similar enough to make comparisons of their practices meaningful.

Where this problem explicitly comes to light is when a company, deemed as a best-practice firm, is put into the benchmarking pool without a careful assessment of its underlying drivers. Best practice in the paper industry may provide little or no information for a company that earns its keep by fixing computers. Depending on the type of function being explored, and the impact upper level constraints have on it, the benchmarked process may or may not be comparable in the two settings. Best practice, then, is defined by the constraints or performance drivers that surround it. A highly regulated environment brings with it a completely different set of constraints and issues than those faced by a firm competing in a global marketplace with limited restraints on its policies and practices.

The constraints identified during the internal assessment process, then, isolate the list of criteria for the choice of the benchmarking target sites. This makes the final choice much easier; potential candidates can be rapidly sorted into feasible and infeasible groups. The better the "match" or consistency between the constraints faced by the benchmarking target and the sponsor firm, the more rapidly and effectively the results can be employed.

As with all concepts, though, performance driver concerns can be taken to unreasonable limits. The end point of the argument would be to throw in the towel on benchmarking because your company is "unique." That goes without saying, but knowledge comes from many sources. An explicit recognition of the key performance drivers will help focus the benchmarking study; it does not constrain it to one industry or a small group of "peer" competitors. Instead, it raises the awareness early on in the benchmarking process that the ability to use the information obtained in the study is a function of comparability. Two brands of apples may be compared in a meaningful way, two fruits in a lesser sense. Comparing a fruit to a vegetable, though, is a more heroic task. The message is clear: make sure that the companies or functions *can* be compared before collecting data from them.

Drivers and the Interpretation and Use of Benchmarking Results

> The second half of a man's life is made up of nothing but the habits he acquired during the first half.
>
> Feodor Dostoevski

Once the measures and focus of the benchmarking study have been defined and the information gathered from the final set of benchmarking sites, little can be done to change it. The task now turns toward interpreting and using the data. Unfortunately, if the performance drivers have not been well defined in earlier stages, they come back to haunt the benchmarking team at this point. If incomparable data have been collected, the analysis and application of the results is impossible. While a few hints for improvement opportunities may be squeezed from the study, little substantive knowledge can be gained.

Obviously, the less comparable the underlying benchmark sites are to the sponsoring firm, the more difficult it will be to develop an action plan to reach their level of performance. The differences can be so great, in fact, that action becomes unlikely if not impossible—that is, unless the action is to throw the study away or redo it with a more representative sample. In either case, the lessons learned will not be the ones the company set out to master.

On a more positive note, the more comparable the benchmarking sites are to the core features of the sponsoring company, the faster an action plan can be developed to take advantage of the data. Being able to match the key drivers for the companies eliminates much of the analysis and interpretation necessary to make the practices uncovered at the target sites fit the structure of the benchmarking firm.

Comparability at the higher levels of the performance driver hierarchy, then, shortens the time required to implement action plans to incorporate the acknowledged best practices, as well as raising the probability that they can be implemented. If the driver "mismatch" is at the strategic commitment level, by definition it will take five or more years to enact the needed changes. On the other hand, if the improvements are focused at the operational level, benefits can be reaped almost at once. The higher the level of convergence in practices or drivers, the more difficult it will be to get an action plan in place.

Constraints Set the Tone

I don't know whether I am getting very wise or very silly, but the only comment I seem to be able to make about anything is, "All is well," or "So be it."...There is no such thing as a definite conclusion. Everything must be followed by a question mark. All I can do is act according to my deepest instinct, and be whatever I must be.

Katherine Butler Hathaway
*The Journals and Letters
of a Little Locksmith*

Do constraints set the boundaries of a problem? Or is a problem defined by the constraints a person places around its resolution? Quite likely both conclusions are true. Innovative practice often comes from stepping outside the existing boundaries of the problem. If that were not the case, companies wouldn't be so rapidly and effectively employing best-in-class benchmarking. A BIC study, by definition, requires a shedding of industry boundaries and a focus on comparability defined by the objective or nature of the system or business process, rather than the organization that surrounds it.

A careful examination of performance drivers, then, informs the benchmarking process. It is a critical facet of industry and competitive analysis, but takes on a much different meaning when set in a best-in-class framework. Comparability is defined in a different way, then, for every type of benchmarking approach. A benchmarking target may be quite relevant for a BIC study and totally irrelevant for an industry analysis. In fact, that should be the case. If the same companies show up in both cases, something is wrong. Industry practice is seldom "best-in-class" across the board. For mail order businesses, L.L. Bean's distribution system is of interest; it is less likely that its accounting procedures (for example, days required to close the books) are also the best for the broader set of industries that might be of interest.

If comparability is ignored, the benchmarking process is unlikely to yield usable results. Serendipity can at times enter to save a company from disaster, but it can't be counted on as an ongoing event. The design and execution of an effective benchmarking project starts with a comprehensive internal assessment and ends with the development of action plans that target identified constraints for change. Careful planning may take time, but it provides benefits throughout the benchmarking process.

Perhaps the most valuable result of all education is the ability to make yourself do the thing you have to do, when it ought to be done, whether you like it or not; it is the first lesson that ought to be learned; and however early a man's training begins, it is probably the last lesson that he learns thoroughly.

Thomas Henry Huxley
Technical Education

14: USING BEST-IN-CLASS BENCHMARKING TO GAIN FOCUS: AT&T AND THE WORLD-CLASS CHIEF FINANCIAL OFFICER

Type of Benchmarking Used: External, Best-in-Class
Purpose for Use: Rapid changes in the overall structure of AT&T had radically redefined the demands on, and role played, by the Chief Financial Officer (CFO). Decentralization of the financial function had made it quite difficult to determine exactly what the financial function should be doing at each defined level in the organizational structure.
Area Examined: Functions encompassed by the CFO

Lessons Learned:

Rapid structural changes in the corporation create a defined need to reassess the functions and responsibilities of major business units.

The role of the world-class CFO is to enable, and facilitate, other groups in their pursuit of continuous improvement.

The CFO functions as an early warning monitor for the likelihood of achieving success. The effectiveness of this early warning system is a function of the quality of information and linkage between financial and operational data.

The CFO serves a vital advisory role in operational and strategic decision making throughout the organization.

The traditional "scorekeeper" role continues for the CFO function, but it is de-emphasized in world-class companies as new business advisor roles and responsibilities are taken on.

THE SETTING

The AT&T story is well known to the business community. Judge Green's decision in the early 1980s to force the breakup of "Ma Bell" is still having repercussions on the American telecommunications industry. Any repercussions felt by the industry are minor, though, compared with the upheaval AT&T's organization has experienced as the protective walls of a regulated monopoly were smashed to meet the realities of the competitive marketplace.

The evolution of AT&T's internal structure, since divestiture in 1984, reads like a Kafka-esque play of radical upheaval and temporary stability. The first post-divestiture organization structure was influenced by restrictions placed by Judge Green in order to curb AT&T's competitive advantage. Two lines of business were established: Communications and Information Systems. This dual product line was pursued for approximately two years.

In 1986 Judge Green, in reviewing the marketplace and his prior decisions, lifted the restriction requiring AT&T to maintain separate product lines. This led to the era of "one enterprise."

The realities of these shifts at the highest level of the driver hierarchy were enormous. Functions, such as the financial organization, that had gained an understanding of what types of activities, systems, procedures, and measurements would be needed to support the "dual entity" concept were now told to unify the two systems into one.

Two more years passed, and to better position its products and services in the market, AT&T decided to decentralize into business units. The now-integrated processes and systems were once again asked to splinter their operations into different and smaller configurations. This redirection of the company was to achieve three objectives:

1. To enable the company to maintain its current customer base
2. To grow AT&T's system business
3. To broaden AT&T's international business

This sequence of events might be easily absorbed over a century of operations; less than a decade is an impossibly short period for making such major changes. Jim Meenan, Vice President and CFO of the Communications Services Group, describes the process in the following way:

> When you try to take a $34 billion company that's been functioning in a regulated environment, with all the mindsets associated with regulation, and convert that company...into a competitive business where you have to know product-specific costs and revenues, that's a mammoth job....Forget that we didn't have any systems, forget that our systems were broken...we didn't have receivables, etc. Forget all of that. That's just a little problem, a small blip out there. In addition we were faced with a massive culture change. We had a monopoly in the business and suddenly we were entering a very competitive marketplace.[1]

WHAT IS THE ROLE OF A CFO AT AT&T?

The rapid unfolding of events created a quandary for the financial executives at AT&T (see Figure 14.1). There were now three to four levels of financial staff: corporate, groups, business units (BUs), and strategic business units (SBUs). While some basic tasks or responsibilities had been defined (e.g., treasury function would be focused at the corporate level), there was very little clarity about the boundaries between the group, BU, and SBU financial executives. Jim Meenan continues:

> After the latest round of changes, I found myself sitting at my desk and asking "What is the role of all of these various CFOs? What's my role and what should I be aspiring to?" I knew that the environment around me was changing, but I was unclear about what I should be focusing on, and what changes we should be instituting in our financial services group.

While the company had adopted a goal of "world-class financial organization," it was difficult to translate that into daily practices and ongoing policies. This definition issue and concerns

Issue  **What is a World-Class CFO?**

Situation **Vision to be world-class financial organization**
Transition issues from centralized to decentralized
Company reorganized to decentralized business units
Redefinition of financial roles and responsibilities

Research/
Findings

Key Interviews
- **Academics**
- **Financial Associations**
- **CFOs**
- **CEOs**

Measurements
- **Background of individuals**
- **Environmental factors**
- **Focus of words**
- **Relationship with working senior management**

Changes
- **Assessment against straw man**
- **Development of training program**
- **Greater communications**

Figure 14.1 AT&T best-in-class benchmarking objectives.

about the need to develop a vision for the financial function led Jim Meenan to undertake a best-in-class benchmarking project to answer the following questions:

- What does it take to compete in this new competitive world?

- How will the decentralized financial organizations within the communications group support the achievement of those objectives?

- How do we define and implement a world-class structure?

- How have our traditional roles in the financial function been changed? What is a world-class CFO's role within our business unit structure? How can we get there?

- What types of decision-making processes will we be asked to support?

- How are we going to deal with the people issues (e.g., training, promotion, and motivation)?

- How can we instill a proactive, decision-making partnership role into the culture of the financial group?

WHO IS BEST-IN-CLASS?

To set the vision of the world-class CFO, the first question that had to be addressed was who was best-in-class. This question was posed to three knowledgeable groups: the academic community, financial associaitons, and the Coopers & Lybrand Partnership. All were given a free license to interpret "best-in-class" and not be limited to an industry and/or national.

The screening criteria that resulted from these three groups included the following:

1. Company executive management (i.e., CEO, CFO) was recognized as being among the most dynamic and forward-thinking leaders in their particular industry segment.

2. Companies had demonstrated success in developing management approaches and philosophies and in being responsive to new opportunities and other business drivers.

3. They had a consistent record of product and service innovation, in addition to marketing and financial excellence.
4. They had pioneered decentralization of critical management functions to the lowest levels of organizational
   structure possible, thereby instilling entrepreneurial vision
   across all management segments.

In addition to these company-based criteria, it was critical that in
the target firms the financial managers maintained a broad role
as "primary business advisors" in additon to their financial management role. The financial function itself had to be innovative
and creative and be rewarded for a proactive stance in directing
the activities to support the company's responses to competitive
demands.

In the end there were 24 companies that appeared on all three
lists, which was the definition, in this engagement, for best-in-
class.

A TWO-PHASED APPROACH

As a first phase, 10 of the 24 companies were interviewed in order to develop a straw man model of the world-class CFO. The
interviews were complemented by a discussion of key concepts
and trends in the CFO function with experts in the area, as well
as an in-depth literature search to see what types of changes were
being reported in the popular press. Compiling this information
led to the following findings:

1. The vision to be world-class must be empowered by the
   corporation.
2. The CFO is a partner with the CEO.
3. The CFO's role varies widely from traditional to world-class
   (see Figure 14.2).
4. The CFO's role in the enterprise should determine the
   division of functional responsibilities. For instance, tax,

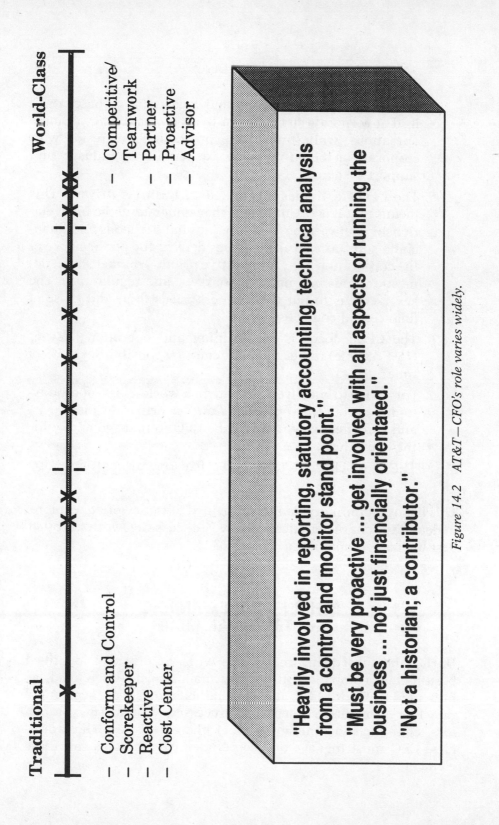

Traditional

World-Class

- Conform and Control
- Scorekeeper
- Reactive
- Cost Center

- Competitive/ Teamwork
- Partner
- Proactive
- Advisor

"Heavily involved in reporting, statutory accounting, technical analysis from a control and monitor stand point."

"Must be very proactive ... get involved with all aspects of running the business ... not just financially orientated."

"Not a historian; a contributor."

Figure 14.2   AT&T—CFO's role varies widely.

treasury, human resources, and legal tend to be central-ized at corporate since they have an impact on all business operations, while transaction processing can reside with corporate or the business unit, depending on industry and support systems.

5. The CFO's activities are linked to business drivers. This means that it is essential that they understand the interrela-tionship between business/operational decisions and finan-cial results, as well as the issues driving the performance of the corporation (e.g., competitive pricing, market share, do-mestic versus international markets, and regulations). The key factor is to put the business needs first, and those of finance and control second.

6. The CFO's focus is on planning and operational issues (75% of time) rather than fiduciary responsibilities (25% of time).

7. For a CFO to effectively operate in a world-class mode, day-to-day accounting operations and information must exist and run effectively to allow the CFO to manage and guide the operations.

8. The most effective CFOs have had operational expertise.

This list of preliminary findings provided a framework to explore, in detail, the characteristics of the world-class CFO with the other best-in-class companies.

REFINING AND EXPANDING
THE STRAW MAN MODEL

During the subsequent discussions with the other 14 identified best-in-class companies, the straw man model was refined, as presented in Figure 14.3, and the characteristics were segmented into four elements: cornerstone processes, critical success fac-tors, enabling, and mission-critical characteristics. The world-class CFO must manage and sometimes stretch across all these elements.

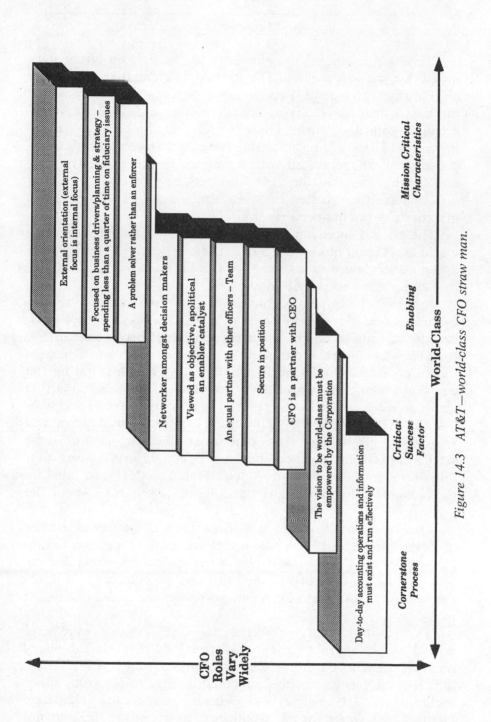

Figure 14.3   *AT&T—world-class CFO straw man.*

Reviewing some of the elements in the revised straw man model for the world-class CFO, it became clear that day-to-day accounting was a critical cornerstone process. Originally raised in Phase I interviews, day-to-day accounting took on greater and greater significance during Phase II. It included reporting requirements being stable, processes and systems being enhanced or improved, and financial staff with strong analytical skills. The general feeling was that the CFO who gets bogged down in detail doesn't have time to step back and understand the business implications of the financial results.

The critical success factor remained constant: the vision to be world-class must be empowered by the corporation. This empowerment was viewed as a license for the CFO to assume a broader role and greater responsibilities.

In the enabling area a number of additional factors, besides the unique relationship between the CEO and CFO, were identified during this second round of interviews. It became clear that the CFO was being asked to join the management team. This participation was to be focused on networking and facilitating the decision-making process of the other officers. In performing this catalytic role, the CFO was expected to remain objective and apolitical; the infomration being provided must be viewed as fair and trustworthy. To achieve these objectives, then, the CFO must be secure in his or her position and must be free from a concern that telling the truth might lead to dismissal. The CFO also must be the recognized financial expert and be knowledgeable about the process.

Finally, it was clear that achieving this mission would require an open mind, focused on business drivers, planning, and strategic issues—an abandonment of the traditional scorekeeper role. The world-class CFO had to shed the historic enforcer role in order to become an effective problem solver and provide an outward focus.

The results of this revised straw man analysis were supported by a separate review performed by Keating-Jablonsky for the Financial Executive Research Foundation (FERF), which detailed the trends in the financial function of six companies, including AT&T (see Figure 14.4).[2] It was clear that the challenge facing AT&T was its need to continue to transition its financial

Financial Organization Norms		
Conformance	**Command-and-Control**	**Competitive Team**
Predominant Mind set of Financial Function		
External accountability	Oversight	Leadership/Service
Criterion of Success		
Technical compliance	Operating efficiency	Value-added involvement
Primary Role of Financial Person		
Bookkeeper/administrator	Controller/cost accountant	Financial professional/manager
Primary Source of Status/Legitimacy		
Technical knowledge of rules	Position in hierarchy as steward of corporate resources	Business judgment and financial expertise
Custodian of accounts	Independent third party	

Figure 14.4 Changing roles of financial management.

management group from a conformance mentality past a command-and-control mentality to a competitive-team orientation. As suggested by Keating and Jablonsky, this change required a major cultural transformation in the financial community:

> To shift toward the competitive-team orientation, people have to change the way they think about how they contribute to the success of their firms. This means they move away from being an independent third party or custodian of accounts and become a client-oriented professional (both internal and external clients) with an in-depth knowledge of the business.... To make the transition to a team-oriented financial organization...[the company] must reorient the financial function; it must make interrelated changes in the norms of success.[3]

Implementing and Reflecting on the Findings

The movement toward world-class CFO stature is under way at AT&T. In order to get upper management on board, Jim Meenan initiated a series of assessment exercises that would score the CFOs against the straw man criteria. There were three parts to the assessment process:

1. Self-assessment by the business unit CFOs
2. An assessment of the group CFO, by Meenan, who maintains a "dotted line" reporting relationship with the Communication business unit CFOs
3. CEO assessment of their direct report CFOs against the straw man criteria

This approach gave the CFOs an opportunity to discuss where they were and identify roadblocks to achieving world class.

The final model has been shared with the entire AT&T financial and management group. It has led to the recognition of the need to continue the strong financial community and shared corporate vision of the role of the CFO in achieving it. Maintaining the financial community intact appears to be facilitating the transition to the BU/SBU structure, the development of a shared

- **Group structure – positive influence**

- **Process improvement – high priority**

- **Outward focus critical**

- **Criteria of success and reward for financial staff needed**

- **Vision and roadmap different for each business**

- **Be prepared to foster "discontinuance" change – revolutionary change versus evolutionary change**

Figure 14.5   AT&T—Observations

value set, and the means for the financial group to achieve legitimacy across the corporation. Other observations that needs to be addressed are summarized in Figure 14.5.

Of all the changes being put in place, it is clear the process improvement needs to be given a high priority. The competitive environment is constantly eating away at the corporation's profits, leading to an intensified concern with cost reduction. Only by being close to the business can the CFO help the management team prioritize and select those cost reduction opportunities that will support the long-run success of the enterprise. Where investments are needed, the CFO is to take an active role in making sure that all possible sources and approaches are examined before action is taken.

The marketplace is beginning to permeate the daily activities at AT&T. This is leading to a need to adopt an outward focus and to continue benchmarking to identify those areas where improvements in the nonfinancial aspects of the business are needed.

While the roadmap for achieving these goals will differ across each group and business unit, the message is clear: the CFO is being asked to provide a value-added service to the management team. The goal is to provide financial leadership; the challenge is to overcome tradition and training in the process.

Instead of imposing financial controls over other managers, financial executives are being asked to provide more financial leadership. There is an increasing need for financial executives to help form and implement competitive strategy at the business unit level, as well as at the corporate level. ...When managers fail to balance knowledge of the business with analytic sophistication, and when they rely almost totally on the numbers, they undercut their commitment to the innovation in product and process that is essential to long-term competitive success.

Keating and Jablonsky
Changing Roles of
Financial Management

15: PEOPLE ISSUES IN THE BENCHMARKING PROCESS

Every individual has a place to fill in the world and is important in some respect whether he chooses to be so or not.

Nathaniel Hawthorne

Benchmarking is not another fad or an additional technique to master in addition to continuous improvement–based methods; it is the means to implement these concepts in an objective, meaningful way. In defining performance expectations against external targets, benchmarking takes the guesswork and politics out of the development of continuous improvement goals. The benefits that can accrue to the benchmarking organization are numerous, extending beyond a concern with continuous improvement to encompass sound business practice, no matter what tag is used to describe it.

Making the Change Process Objective Through Benchmarking

Everything keeps its best nature only by being put to its best use.

Phillips Brooks
Visions and Tasks

BENCHMARKING

People like to know exactly where they stand and what is expected of them. If the measures used to guide or evaluate their performance are vague, individuals will translate, modify, and adapt these concepts into a workable and actionable framework. The problem, of course, is that this framework may not be exactly the one management had in mind. But given that no one really communicates displeasure (customers seldom voice their complaints), and that there's really no clear idea of what the individual was supposed to do in the first place, let alone why, the practices institutionalize themselves. For instance, an inventory clerk who refuses to release materials badly needed on the plant floor because the required forms haven't been filled out right may know, deep in his or her heart, that the materials should be released, but this doesn't make the risk of getting disciplined for stepping outside the rules any easier to accept. It's easier to say "no" than to face the risk. This is the heart of "bureaucratic creep."

Now say to this very same person, "I want you to pursue continuous improvement; take this job and restructure it if you must, but get better at it. We are all in this together." What does the individual hear? "You're not going fast enough. Speed up or else." No one has leveled a specific complaint or identified an area to focus this "continuous improvement" stuff on, so the outcome of the change process, if it can be called that, is spotty. Some individuals find ways to really improve their performance; others simply change the tabs on their file folders.

Effective continuous improvement efforts start from an analysis of the process flows—an understanding of what work needs to be done and why. In the next stage of this change process, the worker is asked to figure out who gets the reports he or she produces and whether they meet their "customer's" needs. The response? "Customer...I never see a customer. I don't know what they're talking about, but I'll ask Ben if the reports are okay." The question is asked and quite likely met with a blank stare. "Is there something wrong?" Ben may ask. "No...but I'm supposed to ask you anyway." Ben scratches his head, pulls the report from underneath a huge mound of paper, glances at it quickly, and says, "Looks good to me." Phase II completed.

Sound ridiculous? It really shouldn't, because it happens again and again. Management, fired up by the concept of continuous improvement through employee involvement, sends a clear

15: PEOPLE ISSUES IN THE BENCHMARKING PROCESS

message that change should occur, but what exactly is wanted and when is hard to say. The employee, unaware of what the ultimate goal in pursuing change is, goes through the motions but doesn't really change.

This problem is best understood through an example. Johnson Soap Works, a small specialty soap manufacturer, recently decided to implement total quality management (TQM) to improve the quality of its output in the face of excessive returns and customer complaints. Everyone was sent through the quality training process; posters were put up throughout the building; QIP (quality improvement process) teams were established; and so on. The organization looks as though it is changing. In reality, though, very few of the top management group has bought into the employee involvement or trust aspect of the TQM process. Management is defining what types of measurements, process changes, and operating procedures the "group" needs. Comments like, "They really don't have the ability to do this on their own" can be heard in scattered conversations.

The management team, while going through the motions to change, has not really accepted that the ultimate goal is for them to relinquish daily control to the workforce and to take on a leadership role instead. While the organization is not currently reaping the benefits of the quality process, there are indications that one by one, the management team is making breakthroughs. Once they can establish a leadership position, giving clear direction (but not orders) to the workforce, the quality process will be secured. Until then, everyone, from the top of the organization to the bottom, is going through the motions of pursuing continuous improvement.

Unfortunately, this cycle of unfocused and uncommitted change can deteriorate into a fistfight of sorts. Management, frustrated with the failure to see results, begins to pressure workers to improve. This is what they expected all along. Management wants them to work faster. They do, but not without consequences. Errors increase, attitudes deteriorate, and the very people critical to the improvement process become increasingly alienated. This phenomenon was documented by Mike Parker and Jane Slaughter at the Nummi plant in California. They note:

> Thus no matter how well the workers learn their jobs, there
> is always room for *Kaizen*, or continuous improvement.... This

is how management by stress differs from Taylorism. Taylor believed that management's engineers could capture workers' knowledge of the production process all at once, after which workers would revert to being nothing but hired hands. Management-by-stress managers understand that workers continue to know more about the actual performance of their jobs than higher management does, and so make the process of appropriating that knowledge a never-ending one.[1]

This story is not particularly positive on the practice of management for continuous improvement; unfortunately, it is the game being played today in many organizations. If you read between the lines, what is evident is that the authors are not describing a cooperative workplace, working toward meeting customer expectations, but instead an internally focused process in quest of higher levels of efficiency.

Unlocking the Gates to Progress

> You've got to be a fool to want to stop
> the march of time.
>
> Pierre Auguste Renoir

Benchmarking unravels this deadly game, replacing it with an objective measure of the level of performance that is needed from the individual and why it is needed. By establishing an external measure or standard, it stabilizes the improvement process by clearly defining the rules of the game. Revisiting our employee, let's now suggest that management has done a survey, and customers overwhelmingly agree that it simply takes too long to get an order through the red tape in the order-processing department. They note that the number of forms required, the fact that each order is handled as though it's a new customer, and the need to have a signed purchase order in hand before any action will take place to fill it, all add to the delay and frustration facing the customer. Some customers go so far as to say they won't do business with the company because of this problem.

These are clear signals of customer problems and expectations. They're really not "speed up" messages, but rather a plea to simplify procedures, eliminate paperwork bottlenecks, and institute different order-processing procedures for established vs. new customers. These are tasks that resources can be committed to, with measurable results. The vague "get better" message has now been clearly focused onto specific characteristics and processes that are damaging customer relationships.

This focused change process also helps lay out a clear path to improvement. It details the measures of success and makes it easier for the employee to understand and accept why changes are needed. It's one thing to change because "the boss says so, that's why," and a totally different one when the change process is driven by customer requirements. Finally, the benchmarking process makes it clear that the types of changes being implemented *fit* the problem. It's difficult to justify the "that doesn't apply here" mentality when the change is being driven by the very people the organization exists to serve.

Benchmarking holds the key to unlocking the individual's defenses, creating a logical and achievable path to excellence. As suggested by Rosabeth Moss Kanter,[2] "The degree to which the opportunity to use power effectively is granted or withheld from individuals is one operative difference between those companies which stagnate and those which innovate." Unlocking the power of motivated and focused individuals and teams is the basis for organizational innovation.

DEPERSONALIZING THE CHANGE PROCESS

> What plays the mischief with the truth is that men will insist upon the universal application of a temporary feeling or opinion.
>
> Herman Melville

In organizations change is usually triggered by a change in management or the foraging of the company "explorers," who, never content with the status quo on any front, constantly search for the latest gimmick and the next management panacea. In either case, the change process in these situations is dependent on one person or a small group of people. As their commitment and availability wavers, so does the change process itself. So, the sage "settlers" (that is, most unit managers and staff) sit back, watch, and wait to see the result of what the explorer brings back from the latest conference; but they never really embrace the change process itself.

Each organization can be broken into four distinct groups, with different risk profiles and criteria for change, as suggested in Figure 15.1: the "explorers," the "scouts," the "settlers," and the "dead enders." Explorers seek change for change's sake, while scouts are focused on identifying opportunities that will help the rest of the organization along. Explorers and scouts work closely together. The scouts take their lead from the explorers. If the explorers seem to be onto something, the scouts will chart the "fertile valley" the explorer has discovered traveling through the management tools frontier.

A good idea is really not enough. If only the explorers and scouts embrace the concept, whether continuous improvement,

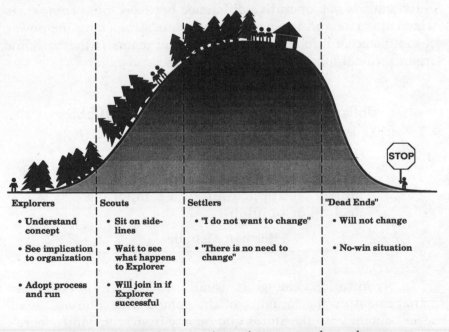

Explorers	Scouts	Settlers	"Dead Ends"
• Understand concept	• Sit on sidelines	• "I do not want to change"	• Will not change
• See implication to organization	• Wait to see what happens to Explorer	• "There is no need to change"	• No-win situation
• Adopt process and run	• Will join in if Explorer successful		

Figure 15.1   Employee analysis–desire to work on change.

JIT, TQM, or any other implement of change, the idea will not take root in the company. Instead, it will become another topic of endless meetings before it dies out due to lack of interest on the part of the organizational majority—the settlers.

Settlers, of course, are looking for new lands, but there's only so much risk they're willing to accept along the way. They're bringing the family along, remember, and so more is at stake than an idea. As long as the explorers and scouts are unable to prove the benefits of their ideas, the settlers will hang back. After all, Mary's department took that route two years ago, and there's hardly a soul left "alive" to talk about, let alone cheer the project on. With a long history of failures and massacres when an ill-conceived journey was undertaken, the settlers require more than a good speech to get them moving—they need proof.

Benchmarking provides this proof by laying out, in externally defined (by the customer and market) and objective terms, what types of change are needed, and the consequences of *not* taking the path toward improvement. Customers, voting with their feet and their pocketbooks, establish clear expectations that few can dispute, even the "dead-enders."

The dead-ender is every manager's nightmare. The terminally placed employee with no desire to change, no desire to achieve any further recognition, promotion, or raise, is unlikely to leap to the front of a charge toward continuous improvement. Unfortunately, the fact of the matter often is that they'll work hard and long to convince the settlers that the path ahead is far too dangerous to tread. If they simply resist changing themselves, the implementation can proceed around them. If these individuals take an active role in undermining the improvement process they can delay the project, destroying the momentum needed to get the settlers forging ahead.

By establishing the continuous improvement process within a clearly defined framework that matches customer expectations against existing performance, benchmarking depersonalizes it. Naysayers can neither table it as a fad nor undermine it through politics. The externally derived benchmarks clearly link the change process to the marketplace, provide an objective goal as well as measurement of how well the organization is currently functioning against the competition, and help organizational members see beyond the "activity trap" to embrace new methods that ensure long-term competitive success. Richard Schonberger reflects this fact in the following statement:

> Increasingly, companies are coming to the same realization: that they have been leaving the customer—and the competition—out of strategy setting. An approach pioneered by Xerox Corporation, called competitive benchmarking, has helped some firms correct that weakness. The idea is to put numbers on best performances: average time to respond to a complaint, number of suppliers, defect rate, and so forth. The narrow approach to benchmarking is looking at the best in the industry; the broader, the better, approach is looking at the best in any industry.[3]

Integrating the Organization

Benchmarking starts from a careful analysis of existing activity networks. In order to assess how well the organization stacks up against its competition, the current process must be documented, attaching time, distance, and performance measures to the detailed process map (the list of activities performed to meet a customer request). Activities span the functional silos of the organization; they capture the workflows that start with a customer request and terminate with its fulfillment. One department cannot serve a customer on its own. Marketing may take the order, but this simply sets in motion an entire sequence of events throughout the organization before the order is fulfilled.

As benchmarking gets underway, detailed process maps serve as the basis for objective measurement of existing performance and for establishing a clear-cut path to improvement. In addition, the participation of customers and suppliers in joint problem solving and the empowerment of these teams to identify, analyze, and resolve any problems creates commitment to the change process, as well as moving the focus from "who messed up" to "what needs to be changed in the way we do things." The team may decide to eliminate tasks totally rather than streamline them.

This type of decision would seldom be made by an individual in a vast organizational web, but it can and does occur when suppliers and customers link up to jointly address an issue. Why? In addition to issues of power and influence within the organization (in other words, the "right" to undertake such a change), the reality of changing one part of a complex web of activity networks that have been built up over time and modified again and again on a piecemeal basis to meet the demands of different projects and different managers, is that unraveling the mystery of traditional company "work" is close to impossible. A team of individuals with various perspectives stands a fair chance of getting to the heart of a process or activity network, establishing its value (or lack thereof) to either the company or the customer, and straightening out the "kinks" in the flow linking tasks together into the activity network.

Integrating the organization is the result of common knowledge, shared beliefs, and open communication between individuals. Continuous improvement concepts are built on this integration and on the linkage of individuals and tasks across traditional boundaries. Achieving the level of process understanding necessary to do an effective benchmarking project is not a one-time project with little benefit; it serves as the basis for choosing and charting the path the company takes toward excellence.

The original Organization Assessment Process (OAP) was created by the Air Force Leadership and Management Development Center. It has been validated by experts from Harvard, the Massachusetts Institute of Technology, the University of California—Los Angeles, and industry. About 300,000 employees in 120 government and private organizations have participated in the survey. These results are stored in a national computer database and are used to make comparison benchmarks. To ensure confidentiality, the names of the employees and organizations are not in the database.

The OAP has about 110 questions answered on a Likert scale of one to seven. You can add or subtract some questions, but core questions remain the same. The survey is given to samples of employees, supervisors, and managers from different work units.

Results are used to answer these questions:

- Do your workers understand what the organization wants from them now that things have "changed"? Are they getting the kind of training and direction they need? How involved and committed are they? How well do they function as a team?

- Are your supervisors giving the right kind of feedback and evaluating performance in a constructive way? Are they promoting a shared sense of responsibility? What bureaucratic obstacles are holding things back?

■ Are your managers giving only lip service to change? Do they have the skills to lead and direct necessary innovation? How customer-oriented are they?

Results analysis begins with external and internal comparisons. You compare your results to selected components from the 300,000-respondent database: groups whose characteristics are similar to those in your organization. You can compare results from your clerical workers, engineers, senior managers, and others to those of people in the database with similar job descriptions. Also, you can make comparisons to the organization in the data base that has the highest positive scores in functional areas similar to yours.

When you make comparisons among your internal groups, you will often find that units and groups of managers and employees have different perceptions about your organization's culture, ability to innovate, and other issues important to introducing continous improvement management. This helps you determine where you will focus your attention.

Taking action on OAP or other survey results is a multilevel procedure. The data are used to describe organization-wide obstacles and opportunities for introducing new quality practices or other changes. They also may lead leaders to focus attention on specific units or types of managers or employees.

During the implementation phase, different units and groups review their results in a team setting. They form action plans to overcome any obstacles shown. This procedure is repeated at lower levels until the entire organization is actively pursuing changes that will lead to a better quality environment.[4]

Prioritizing Improvement Opportunities

> To profess to have an aim and then to neglect the means of its execution is self-delusion of the most dangerous sort.
>
> John Dewey
> *Reconstruction in Philosophy*

15: PEOPLE ISSUES IN THE BENCHMARKING PROCESS

When individuals approach a complex problem, it's difficult for them to separate cause and effect. If they push one button in a long sequence of buttons, will anything happen? Will the right thing happen? Who knows? People have created organizations or systems far more complex than they can visualize and manage on their own. While it is generally understood that the sum of the parts of a system is usually superior to the parts taken alone, there is still a need for someone or some way to be able to understand and direct the complete chain of events.

The fluid organization of the 1990s merges a series of activity networks into one whole that addresses the needs of its constituents, both within and outside the organization, on a number of levels. Learning "loops" must be put in place alongside traditional maintenance-oriented control systems to promote a commitment to change as well as the assurance that critical activities are performed with consistent high quality. In other words, each activity network must maintain a certain level of performance to ensure the survival of the whole organization, yet the interrelationships and specific objectives of the company must be constantly changing in response to customer needs and competitive demands.

This view of the organization is fast becoming the basis for analyzing and managing the development of organizations. A bottleneck is, quite simply, a problem in an activity network or subsystem that is impairing the performance of the entire organization. While certain actions can be taken to keep the organization healthy in general (such as good cash flow management policies), improving its health means that a specific problem has to be identified and repaired. The pursuit of continuous improvement requires the active, ongoing search for bottlenecks—for activity networks that are not functioning as well as possible.

Benchmarking helps prioritize the many opportunities for improvement, much in the same manner as bottleneck analysis, with one major difference. In looking for bottlenecks, management's eyes are turned inward. When performing a benchmarking project, all eyes turn outward, looking for clues from the environment to fix the problem. Benchmarking provides the information needed to eliminate the problem, to restructure the situation, and to ensure continuous improvement.

There's another way that benchmarking helps prioritize areas for change. In discussing roads for improvement, every aspect of the organization comes under the microscope in the benchmarking process.

A best-in-class food manufacturer undertook a benchmark study to better understand cost and profit influences in preparation for increased competition in both the U.S. and European marketplace. The study included development of a framework for linking activities to the use of resources and the establishment of revised performance measures. This framework was then augmented with customer service and sales performance measures and contrasted against other manufacturers' performance.

Based on the analysis, several immediate cost reductions and improvements in customer service were identified. In addition, the application of "state of the art" technologies focused on those areas that provided the greatest overall business improvement. The company also issued specific directives on products contributing the most to market share and profits while adjusting sales promotions on those products having a significant impact on manufacturing and distribution.

In the benchmarking process this area immediately surfaced as a major gap in performance. Not only were resources being wasted, but unnecessary cost and delay was being added to every order received. There was no need for continuous improvement in this area—radical surgery was required. Once the impact of this failure to integrate the information systems was documented, management took the actions that were indicated. The two MIS groups were merged into one department; excess staff and resources were dispersed in the rest of the company, or eliminated where necessary. This both reduced the cost of ongoing information systems and provided a more coordinated and responsive department. The objective benchmarking process had stripped away the politics and emotion from the issue, providing a stark picture of how the poor performance in this area, which was due to structural problems and not employee effort, was hurting everyone.

Overcoming the Resistance to Change

Without resistance you can do nothing.

Jean Cocteau
Writers at Work

15: PEOPLE ISSUES IN THE BENCHMARKING PROCESS

In facing change, people undergo anger, denial, and a range of other emotions before final acceptance is achieved. Change is like death in this manner—each change brings with it a death of the old ways of doing things, setting in their place the unknown. People resist change not because they love the status quo, but because they fear the uncertainty that lies just around the bend.

An organization that employs benchmarking to guide the adoption of continuous improvement-based techniques helps eliminate some of the uncertainty and fear that change creates. It does this by providing a clear-cut objective, examples of how other companies and individuals have addressed the problem, and defined guideposts along the way to ensure that everyone is staying on the right path.

The benchmarking process identifies the critical path to improvement and provides the means to measure the progress made along the way. In looking outside of the organization for clues and experience, benchmarking provides new insights, better information about the potential problems that may be encountered, and serves to provide the settlers with a list of provisions they should take along on the journey. When moving toward continuous improvement, therefore, the goal is not to leave everything behind and start out empty-handed for the brave new world, but instead to take along the best of the past. Elting Morison underscores this fact:

> The institutions that survive and prosper are adaptive in that they select judiciously from the ideas and material presented both by the past and the present and...throw them into a new combination. They neither abandon their traditions nor cleave to them with blind obedience. They muddle along with a kind of resilience that...enables them to accept fully and easily the best promises of changing circumstances without losing their sense of continuity or essential integrity....they change in order to conserve.[5]

The incremental change that typifies continuous improvement builds on the strengths of the organization and the opportunities that it faces in the marketplace to create a dynamic for success.

Creative Modes for Continuous Improvement

> It is the function of creative men to perceive the relationship between thoughts, or things, or forms of expression that may seem utterly different, and to be able to combine them into some new forms—the power to connect the seemingly unconnected.
>
> William Plomer

The final benefit benchmarking provides is the ability to place a new lens on the camera used to view external events and to evaluate and organize internal processes. Specifically, "best-in-class" benchmarking practices provide the basis for creative reorganization of existing resources into unique combinations that provide a competitive edge. For example, ongoing education is a major activity in most major corporations today. While most companies see this as a function unique to corporations, in fact, large-scale training and education programs in companies are comparable to university settings. The training group, faced with limited resources and a "public" that decides whether or not they will attend one, or several, classes, has to manage schedules, provide ongoing support, and create the incentive for "students" to attend their "university." The best place to find out how to do this is at a successful university. The ability to move outside of the current boundaries of a problem is the hallmark of creativity that benchmarking practices make possible within an organizational setting.

Adopting a new perspective brings with it new horizons. Just as an athlete hopes that more practice or a new coach will provide the impetus to excel beyond current abilities, benchmarking in an organization supports the attainment of goals that weren't recognized before. Even if existing practice appears to be the best it can be, looking outside to other types of organizations for an edge on how to do it a bit better, how to combine resources to raise the standard of performance pursued, is a value-added activity.

15: PEOPLE ISSUES IN THE BENCHMARKING PROCESS

With benchmarking there are few limits to growth except the collective imagination of the organization. Whether on the plant floor or in the boardroom, each individual contributes to the efforts of the team. Sometimes the team will exceed the abilities of its best athletes; at other times the leaders will help clear new ground. In either case, benchmarking exercises, by providing a new set of criteria for objectively evaluating existing practices, is the starting point to world-class competitive capability.

The only place where success comes before work is in a dictionary.

Vidal Sassoon

16: EXCELLENCE IN RESEARCH AND DEVELOPMENT: A BENCHMARKING STORY

Type of Benchmarking Used: External, Best-in-Class

Purpose for Use: Success in a competitive market is defined on the "yield" in Research and Development (R&D), or getting more new products to market for the same number of developmental dollars. Rapid declines in product life cycles demand an acceleration of the product development cycle. Products must be moved through the R&D pipeline faster and more effectively.

Area Examined: Research laboratories in diverse industries. Specific focus on the commercialization of basic research into marketable products.

Lessons Learned:

Best-practice firms, in deploying the R&D function to enhance company profitability, have well-defined corporate and business unit strategies that are clearly communicated to the R&D organization.

The R&D function in best-in-class (BIC) firms is structured around core technologies, which are defined using analytical decision support techniques and developed in conjunction with R&D.

Best practice suggests that optimal R&D performance is gained when the basic research component is funded from corporate funds and development work by the business units that will benefit from it.

Investments are made in multinational R&D capabilities.

Formal mechanisms need to exist for regular interaction between scientists within R&D and between R&D and other functions within the organization.

Knowledge gained is applicable to all industries and companies that sustain R&D facilities for product development.

THE SETTING

Research and development (R&D) is the renewing of an organization. It sets the boundaries on a company's ability to compete in the marketplace and to gain a competitive advantage. Not all R&D projects are created equal, though. R&D can only be a competitive weapon if it consistently yields new products that gain acceptance in the marketplace. While research for research's sake (such as basic research) can provide long-run advances for people in general, it is a luxury few companies can afford. In a corporate setting, then, effective R&D means successful commercialization of new products.[1]

A Challenging Environment

As in all facets of business, worldwide competition has redefined the basic nature and definition of effectiveness in the R&D function (see Figure 16.1). The transition has been dramatic; yesterday's bases of competition have become today's price of admission. In addition, new ways of competing have developed. Traditionally, R&D effectiveness has been measured by the functionality and cost of the development. Management felt that if they hired good people, provided them with the best facilities available, let them work on whatever project that interested them, and waited patiently, success would be ensured. Some have called this a strategy of "hope" in managing R&D.[2]

As global competition heated up in the 1970s and 1980s, functionality (a focus on practicality or usefulness) became a price of admission for the R&D area. Competition was no longer based

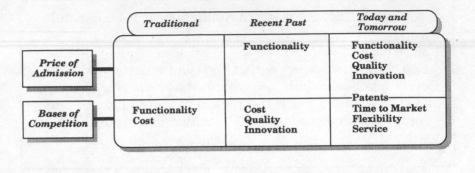

	Traditional	Recent Past	Today and Tomorrow
Price of Admission		Functionality	Functionality Cost Quality Innovation
			─Patents─
Bases of Competition	Functionality Cost	Cost Quality Innovation	Time to Market Flexibility Service

Yesterday's Bases of Competition Have Become Today's Price of Admission and New Ways of Competing Have Developed

Figure 16.1   Research development competitiveness: the bases of competition.

on having a comprehensive and well-supported R&D effort but rather on the cost, quality, and innovativeness of its outputs. R&D could no longer be viewed as an overhead item that would yield fruit somewhere downstream; instead, this phase in the development of R&D as a strategic weapon made it very clear that "hope" had to be replaced with reality. Companies couldn't afford the luxury of waiting for a spontaneous "aha" in the R&D group. Instead, they had to focus the efforts of their R&D groups; products were needed, not pipe dreams.

This increased pressure was initially focused on steamlining the design-to-manufacturing phase of product development. While tremendous improvements were gained, management still felt its R&D efforts could be more effectively utilized. Why? Because the competitive pressures were continuing to mount, increasing the stakes: functionality, cost, quality, and innovation had become the price of admission for R&D. The traditional R&D objective, an increased number of patents, was no longer enough. Instead, the bases of competition were being redefined on time to market, the flexibility of the R&D group, and their ability to service the ongoing needs of the rest of the organization. R&D had to be managed as an integral part of the organization.

Effective R&D in today's global market means getting ever higher yields (research to commercially viable products), at an ever increasing pace, with an ability to respond to rapid changes in the marketplace. If a company isn't first to market with an inno vation, it has to be able to replicate the innovation in a very short period of time. Driven by the realities of ever-shortening product life cycles, management has to find new ways to motivate and support the efforts of their R&D group to ensure flexibility and responsiveness. In addition, there's little or no time for missteps; "over the wall" approaches mean lengthy implementation cycles. These delays consume resources and damage the company's response to market demands, potentially destroying its ability to compete. Patents and products have to flow smoothly from the lab to the plant floor to the customer in record time, or the competitive advantage is lost. Effective R&D management in today's fiercely competitive environment cannot be based on hope or demands; it is the result of actively integrating R&D into the corporation.

Dollars Aren't Enough

The amount of money spent on R&D has little correlation to the number of commercial successes gained. Throwing money at the problem, it seems, is not the answer. Instead, what is needed is more effective management of the R&D process. This fact is underscored in a recent book:[3]

> The R&D imperative for industry has never been more compelling. Virtually all industry feels the impact of both increased competition—much of it technically based—and the accelerated pace of technological challenge and change.
>
> Many companies cannot increase their R&D investment fast enough to compensate for the international R&D challenges they face. The answer cannot simply be to spend "more" on R&D, because more can never be enough. The solution, rather, must be to deploy R&D investments more effectively—that is, more strategically and more efficiently.

Understanding these trends created enough stress at the benchmarking sponsor site to undertake the best-in-class study. Driven by the knowledge that current practices would not ensure future success, management embarked on a path to gain knowledge on *how* other companies were managing their R&D function.[4]

PURSUING BEST PRACTICE

The study began with an internal assessment of existing practices at the sponsoring firm. The sponsoring site was the centralized R&D organization of a Fortune 100 company that was highly respected in the R&D community for its past record of significant achievement. The study was motivated by the fact that current R&D results were slow in coming. Top management was increasingly concerned; the company was, like many of its competitors, "starved" for new products. Facing increasing competitive pressures and management expectations, the R&D director wanted to define a direction or strategy for improvement.

The internal assessment focused on the key elements of the organization and culture of the R&D function at the sponsoring site. The specific areas addressed included the following:

1. Current criteria for rewards and recognition
2. Extent and type of teamwork employed
3. Communication patterns within the R&D group as well as between R&D and the rest of the organization
4. Resources currently committed to R&D
5. Level and type of supervision used
6. Leadership (availability and source)
7. Decision-making patterns (such as who selected projects and how)
8. Level of productivity (patents/dollars spent)

Information on these items was collected by interviewing personnel at all levels of the R&D group, grading the company's current performance against these criteria, evaluating the results, and identifying and analyzing areas where performance gaps appeared. The "straw man" used to score the area was provided by the outside facilitator, who actually conducted the internal assessment and subsequent benchmarking study.

The internal assessment further focused on issues that were impediments to shortening the R&D process. The R&D process was mapped and documented so that areas in need of improvement were clearly visible.

16. EXCELLENCE IN RESEARCH AND DEVELOPMENT

The Culture of R&D

While several cultural performance gaps were identified, one area proved to be of major concern: the values of the laboratory were based on traditional research science criteria, which had little or nothing to do with the commercialization, or business side, of the issue. The identified goals of the research staff focused on the scientists' ability to

- Create "new science"
- Gain patents for new concepts or products
- Publish in learned academic journals
- Gain the respect of their "intellectual peers"

The ongoing success of the company, though, was not reflected in these objectives. To gain competitive advantage, the company needed *effective* R&D, as defined by the speed, flexibility, and success rate of the R&D group in transforming new scientific and technological ideas into commercially viable products. Patents might or might not result in new products. And while the company prides itself on the credentials of its research staff, expertise alone would not ensure profits. Every stakeholder within the organization depended on R&D to discover new products and processes and turn them into viable commercial ventures.

The key performance gap, then, was identified during the internal assessment by comparing the objectives of the organization and the needs of its stakeholders against the defined goals of the research staff. The "expectations gap" was evident; knowing it, though, did not provide the information needed to narrow it. The decision was made to embark on a search for best practices (in other words, best-in-class benchmarking). The objective was to seek out those companies that were known for their success in commercializing their R&D efforts and to explore the values of their research scientists. Best practice would be focused on, and defined by, the *management* of the R&D process.

The Benchmarking Process

The internal assessment, analysis of the R&D process, and identification of performance gaps provided the benchmarking team[5] with the list of organizational performance and cultural characteristics that would be obtained from the target sites. This list of desired characteristics was transformed into a questionnaire that would provide the detailed information needed to identify best practice and to determine what initiatives were necessary to implement them at the sponsoring firm.

Once the scope and focus of the BIC benchmarking study were decided on, target sites needed to be identified. Working together, the sponsoring firm and facilitators developed a comprehensive roster of companies that had a reputation for excellence in their R&D function. "Excellence" did not necessarily mean that the companies were successful at commercialization. In fact, the team decided it would collect information from a very diverse group of companies to home in on the practices used by firms successful at commercialization vs. the practices pursued by reputedly "excellent" R&D functions. The results, then, would provide the benchmarking team with the ability to discriminate between R&D excellence in a traditional model vs. excellence in a model focused on effective commercialization.

The selection of the sites, then, was aimed at diversification of the sample group. Several sites were chosen as being direct competitors of the sponsoring firm; others because of their general R&D reputation; and a third group based on public knowledge of their effectiveness at commercializing R&D (see Figure 16.2). Variety would increase the probability that new knowledge (in other words, innovative practice) would be uncovered. In addition, participants were chosen from both domestic and international firms to ensure that "best practices" didn't mean "the American way."

Given the sensitive nature of the study, it was imperative that a "double blind" be used to screen the sponsor from the participating firms and vice versa. The benchmarking facilitator therefore picked the group of target firms in isolation from the sponsoring site. Only the facilitator would know the true identity of the participants. Armed with this level of credibility, the facilitator easily obtained agreement from the target sites to conduct the study. As usual, each firm was guaranteed a copy of the final results for its own use.

Several factors ensured the success of the study, then:

1. Guaranteed confidentiality, including screening the sponsor's knowledge of target sites

- **Participant's Characteristics**

    - Pursue Significant R&D Activity -- Basic Research, Applied Research and Development
    - Known for R&D Success
    - Compete Globally
    - Sales Between $1,000 Million to $71,000 Million
    - R&D Expenditures from $80 Million to $5,000 Million

- **Geographical Mix of Participants**

    - Twelve United States
    - Two Germany
    - One Japan

Figure 16.2   Profile.

2. A focus on the *management* of the R&D process, rather than any technical details associated with the projects and products being pursued
3. Low cost of participation vs. judged value of knowledge gained
4. Access to an objective "straw man" for effective (that is, high commercialization ratios) R&D management and practice

Gaining the knowledge that would be uncovered by the study would help everyone; it was a win-win situation. The fact that the study would yield a "model of excellence" for R&D practice that was clearly linked to organizational and cultural factors meant that each participant could score itself on the key items and identify opportunities for improvement.

Getting the Data

A questionnaire served as the basis for the data collection phase of the study. The survey was not immediately mailed to participants, though. Instead, the facilitating team directly contacted each participant before the survey was even mailed and explained the process, benefits, and safeguards that were associated with the study. Once initial interest was confirmed, the target companies were mailed the survey and reviewed it to determine whether or not they still wanted to participate—which they did, across the board. The participating companies, then, were in control of the process; they could back out of the project at any time, no questions asked.

Once the surveys were distributed, the facilitator conducted a second round of telephone calls, this time to collect the actual data. The survey served as the basis for a telephone interview. While the individual survey items were answered by all, what added value to the approach was the anecdotal information that was obtained during the interviews. Given the nature of the study, the qualitative data or comments given by the respondents were critical to making sense of the results. The key question that framed each interview was "What are your criteria for success in the R&D area?" Each company defined its own measures of success. After the study was completed, the facilitator was then able to sort the respondents, based on their defined critical success factors, and compare the practices of those firms focused on commercialization with the practices pursued by other participants.

The study triggered self-analysis at each of the sites contacted. Gaining "buy-in" was the least of the facilitator's problems:

> The participants got wrapped up in the study. They wanted to do a good job and to make sure that they were giving us what we needed. It wasn't seen as a chore; they were active participants in improving their profession and its long-term viability as well as that of their firm.

The fact that the benchmarking study would provide long-term value to everyone involved ensured its success.

BEST PRACTICE: THE STRAW MAN MODEL FOR R&D

Before analyzing the data, the benchmarking team had to develop a list of criteria or discriminators for judging the effectiveness of the R&D process. Two factors framed their analysis: revenue enhancement capabilities and cost containment strategies. These were universally agreed to as criteria by all the participants. To be an effective strategic tool, R&D has to yield viable products that can garner revenues for their firm. The four elements of performance chosen to capture effective R&D revenue enhancement were

1. Percentage of basic research projects that progress to applied research

2. Percentage of applied research projects that progress to development

3. Percentage of development projects that progress to *profitable commercialization*

4. The level of contribution of R&D to the profitability of the company

The cost criterion used was simpler: the ratio of the R&D budget to the number of scientists.

High-performance companies were then identified as those that met the following criteria:

■ Their progression from basic and applied research to commercialization is well above that of other participants.

■ R&D contributes to more than 50 percent of the company's profitability (via successful new product launches).

■ Total R&D budget per scientist was lower than other participants.

Two of the companies (and perhaps a third) qualified as high performers on these criteria. Looking across the common factors that might explain their success, thirteen best practices (the straw man) emerged. These practices spanned the strategic formulation and communication area, financial perspectives, culture and organization, evaluation and performance measurement, resource access and retention, and identified alliances and relationships (see Figure 16.3).

BENCHMARKING

STRATEGY FORMULATION AND COMMUNICATION

- Corporate and business unit strategies are well defined and clearly communicated to the R&D organization.

- Core technologies are defined using analytical decision support techniques and communicated to R&D.

FINANCIAL PERSPECTIVE

- Funding for basic research comes from corporate sources and funding for development comes from business units.

- Investments are made in multi-national R&D capabilities.

CULTURE AND ORGANIZATION

- Formal cross-functional teams are created not only for development projects, but also for basic and applied research projects.

- Formal mechanisms exist for regular interaction between scientists, and between R&D and other functions.

- Basic and applied research are performed at a central facility of a small number (2 or 3) of facilities, each focused on a particular science or technology. Development is performed at distributed sites, co-located with business units or manufacturing plants.

EVALUATION AND PERFORMANCE MEASUREMENT

- Analytical tools are used for project selection, on-going project assessment, as well as for R&D portfolio balancing.

- Technology transfer to the business units is the most important metric of R&D performance.

RESOURCE ACCESS AND RETENTION

- Effective career development is in place for all levels in the R&D organization.

- Recruiting of new graduates is from universities at large and other companies when specific skills are required that would take too long or cannot be grown internally.

ALLIANCES AND RELATIONSHIPS

- Formal mechanisms are in place for monitoring external R&D activities.

- Some basic research is performed internally, but there are also many university and third party relationships.

Figure 16.3   Best practice in Research and Development.

Best Practice in Strategy Formulation and Communication

Effective R&D deployment was tightly tied to the clear definition and effective communication of corporate and business unit strategies to the R&D group. Each top-performing company had established mechanisms for communication between R&D and management as well as a practice of placing a premium on the use of this communication channel by both sides of the "house."

The clear definition of strategic objectives was reinforced by the practice of evaluating the ongoing effectiveness of the R&D function against these objectives. Best practice in R&D, then, began with developing a shared vision of what the company was trying to accomplish in the marketplace.

A second major thrust in the strategic area for best-practice firms was the definition of "core technologies" at the corporate level, using analytical decision support techniques. Core technologies reflect an underlying performance characteristic, or common set of major components, for the company's products. Honda defines "internal combustion engines" as one of its core technologies; each of its products uses a Honda engine that is designed to meet rigorous performance criteria. These core technologies were defined in conjunction with R&D in best-practice firms, not by individual scientists. Research expertise was accumulated around those technologies that were chosen by the company for their strategic merit. These core technologies were used to set the direction of the R&D efforts as well as to link R&D and business unit activities.

Financial Metrics of Best Practice

A second major element of best practice in R&D is the firm's R&D investment strategy. Best-practice firms, for the most part, were taking a global perspective in defining their R&D capabilities, focusing on developing excellence in international communication and teamwork. If a core technology was being perfected outside of the United States, the R&D function was encouraged to follow it.

Relatedly, best practice from the financial perspective indicated that funding for basic research would come from corporate, while development costs were being borne by the business units. While all units in the corporation could benefit from basic research into the core technologies, the application of those discoveries were more clearly defined at the business unit level. In order to encourage increased teamwork between R&D and the business units, best-practice firms tied their destinies together.

Culture and Organization

Three key practices were uncovered in this area. First, top-performing companies had created formal cross-functional teams for all R&D projects, whether basic or applied in nature. This cross-fertilization helped define those projects with high commercialization potential and led to rapid transference of the innovation into a marketable product. The cross-functional approach provided an enhanced creative environment for identifying, choosing, and maximizing the value of R&D's projects.

Formal cross-functional teams translated to formal mechanisms for regular interaction between the scientists within the R&D group as well as between R&D and the other functions. In best-practice firms this interaction was not left to chance; structured procedures were put in place to force the process. The knowledge-generation process was not seen as solely a high-level management concern; instead, all organization levels of the R&D and business unit group were actively involved in identifying and implementing research results.

In line with the financial and strategic practices of the best-practice firms, basic and some applied research was done in centralized locations that would maximize the interaction of scientists involved in major projects. Most of the applied research and the development work, which entailed getting the new products into the marketplace, were decentralized around the location of business units or major manufacturing sites. This approach retained the structure of the core scientific community while ensuring that the output of their efforts could be put to work in the individual sites.

Evaluation and Performance Measurement

Tightening the ties between R&D and the business units they served led best-practice firms to use analytical techniques for project selection, ongoing project assessment, and R&D portfolio balancing. This was in direct contrast to traditional approaches in the United States, where projects were chosen and developed by "stars" in the R&D group. Since the business units were paying for the development of marketable products, not simply neat ideas, they wanted to make sure that projects were selected based on objective estimates of their relative market and profit potential. By employing decision support tools that assessed the profit potential over the life cycle of the various projects, the assessment of the R&D process was formalized, and the involvement of many different business functions in ongoing selection and assessment of projects was assured.

This policy was enforced by making technology transfer the most important metric of R&D's performance. Patents and publications were given a secondary role in the performance evaluation process, giving a clear signal that the scientists were expected to work toward institutional goals before personal and professional ones. With analytical tools (which were well tested for effectiveness) available to help forecast the likelihood of success, R&D was given maximum support in achieving its technology transfer objectives.

Resource Access and Retention

A fifth dimension of best practice in R&D deployment revolved around the acquisition and retention of research staff. Two areas of interest surfaced in this respect: career development and the recruiting of employees from the outside. Top-performing R&D groups had effective career development strategies that served to reinforce a spirit of cooperation at all levels in the organization. Technicians, rather than being treated as second-class citizens, were valued and provided with the support and opportunity to move upward in the R&D group. In addition, expertise was not defined by the number of degrees a person held; each employee was actively engaged on development teams. Innovation was the goal—creative ideas were being fostered at every level in the research group.

Maintaining a policy of promoting from within did not keep best-practice firms from recruiting from outside sources. External recruiting, though, was done in a targeted manner, when specific skills were required that would take too long or simply could not be developed within the existing staff. In this manner, best-practice firms were able to maximize their exposure to new forms of basic research that were being developed at other companies, in other industries, or on university campuses around the world. The objective in employing external recruiting on a selective basis was to learn from the best, not steal trade secrets.

Alliances and Relationships

The final element of best practice involves the relationship of the R&D group with external research groups. While tremendous growth can be fostered within the corporation, it is tantamount to suicide to ignore emerging practice in the external environment.

Best-practice firms, then, had formal mechanisms in place for monitoring external R&D activities. Gathering this knowledge was a key element in the constant evaluation and redeployment of R&D as a strategic weapon.

The final best practice identified in the BIC study was the fact that while top-performing firms conducted some basic research internally, they also maintained strong ties with universities and other third parties in this area. Basic research is a much riskier undertaking for a corporation; while significant innovations may be uncovered in its laboratories, the company's ability to commercialize the breakthrough is not guaranteed. Often the product of the basic research project, a new technology or product, has to be licensed or sold by the company that develops it, because it simply can't effectively commercialize or market the innovation. By focusing its basic research in a few vital areas and keeping open communication channels with universities and research firms that have ongoing basic research projects in place, the best-practice firms are able to reap the maximum benefit from each R&D dollar expended.

Understanding and Implementing Best Practice

The list of best practices is the starting point in the process of improving a company's performance. Once the benchmarking study was complete, the results were shared with all participating firms, but only the benchmarking sponsor had the added benefit of directly comparing its structure and approach to the straw man model in an effective manner.

Looking across the list of best practices, the anecdotal information, and the combined expertise of the benchmarking team, four key elements for successful commercialization of R&D emerged:

1. Clearly defined, long-term corporate business strategy was communicated to R&D and the business units.
2. Defined core technologies were communicated to R&D and business units.
3. Formal cross-functional teams for staffing research and development projects were employed.
4. Technology transfer became the primary metric of success.

For the sponsoring firm, the most significant internal cultural components proved to be the clear communication of corporate direction and strategy, increased delegation of authority and decision making, and increased emphasis on research productivity (timeliness, cost, and results). Given that the most successful firms proved to be those that rewarded their research staffs on the number of projects resulting in commercialization, it was obviously important to reinforce the shift in emphasis with appropriate evaluation procedures.

As with many research facilities, the sponsoring firm is facing a major cultural change away from development in isolation, described as "pushing food under the door to the sequestered scientist," to the model of best practice: close proximity and communication between the producers and consumers of innovations in the firm. Relatedly, moving the R&D world in the United States away from a "superstar" model to a team orientation will require major changes in the structure, practice, and training policies of research groups. In seeking rapid innovation and the application of ideas to practice, more minds are better than fewer. The creative process may occur in isolation, but the development and application of the innovation cannot. Commercialization affects every stakeholder in the firm.

The results of this BIC benchmarking study reflect a growing consensus in the United States that Americans are great at discovering new technologies and products but very poor at managing the R&D process for maximum commercial benefit. The joy of the hunt may be culturally defined, but the competitive environment is not. The straw man developed by this model, because it reflects best practices in R&D and not industry practice, can provide the basis for refocusing development efforts in any company. That is the essence of BIC approaches: they create knowledge that can be used to improve practices in many companies, across many industries. Learning from the best is the first step in becoming the best.

As the world becomes more interconnected and business becomes more complex and dynamic, work must

become more "learningful." It is no
longer sufficient to have one person
learning for the organization, a Ford
or a Sloan or a Watson. It's just not
possible any longer to "figure it out"
from the top, and have everyone else
following the orders of the "grand
strategist." The organizations that
will truly excel in the future will be
the organizations that discover how to
tap people's commitment and capacity to learn at all levels in an organization.

Peter M. Senge
The Fifth Discipline

17: IMPLEMENTATION OVERVIEW

The work will teach you how to do it.

Estonian proverb

It isn't so much a man's eminence of elementary faculties that pulls him through. They may be rare, and he do nothing. It is the steam pressure to the square inch behind that moves the machine.

William James

True learning comes from applying the lessons embedded in a lecture or a book. This fact holds in benchmarking as in every other challenge in life: experience has to be earned; it cannot be imparted through words or diagrams. Multiple examples have been used to convey the essence and objectives of benchmarking. The approaches used and lessons learned by companies in diverse industries, looking at a wide variety of functions and processes, have underscored the flexibility and value of benchmarking for defining and achieving best practice and for instilling continuous improvement inside an organization.

Benchmarking's value lies in its objectivity, focus, and degree of comparability between the benchmark targets and the sponsoring firm. It is objective, because it looks to outside sources to define excellence; internal company politics plays little or no part. By its very nature, a benchmarking study has to be focused; it is impractical to try to collect every ounce of information on every task performed in your own organization, let alone others. In clearly defining a purpose for the benchmarking exercise, a company sets the boundaries on the types of firms or units that can be analyzed. Without this focused effort driven by comparability, benchmarking is a resource drain rather than a source of competitive advantage. Benchmarking starts, therefore, with a clear knowledge of its destination.

Defining the objectives of the benchmarking process is only one critical factor in its success. A second major issue in effectively implementing benchmarking is a willingness to accept criticism and to learn. Benchmarking lays out, in graphic terms, the strengths and weaknesses of a company or function. The facts can't be avoided once collected; if they are, then the process of natural selection takes over. In the economic world as in nature, only the fittest survive. Benchmarking defines the competitive arena; it cannot force it to be acknowledged.

Effective implementation of benchmarking requires even more than clear objectives and a willingness to learn. It requires careful planning, open communication, participation from the entire management group, and the establishment of a clear action plan for achieving best practice. At its core, then, benchmarking is intricately tied to the process of continuous improvement and to the techniques and philosophies that surround it. Benchmarking is the key to creating the learning organization.

The Implementation Sequence

> We must forget what is behind. If we cease to originate, we are lost. We can only keep what we have, by new activity.
>
> William Ellery Channing
> *Dr. Channing's Notebook*

The myriad examples used in the preceding pages have a common implementation approach embedded in them. Much like scientific research, effective benchmarking comes with a set of defined objectives and rules for collecting and analyzing data from the field. The implementation sequence that has been followed in each of these examples is as follows:

Phase I: Internal data gathering and assessment
1. Identify an area or problem for study.
2. Create a benchmarking team.
3. Conduct an internal assessment of existing work practices, including a detailed list of the performance drivers/constraints for the organization and the area being examined.
4. Define desired internal performance levels using a straw man model, or aggregation of existing practice, across the organization.
5. Identify performance gaps, or areas where existing practice is unsatisfactory.
6. Fix the easy problems.

Phase II: External data gathering
1. Choose a benchmarking approach.
2. Develop a questionnaire, interview document, or related data collection tool.
3. Identify candidate participants (organizations and people).
4. Solicit candidates.
5. Send questionnaire to participants.
6. Interview participants.

Phase III: Analysis of benchmarking information
1. Compare benchmarking data against original performance drivers and note similarities and differences for your firm and the benchmarking participants.
2. Classify and analyze the quantitative data.
3. Review qualitative data (interview comments) to identify innovative concepts and unique approaches.
4. Confirm findings where needed.
5. Reanalyze the quantitative results in light of the anecdotal information (interview comments).
6. Develop a straw man model of best practice for the area under study.
7. Communicate the basic findings to all benchmarking participants.

Phase IV: Implementing an action plan

1. Establish an implementation team to supplement the benchmarking team.
2. Score internal operations against the benchmarked straw man.
3. Sort the identified performance gaps based on their relationship to the underlying strategic plan of the company.
4. Prioritize performance gaps based on your firm's strategy, the impact of the change on stakeholder satisfaction, and relative cost versus ease of implementation.
5. Have the implementation team begin facilitating the change process by holding meetings in the affected groups, taking suggestions for developing an action plan, and encouraging active involvement.
6. Create clear objectives that will provide short-run signals of improvement to reinforce the change process and motivate behavior.
7. Establish measurements that reflect improvement, or failure to improve, on the key straw man measures.
8. Communicate the results in a positive manner.
9. Work with affected groups to establish long range plans for gaining parity with benchmarked best practice, and for accelerating the learning process.
10. Reinforce, learn, and change on an ongoing basis.
11. Benchmark again to recalibrate best-in-class.

These four phases represent a structured learning process that provides clear, objective data on the company's relative performance against its competitors or best-in-class firms.

Defining the Problem: The Essential Role
of Internal Assessment

Very often a change of self is needed
more than a change of scene.

A. C. Benson

Very few benchmarking studies adequately describe the need to perform an internal assessment of existing practice prior to turning to external sources of data. If existing practice is not understood, how can a company or function learn from how someone else does the work? Internal assessment is the key to effective benchmarking, and yet it is the most difficult lesson to learn.

Internal assessment runs counter to the American approach to problem solving. The apparently meaningless process of writing down what you already know is a hard sell to a culture energized by action. Introspection can foster action, but only after the requisite level of honesty and disappointment has been reached. Whether rightly or wrongly, management usually believes that it already knows how its company works; why should it spend valuable time and resources writing it all down? The answer is quite evident: practices evolve over time. Even if everyone "knows" how a certain area performs its work, it's quite likely they don't know all the things that are done that no one asked for. How could they? If they never ask for the output of that chain of activities, how would they know the work is performed?

Internal assessment, then, is useful in and of itself. It reveals areas for improvement in existing practices that can eliminate non-value-added work and streamline the value-adding components. The need for internal assessment doesn't end there, though. To gain the maximum benefit from benchmarking, an organization has to know that the benchmarking firms are comparable on key performance drivers (or constraints) and that lessons learned from them can be adapted to fit internal operating characteristics. Benchmarking's effectiveness is defined by the level of *comparability* between the benchmarking participants and the sponsoring company. If comparability is low, the usefulness of the benchmarking data will also be low. Designing, conducting, and implementing the benchmarking process starts with understanding those unique features of your organization that cannot be changed, the strategic objectives being pursued, and how external constraints limit the alternative solutions that can be used to improve performance.

As suggested earlier, Avon Products has used internal benchmarking to standardize its operations. This is another benefit of the internal assessment process: the company can actually apply the benchmarking results across multiple internal units. As the internal assessment is conducted, communication channels are opened up between groups in the company that can learn from each other and that share solutions to common problems. Significant changes can be generated through standardization of internal practice and by creating internal competition for best practice.

Internal assessment, then, is not an optional stage in the benchmarking process or a separate technique that only fits limited situations. It is the basis for all forms of continuous improvement, whether the goals being pursued are based on internal or external criteria. In addition, it generates momentum and an acceptance of the need for change. By triggering the improvement process using internal criteria, the "blow" is softened and many of the traditional barriers to change are eliminated (such as the "not created here" syndrome). It opens a dialogue between the explorers, scouts, and settlers, suggesting that there may be greener pastures on the other side of the mountain (outside the firm). Once this momentum is set in place, the benchmarking team can turn its attention to the outside.

> There is only one way in which a person acquires a new idea: by the combination or association of two or more ideas he already has into a new juxtaposition in such a manner as to discover a relationship among them of which he was not previously aware.
>
> Francis A. Cartier

CHOOSING A PROJECT: MOVING BENCHMARKING TOWARD ACTION

> An idea is a feat of association.
>
> Robert Frost

Choosing a benchmarking project can precede the internal assessment or follow it. Often, management knows exactly what areas it needs to improve in order to gain competitive advantage; in other cases it simply knows it wants to get "better." Even if the general area that is to be benchmarked is known from the beginning, the internal assessment process brings it into sharp focus. For instance, if Jannsen had not done an internal assessment of its administrative function, it quite likely would not have identified the need to review Research and Development.

Choosing a benchmarking project, then, starts with the identification of the critical success factors for the organization and the isolation of those parts of the firm that are not meeting stakeholder expectations on a consistent basis. This performance shortfall, though, need not be the only trigger for choosing a benchmarking project. Often the functional management group knows it needs to make improvements, or it simply wants to get fresh insights on how it could improve its performance. In fact, an area that has been designated as a key strategic weapon can often benefit the most from the benchmarking process, as management isolates how effectively it is deploying its resources in this area and what further improvements it should be implementing.

At a major speciality chemical manufacturer, the study focus centered around the infrastructure to sell, manufacture, and supply a new food additive. The product was initially to be manufactured by subcontractors at multiple sites. Under this plan, coordination and shipment became critical to meet production demands influenced by custom service. The benchmarks were designed to identify

- How technology can be applied to ensure quality, consistency, and on-time delivery

- The barriers in applying the technology

- Steps that could be taken to minimize the risks and costs

As a result of the study, alternative strategies were implemented to ensure on-time product delivery, and a training program was also developed.

In contrast, a leading service company that recognized the growing importance of effective order management in maintaining customer satisfaction and controlling operating costs benchmarked the process prior to restructuring. To determine operational characteristics that were common to companies recognized as best-in-class, the company developed a four-part framework for understanding and comparing key elements:

- Process

- Human resources

- Organization

- Automation

Based on the study, ten key process characteristics were identified along with resource performance levels. This information was used in the reengineering efforts.

Sometimes the internal assessment process is not needed to identify the right projects but rather to ensure that the right questions are asked once the study is undertaken. Here the company isn't really choosing a "project," but it is clearly defining the boundaries and objectives for it. The underlying process becomes one of isolating what performance measurements should be chosen, what factors are responsible for customer satisfaction, and related issues.

The selection of a benchmarking project, then, is driven by competitive pressures that target a low-performing area or that suggest that the rules of the game are being redefined (for example, customer expectations are being raised). Likewise, an area can be selected for benchmarking because it consumes a major portion of available resources or affects the performance of a significant number of downstream activities.

The bottom line in choosing a project, then, is management's belief that the benefits to be gained from improving the performance in that area will outweigh the cost of doing the benchmarking study. Gathering data, analyzing data, and implementing change are all costly events. For these costs to make sense, they must lead to an enhancement in the value or competitive position of the company. Change for change's sake is not the objective;

gaining strategic advantage through effective resource deployment is.

DATA GATHERING: LESSONS FROM THE OTHER SIDE

Man is not a machine in the sense that he can consistently maintain the same output of work. He can only meet the demands of outer necessity in an ideal way if he is also adapted to his own inner world, that is to say, if he is in harmony with himself. Conversely, he can only adapt to his inner world and achieve unity with himself when he is adapted to the environmental conditions.

C. G. Jung
Psychological Reflections

Data gathering is the phase of benchmarking that attracts the most attention. Many companies are not accustomed to asking competitors or strangers for detailed information about how they perform tasks or evaluate results. And these external sources have probably not made it a practice to share this type of data. Benchmarking is a learning process for both the sponsoring company and the benchmarking firms; both need to open their minds to the fact that someone may have a better way of working, or a different slant on solving an ongoing problem.

A research design is the first step in this process. It is a detailed plan of action that defines the how, when, where, what, why, and who for the benchmarking project. The key facet of this definition is a clear statement of objectives—what question is the benchmarking project going to try to answer? Focusing the benchmarking study starts with an idea of where you want to end up and what benefits the journey will yield. It's also important to detail the financial constraints for the project; few companies can afford to spend unlimited sums in gaining benchmarking information.

Developing the right type of questions is so critical to the benchmarking process that an entire chapter will be devoted to it. If questions are poorly stated, are vague, or fail to focus on the core issues under study, they are unlikely to yield the needed data. Also, vague questions can frustrate the well-intentioned participants, changing their initial enthusiasm to dismay and potential rejection. The way questions are worded, the level of detailed knowledge required to answer them, and their relevance to the issues at hand are all critical dimensions of successful surveys. Management's buy-in to the benchmarking process, instruments used, and chosen performance measures underlies this entire process.

In addition to the survey itself, significant thought has to be given to the mode used to obtain the data. Are the surveys going to be mailed, filled out by the participants, and returned without any direct contact? Should phone interviews supplement the survey or be used to guide the participants in completing them? What kind of information is needed to develop a straw man model and ensure that the benchmarking study results in the types of improvement the sponsoring company wants? And can the desired data be realistically gathered directly by the company, or are they so sensitive that an objective facilitator will be needed to get it?

Choosing Benchmarking Target Firms

> Knowledge is power, if you know it about the right person.
>
> Ethel Watts Mumford

Once the benchmarking team has a clear idea of where they're heading, it becomes time to identify the list of potential benchmarking candidates. Based on the internal assessment and the list of key performance drivers and environmental constraints, the benchmarking team can narrow the list of potential firms to those most likely to yield useful comparative data. Where do the initial list of candidate firms and the final choice of participants begin?

It begins with a careful analysis of the literature to identify companies that have achieved recognition in the area or are attempting to improve their performance; brainstorming within the sponsoring company; discussions with industry experts, customers, suppliers and other advisors; attendance at conferences and association meetings; and examination of other benchmarking projects the firm has participated in or gained access to in some other manner. In other words, the initial list of benchmarking candidates should be expansive (see Figure 17.1). When the necessary criteria, such as driver characteristics, are applied to the sample, it will shrink at an alarming rate. Rather than facing the potential of starting all over again, it's better to err on the side of a large first-pass sample of candidates.

Developing a list of candidates, then, is followed by the elimination of those that fail to meet key criteria identified in the internal assessment. This pared-down group becomes the focal point for the study. While significant diversity can remain in the sample, it's critical that the key structural characteristics and constraints facing the sponsor organization are reflected in the sample selected. It is also important that management understand the rationale for the list of firms and agrees with it.

Figure 17.1   Developing a list of candidates.

Core group in hand, the benchmarking team embarks on the "sales" part of the benchmarking project. Target firms have to be contacted and participation secured. Anyone who has played a hectic game of telephone tag knows that this process can extend days and weeks beyond any reasonable estimate of its time to completion. Often the first several calls to a company can lead to accelerating handoffs, fumbles (that is, disconnects), and false starts. Persistence is one key to success; the other is having a clearly identified list of what you are benchmarking as well as the reasons why the target firm will benefit from participating in your study.

If the solicitation process has been successful, the rest of the data collection process is simply follow-through. Based on the approach chosen, target firms are surveyed via either mailed questionnaires, phone surveys, or site visits. While mailed questionnaires may appear to be the optimal approach, they leave a lot of ground uncovered. There's no way to tell who really filled out the survey or what interpretations they added to your questions before answering them. If they didn't know a fact, did they call someone and find out, or did they simply guess? In using a mailed questionnaire there is significant potential for "slips between the cup and the lips."

Interview data provide a much richer basis for benchmarking analysis and conclusions. Interviewing adds depth to the questionnaire responses and identifies areas that may have been missed in the initial instrument. Additionally, it helps decrease the potential for faulty conclusions, as target respondents help the benchmarking team think through the issues from an alternative perspective. The creative process is escalated from this enriched interaction between the benchmarking team and the target firms.

Analysis: Making Sense of the Data

> The last thing a scientist would do is cling to a map because he inherited it from his grandfather, or because it was used by George Washington or Abraham Lincoln.
>
> S. I. Hayakawa

Analyzing the data is the next major step in the benchmarking process. It entails the focused categorization, measurement, summation, and integration of the quantitative and qualitative components of the underlying information base. To make sense out of raw data, the benchmarking team has to apply analytical techniques to sort the information and identify patterns. This process is laid out in detail in subsequent chapters. The key factor to keep in mind is that data analysis is an art, not a science. The objective is to sort, screen, and interpret the data in order to create new knowledge, gain insights, and formulate strategies for improvement.

There's no one right way to analyze data, although there are scores of incorrect procedures that can distort the results. The key to success is keeping an open mind, a critical and objective stance, a willingness to experiment with several different compilations of the data, and a skeptical view of the suggested results. Confirming the results takes place throughout the data analysis process, as the benchmarking team reworks the data and its models in the search for the best fit between the data and known reality. Finally, the team has to be willing to throw away its own perceptions of what the "right" answer should be. If the company already knows the right thing to do and does it, benchmarking may not be needed. On the other hand, if management has this opinion, it quite likely needs to benchmark.

Moving Toward Action

With the straw man in place, the data analysis process comes to a close and the real work begins. The benchmarking results have to be communicated to management and the stages of mourning experienced. While the list of actions may appear quite objective, anyone who has spearheaded a massive change in the mindset and practices of an organization knows that it is more like standing in quicksand than on dry earth. The path ahead is strewn with visible and invisible barriers to change; the process is subject to snags, miscommunications, and revolution as the message filters its way through the management ranks.

As has been stated repeatedly, this is where benchmarking gives the change agent an added advantage over more traditional change methods especially in light of management's buy-in. The objective, verifiable nature of benchmarking results may lead to denial, but they can't be discredited. The facts speak loudly for themselves. The care taken in designing and executing the study now comes into play. If the study has been poorly done, it will be rejected by the organization. Acceptance and motivation are based in the individual's belief that the data are accurate and objective.

In choosing an implementation path, it's important to focus on a few key measures and objectives for the short term. These measures and objectives should be designed to get the improvement process started and to provide rapid reinforcement of the gains being attained. The vital factor separating a successful from an unsuccessful implementation is momentum: there has to be a defined path of improvement with visible scorecards along the way. If effort is easily connected to results, then more effort can be expected to follow. On the other hand, if effort is neither recognized or rewarded, the improvement process will be short-lived. Benchmarking is designed to create continuous improvement, not one-shot change.

The types of changes put in place will not lead to immediate "best-practice" status. The performance improvements will be gradual. And the target will constantly keep moving; the benchmarked firms cannot be expected to stop innovating. They will continue to improve, making it imperative that the benchmarking company always keep its eye on the future, fighting off the tendency to rest on its laurels once parity is achieved.

CREATING STAKEHOLDER VALUE: THE ULTIMATE GOAL

Man must cease attributing his problems to his environment, and learn again to exercise his will—his personal responsibility in the realm of faith and morals.

Albert Schweitzer

The true test of benchmarking is whether or not the company succeeds in increasing stakeholder satisfaction and value. In implementing a benchmarking study, then, the connection between the study, its results, the subsequent action plan, and the value of the firm cannot be ignored. Benchmarking isn't another fad to make everyone feel good that the company is trying to get better, but is instead the cold shower that makes it very clear just how much they have to improve. Companies are successfully using benchmarking to gain competitive advantage, eliminate non-value-added work, and focus scarce resources on those activities and functions that will yield a competitive advantage.

In a competitive marketplace, every resource has to be used to its fullest. Creating value requires the effective, efficient deployment of existing physical and human assets, as well as the continuous search for improvement. If a company fails to innovate quickly enough, it will lose its competitive edge and face potential decline and death. This is the reality of economics; competition for scarce resources leads to the survival of the best and the elimination of weaker rivals.

Implementing a full-scale benchmarking program cannot ensure that a company will survive the competitive battles it faces, but at least it will know what the score is and where its strengths and weaknesses lie. Knowledge does not ensure victory, but ignorance is a sure path to defeat. A good general would never lead an army onto a battlefield without having extensively studied the terrain, the opposing general's character, and the strength and position of the opposing forces. Armed with this knowledge, the general crafts strategies that are based on historical battles to maximize the potential for success.

Managing a modern corporation is akin to carrying out an intense military field campaign. In both cases fortunes are won and lost and lives irreparably affected. While more than one army may occupy the battlefield, only those that successfully defend themselves from attack survive. And if survival is the only objective, the army's strength will be gradually eroded and finally falter. As is often stated, the only good defense is a strong offense.

Benchmarking provides the strategic advantage and focus necessary to launch a successful campaign to regain lost markets or gain new ones. Properly implemented, it can focus the efforts of the organization on defined critical success factors, unify activities, and initiate long-term improvement. Its benefits, though, are a direct function of the skill used in designing and implementing the study and the careful analysis and evaluation of results.

BENCHMARKING

Skillful use of benchmarking techniques begins with a careful study of what they can do for the firm, clear development of underlying objectives for the analysis, and continuous learning from the data and the process itself. Implementing benchmarking has a beginning, but no end.

I know of no more encouraging fact than the unquestionable ability of man to elevate his life by a conscious endeavor.

Henry David Thoreau

18: DESIGNING AND USING QUESTIONNAIRES

> It is a capital mistake to theorize before one has data. Insensibly one begins to twist facts to suit theories, instead of theories to fit facts.
>
> Sir Arthur Conan Doyle
> *The Adventures of Sherlock Holmes*
> *"Scandal in Bohemia"*

Benchmarking's power lies in its reliance on objective data collected from a variety of sources. In planning and executing a benchmarking study, the published literature is culled, trade association materials and contacts obtained, databases perused, and countless questions generated and asked of experts both inside and outside the firm. While each of these data collection approaches has merit, none replaces the focused collection of original data as a primary source of learning and verifying benchmarking lessons.

When the decision is made to obtain original data, the benchmarking company is committing resources and management time. That means everyone's "homework" has to be done—you don't want to collect data before you're sure that you are asking the right questions. Designing and completing a questionnaire or interview study is the last stage in understanding existing problems, performance gaps, and opportunities for improvement. It should be done carefully and methodically, because it is seldom possible to run the study again if mistakes are caught downstream. Questionnaire design, then, shouldn't be undertaken until the benchmarking team is comfortable it knows exactly what and why it is benchmarking.

DESIGNING A QUESTIONNAIRE

> To treat your facts with imagination is
> one thing, but to imagine your facts is
> another.
>
> John Burroughs

Designing a questionnaire begins with a clear understanding of what it is going to measure, and why. In describing the design process, Floyd J. Fowler, Jr. notes:

> Designing a good questionnaire involves selecting the questions needed to meet the research objectives, testing them to make sure they can be asked and answered as planned, then putting them into a form to maximize the ease with which respondents and interviewers can do their jobs.... A prerequisite to designing a good questionnaire is deciding what is to be measured. That may seem simple and self-evident, but it is a step that often is overlooked to the detriment of the questionnaire (and the study).[1]

Questionnaire design starts with a clear statement or paragraph that details what the survey is supposed to accomplish. The statement of objectives helps the benchmarking team clarify its goals, language, and intentions. It also defines the types of data that will be needed to get desired results and why it is necessary.

This statement later serves as a sanity check and a way to screen and eliminate questions that may be interesting but aren't necessary to get the answers wanted. In many ways, designing a questionnaire is a constant battle to eliminate the irrelevant. The survey is not a garbage can or a mine sweeper; it is a focused document that has to get needed data in an efficient manner.

> In larger things we are convivial;
> What causes trouble is the trivial.
>
> Richard Armour

Gaining Focus—Environmental Benchmarking

During the 1960s there was little discussion of global warming, waste management, or "green" products. Today, the state of this planet is explored in every medium and has become part of our day-to-day lives—and corporations. Since this is a relatively new area for corporations, Coopers & Lybrand's worldwide environmental practice leaders wondered "What are the best management techniques currently being employed to direct and control environmental performance and practices?"

To answer this question, a number of alternative approaches were explored, including environmental audits, surveys, and benchmarking. Environmental audits were eliminated for the following reasons:

■ Because of different regulations in each country and industry, an apples-to-apples comparison would be difficult.

■ Compliance-based comparisons are inherently limited in identifying "Best," because compliance is by definition the minimum requirement.

The survey approach was also eliminated because it tended to be more quantitative rather than qualitative. After a number of discussions, it was decided that a best-in-class benchmarking study would provide the most insight and opportunity for identifying quantum leaps in management techniques. The partner-in-charge of the U.K. environmental practice felt that:

> Best-in-class benchmarking would allow cross-industry comparison that has been limited to date in the environmental area. . . . It is a tool that provides a way to understand the cost/benefit of different practices, and maybe more importantly, the why behind what is being done. In the end it should provide better information on how corporations should manage their environmental performance.

Once the decision was made to perform a benchmarking study, the hard part of the process began. What was meant by directing and controlling environmental issues? What types of questions would provide the information required?

This initial question itself—a definition of directing and controlling environmental operations—caused some unexpected and spirited debates. Everyone had a slightly different perspective in terms of key factors, areas of importance, scope, and depth of analysis. Opinions ranged from a narrow focus on reports from senior management to a broader definition of all environmental information requirements. The partner-in-charge of the C&L Canadian environmental practice stated that:

> Environmental management permeates every aspect of the business—the full life cycle. Therefore, our best-in-class management criteria should be the development and implementation of proactive, quality-driven measures to achieve minimal impact on the environment, e.g., pollution prevention. This means we must identify and compare the tools and techniques at each stage of the process.

In the end, it was decided that the study would review the environmental management systems (EMS) from the CEO's perspective. The CEO's perspective was key because CEOs are responsible for the environmental performance and practices of the corporation—from both a shareholder and legal perspective.

The next step was to identify the drivers for EMS and the CEO. These drivers included product life cycle, management attitude, and historic environmental issues. Once that was agreed upon, defining the questions that would provide the required information proved to be another major challenge. It took three solid drafts before an acceptable version was developed. Earlier versions asked a lot of questions that couldn't pass the "Why do we care about this?" and "What are we going to do with this information?" screens. At first, everything was seen as important. In the end, only questions that would help (1) identify the similarities and differences in management techniques, (2) assess the impact of the corporation's inherent and structural drivers, and (3) develop the final benchmarking measures and a strawman model remained. The director in the U.S. environmental practice reflected:

> Not having a background in the application of benchmarking methodologies, I originally did not appreciate the differences be-

tween a survey and formal benchmarking study questionnaire. Rather than address many issues dealing with environmental management, albeit superficially, the benchmarking study was designed to first develop a set of criteria with which we could identify the "best-in-class" environmental management. What we were seeking in the questionnaire is a profile of the Chief Executive Office's involvement in day-to-day and strategic environmental decision. This one factor was explored in great detail.

Once the questionnaire was accepted, it then went through a series of tests with various internal and external experts for completeness and clarity. This, too, was a learning process as suggested once again by the U.S. director's comments:

Developing and circulating the questionnaire helped crystallize and confirm our thinking about environmental management. It also helped us be more precise identifying word misinterpretations, and questions that could not be answered or did not provide information intended. . . . Finally, it insured that the questions addressed all industries, which was critical in this best-in-class benchmarking study.

Testing and Retesting the Document

The key to everything is patience. You get the chicken by hatching the egg—not by smashing it.

Arnold Glasow

A second major element of questionnaire design is pretesting it using internal personnel, benchmarking team members, and external experts. Once the list of questions has been carefully pruned to a list of essential items, attention has to turn to the wording and structure of the questions. Fowler identifies four practical standards that all questions should meet:[2]

1. Is this a question that can be asked exactly the way it is written?

2. Is this a question that will mean the same thing to every-one?
3. Is this a question people can answer?
4. Is this a question that people will be willing to answer, given the data collection procedures?

Many of these screens can be applied to the survey before it goes out for a formal pretest. Trying questions out on cowork-ers, friends, and relatives is one way to find problems. If they scrunch up their nose or return your question with a blank stare, the question needs to be reworked. Do they look suspicious for a moment, then let down their guard because it's you asking the question? You're headed back to the drawing board. Good survey design requires clear statements in common language with no (or minimal) ambiguity. If people don't understand or like a question, their answers are of questionable value.

Style is effectiveness of assertion.

George Bernard Shaw
Format of the Questionnaire

All the fun's in how you say a thing.

Robert Frost

The sequence and appearance of the questions in a survey can have an impact on the responses made. Many survey design guides suggest starting with easy questions first to ease the re-spondents into the study.[3] There is some merit to this position, but only if the easy questions can be logically drawn together into a free-standing section. A second approach is to put the least sensitive questions up front, gaining commitment from the re-spondent before asking for the hard facts. In deciding upon the sequence of questions, one should sort them into logical groupings (based on querying the same subject), and then arrange them so that early questions lead naturally to the mindset needed to understand and respond appropriately to later ones. Simple questions, then, are those that are immediately understood and have no trace of ambiguity around them. The ideal situation is to make every question "simple." Failing that, it is important to ensure that the question, even though complex, can be easily understood and answered.

Details of formatting the survey include choosing a type style that is easy to read, using consistent wording in key instructions, and clearly demarcating instructions from the questions themselves. Using different type faces for instructions vs. questions is one clear way to keep the two separate and to signal clearly to the respondent that the "rules" for answering the questions have changed.

Each "rule" for answering the questions has to be concisely stated and extremely clear in its message. The first rule to follow is to keep these messages consistent; if different words and approaches are used to ask people to do the same thing, it's quite likely they'll believe you want something else, and you'll get it. If a negative response to one question propels the respondent into another section of the survey, make sure that the message is clear. Every such "leap" through the survey is greeted with relief by the respondents; their only concern is making sure they understand where to go next (maybe the end?). Fowler, a noted expert in survey design, suggests that such "skip" patterns be kept to a minimum and that arrows and boxes that communicate the skip message without the need for lengthy instructions are best (should someone tell the IRS?). Other design hints noted by Fowler[4] include the following:

- A self-administered survey should be self-explanatory. Reading instructions should not be necessary, because they will not be read consistently.

- Self-administered questionnaires should be restricted to closed answers. If respondents are asked to use their own words, the answers are likely to become vague (*Note:* A comments section at the back of the survey can prove to be invaluable; the ambiguity is as important as the focus).

- The question *forms* in a self-administered questionnaire should be few in number. The more the questionnaire can be set up so that the respondent has the same kinds of tasks and questions to answer, the less likely it is that respondents will become confused; also the easier the task will be for respondents.

- A questionnaire should be typed and laid out in a way that seems clear and uncluttered. (*Note:* Shrinking the questions down, or other creative ways to decrease the final page count, actually decrease the response rate, according to Fowler). Use more pages rather than less, spacing questions attractively.

- Provide redundant information to respondents. If people can be confused about what they are supposed to do, they will be.

Fowler provides a good set of comments on the appearance of the survey, as well as ways to minimize its ambiguity. The creative use of question formats (such as running a string of questions together that have the same answer options) and simplifying data demands combine with the use of professional presentation formats to increase the response rate and ease completion of the chosen design.

Pretesting: Gathering Comments Before It's Too Late

A conclusion is the place where you got tired of thinking.

Martin H. Fischer

Sending out a questionnaire that hasn't been extensively pretested may make the benchmarking team feel like they're making progress, but in reality it means they got tired before the race was done. Pretesting a survey entails asking individuals both within and outside the firm to complete the instrument, to time how long they took to finish it, and to note every instance where they were uncertain about either the instructions, the question itself, what they were trying to answer, and so on. A pretest often reveals major holes in the logic or structure of the survey and provides a realistic estimate of the amount of time you're asking people to give you at the target firms.

Once the pretest is complete, the survey can be revised and administered. Whether it is mailed, filled out via a phone conversation, or completed through an on-site visit, the ultimate test of the questionnaire will be the data it collects. If the items are well thought out, clearly presented, and irrelevant questions eliminated, the probability of success is high. Conversely, carelessness will quite likely lead to failure. If in doubt, revise the instrument and pretest it again; never send it out if there is any indication that errors still exist.

Questions That Make Good Measures

Good questions may not lead to the solutions and information desired. As in all things, form over substance is to be avoided at all cost. Fowler provides some final insight on this issue:[5]

> Questions can be poor measures because they are unreliable (producing erratic results) or because they are biased, producing estimates that consistently err in one direction from the true value (as when drunk driving arrests are underreported).
> ... In a sense, each variable to be measured requires research to identify the best set of questions to measure it and to produce estimates of how valid the resulting measure is.

Good questions are ones that are clearly understood by the respondents, that don't lead the individual to choose a specific answer through careless wording, and that carefully focus on a key construct or issue under study. Questions should be categorized and screened against criteria such as the following:

■ Does it relate to one or more of the identified drivers?

- What does the question add to the understanding of critical success factors or key issues?

- Are there an adequate number of questions aimed at each key variable, or have some been poorly developed?

- Will these questions provide the answers we need?

While designing a questionnaire is as much art as science, there are logical rules that prevent the process from spinning off into obscurity. If the questions being asked are nonsensical, irrelevant, or redundant, cut them. If the key questions that motivated the benchmarking study in the first place don't seem to be addressed adequately, add some questions. Continue reviewing and revising the document until it is the best that the group can devise; stopping short of best effort will adversely affect the results.

ISSUES TO NOTE, REMEMBER, AND USE TO GUIDE DATA COLLECTION

Known principles are the barbed-wire entanglements around the detention camps where our intuitions are restrained from going into warfare.

Henry S. Haskins
Meditations on Wall Street

Benchmarking raises a series of issues for both the sponsoring and participating firms. One of the most critical of these is *confidentiality*. Enticing a company with the opportunity to receive benchmarking data is one thing; getting them to "open their kimono" in public is another. Even though most benchmarking data are focused on the process or management of a specific function or role, it can still be perceived as a strategic threat by some potential participants. Reassuring them that their answers are going to be anonymous is one way to get past these reservations, but it brings with it its own problems.

If anonymity is to be preserved, one of several approaches to data collection has to be employed:

- Abandonment of personal interviews
- Creation of expert panels to address qualitative issues
- Inclusion of open-ended questions, and a hope that participants respond to them
- Use of an external facilitator to mask the identities of all benchmarking firms

Undoubtedly other creative approaches to the confidentiality issue can be generated. Unless an external facilitator such as a consulting firm is used, the benchmarking sponsor will be faced with sacrificing some data. It may not be seen as a critical issue, but then again it may drastically impair the benchmarking team's ability to "make sense" out of the data, construct a straw man, and develop process-oriented improvement programs.

The confidentiality issue really stems from competitive concerns. One reason why best-in-class benchmarking is so successful is because it looks outside of the sponsor's industry for insights. In addition, it is always focused on a process or role within the company, not its overall performance, marketing plans, or strategic issues. In designing a benchmarking study, then, keep one fact ever present, ever clear:

Keep all questions objective and nonthreatening.

A platitude? Perhaps, but nonetheless the simple fact is that benchmarking can turn into a competitive assessment initiative, which destroys its essence and ensures that, even if the study is completed, another one won't be.

The objective of benchmarking is gaining knowledge about how to work smarter and better; to improve performance against stakeholder expectations. To gain this knowledge, the benchmarking team needs to explore every avenue open to them, and turn to other companies only when they know exactly what they need to learn and why. If the why is a veiled desire to get "insider information" from a competitor, the benchmarking project not only is unethical—it may teeter on the edge of collusion and anti-trust.

Related Issues and Some Answers

> Action and faith enslave thought, both of them in order not to be troubled or inconvenienced by reflection, criticism, and doubt.
>
> Henri Frederic Amiel

Other issues that arise during data collection and affect the effectiveness of a questionnaire-based benchmarking study include the following:

1. How unique are the drivers and constraints faced by my firm?
2. What kinds of data will be needed to ensure comparability?
3. If only part of the questionnaire is completed, what does it mean, and can it still be used?
4. If mistakes are discovered, what can be done?
5. How can you know if everyone's returned their questionnaire if there aren't any names on them?

The essence of benchmarking is comparability. When collecting data, it's important to constantly review whether or not the target firms are similar enough to your own to ensure that the information can be used. In designing a questionnaire, then, a significant element (for example, a bank of questions) has to be focused around the identified performance drivers, constraints, and critical environmental factors that define the sponsor firm. Each major constraint, each driver, has to be included in the survey. Otherwise, there's no way to effectively sort or use the data obtained.

What if only part of the survey is completed? The issue here is, what was left out? How vital was that information to the study? In dealing with incomplete information, the scientific solution is to either discard the response or set up a series of codes for "missing data." These options are equally valid for benchmarking studies; throw away a response, though, only if there is no alternative. Data are difficult to gather; they shouldn't be lightly discarded. Conversely, if there are gaping holes in the data, they are worse than useless; they can bias the entire analysis. There's no simple answer to this common problem.

Hitting the data analysis stage of the study and finding out you forgot a key element is disheartening to say the least. While suicide may seem a bit drastic, mental flagellation is often undertaken. Mistakes do happen. Careful preparation and multiple iterations and pretesting of the questionnaire can limit these problems, but every study has at least one flaw, no matter how well planned and executed. What to do? Once again, it depends on the severity of the problem. If the key benchmarking question has been adequately addressed, the "hole" should be noted and plugged in future studies.

On the other hand, if the flaw is critical, a second survey can be attempted. Most people keep a copy of the survey they originally filled out; it's not inconceivable that they can simply send a second copy, along with their response to the omitted items. Maybe. In reality, though, going back to the well a second time is difficult; credibility and momentum are lost, and participation is likely to deteriorate. Starting from scratch with a new set of firms is the final alternative; it's costly, and hard to explain to the powers that be. Is it a career-limiting move [CLM]? Hopefully, it's not, but compiling the study's results with known flaws unaddressed may well be a CLM—it can be perceived as tantamount to lying. The only way around this undesirable chain of events is prevention: work, rework, and review the study documents multiple times before using them.

The final issue noted above is the easiest of all to address. When a "blind" survey is being used, the benchmarking packet should include the survey, a stamped return envelope, clear instructions, *and* a return postcard. The postcard asks for the respondent's name, the name of the respondent's firm, and the date the survey was mailed. It may even contain a question like "Would you be willing to discuss this study in more depth?" If the answer is yes, follow-up telephone interviews can be conducted that add depth to the data analysis and benchmarking models developed. This approach assures the participants that you are keeping the responses confidential, and yet it allows the benchmarking team to do a second request or mailing to increase the response rate.

Never attempt to code a questionnaire with some identifying marks if confidentiality has been assured. It's the first thing the respondents will look for, and chances are they'll find it if it's there. If the benchmarking design requires that the identity of the firms be known, ask for it right up front and accept the fact that some firms may refuse. Not all will, though, and the open sharing that can ensue can enrich the study and create a far superior final product.

Benchmarking isn't espionage; it is a focused search for best practice to encourage continuous improvement. Keeping that fact ever present in the minds of the benchmarking team, the participating firms, and the implementation task force that follows will help your company maximize the benefits from benchmarking. It is a tool, and like any other, can be put to good use or abused; effective design and sound execution lay the groundwork for the learning process.

> The fatal tendency of mankind to leave off thinking about a thing when it is no longer doubtful, is the cause of half of their errors.
>
> John Stuart Mill

19: INTERPRETING BENCHMARKING RESULTS

> If a man understands that he is asleep and if he wishes to awake, then everything that helps him to awake will be good and everything that hinders him, everything that prolongs his sleep, will be evil.
>
> Georges Guidjieff

Obtaining the right data is the first step in putting benchmarking to work as a tool for continuous improvement. Sound interpretation is the second stop on the path to excellence, which culminates in an action plan and its implementation. Getting the most from the data starts with careful classification and interpretation of the results, using structured and unstructured approaches.

Establishing the Baseline

The underlying objective in data analysis is to identify performance gaps and isolate best practices, in order to construct a straw man. Before these events can occur, the participating firms have to be reevaluated against the original performance drivers and constraints that were identified in the internal assessment. Companies that are "different" can provide useful insights, but their practices have to be carefully evaluated for the feasibility of implementing them in the sponsor firm.

BENCHMARKING

One of the best ways to get a handle on the level of comparability is by constructing a chart that lists the core performance drivers for the company juxtaposed against the characteristics of each of the benchmarked firms (see Figure 19.1). Several types of classifications can be used to narrow in on the level of comparability:

- Numerical estimate of similarity (exact match = 5; no match = 1)

- General categorical approach (yes/no)

- Ranking of similarity (closest match = 1, next best = 2, and so on)

- Verbal listing of actual site characteristics

The approach taken is a matter of taste. Each of the classification schemes builds from the benchmarking team's *interpretation* of the results (with the exception of the last approach); the final choice is based on the type of decision that is being made.

Scoring the level of similarity between the benchmarked firms and the sponsor provides a way to classify and integrate subsequent data analysis. It also provides an objective way to eliminate (or sideline) responses that have limited applicability. If the benchmark firms are dissimilar in key structural areas from the sponsor and are outperforming it, that in itself is a vital finding.

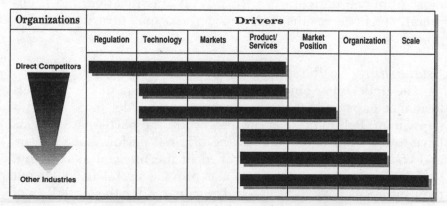

Figure 19.1   Sample basis of comparision.

Another way to gauge the relative structure of the participating firms is by listing the actual responses to key structural questions on the *comparability grid*. It is quite likely that there will be important details embedded in these responses that will be lost if an interpretive scheme is used (such as assigning a "score"). It is also possible to do several comparability analyses, including the detailed listing of characteristics as well as the benchmarking team's assessment of the degree of comparability. Both tables can be used effectively in subsequent analysis and the development of conceptual models of best practice.

Cross-Classifying Key Measurements

True genius resides in the capacity for evaluation of uncertain, hazardous, and conflicting information.

Winston Churchill

For each major measure or each questionnaire item, a cross-classification should be performed that details the response made by each of the participating firms. Significant trends can often be spotted using this basic analytic technique. While more elaborate statistical approaches may look more "precise," they can seldom be effectively used in a benchmarking study, because the underlying sample size (number of participating firms) is simply too small.

This series of cross-tabulations should incorporate the appropriate measures for the benchmarking sponsor. Each such analysis provides an indication of relative performance and can be used to draw preliminary conclusions. It may be even more helpful to transfer related questions and results to free-standing reports or scorecards (see Figure 19.2). Completing this type of analysis moves the benchmarking project beyond data gathering into interpretation and learning.

Another viable alternative for analyzing the data is to create a graph of the firms' relative performance on key dimensions of performance. For instance, in Figure 19.3 the complexity of the

Key Characteristics	Excellent Companies	Company	vs. Others
Automation as a means of coordination	• 100% of companies use automation as the primary method of coordination	• Minimal "Customer Bonding" (EDI for simple orders) • Automated tracking capabilities • Limited systems intelligence (e.g., automated fulfillment) • No automated work assignment or scheduling	<
Single order processing system	• Most use a single ordering system and single interface	• Multiple ordering systems and interfaces	<
Breadth of responsibilities aligned with strategy	• Breadth of responsibility increases with increasing product complexity and emphasis on customer service	• Narrowly focused order processors for all levels of complexity • Broader responsibilities for National accounts than for Commercial and Major accounts	< For Commercials and Majors = For Nationals
Minimization of order processing handoffs	• 77% of processes have two or fewer handoffs between the customer and fulfillment groups	• Three or more handoffs	<

Figure 19.2   Sample scorecard.

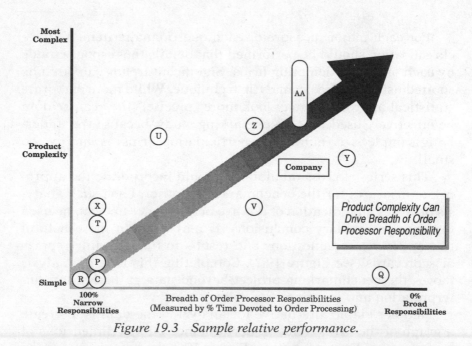

Figure 19.3   Sample relative performance.

products offered by a company are compared against the breadth of responsibilities assigned to its order processing department. What the diagram suggests is that increased product complexity leads to more broadly defined order-processing capabilities. If a product is very complex, the individuals taking the order have to be knowledgeable enough to respond to detailed questions from the customer. If they lack this level of expertise, the customer has to be "passed" to someone who can answer the question.

Frequent handoffs are not the path to high customer satisfaction marks. To prevent this chain of events from occurring, then, companies dealing in highly complex products instill more authority, and hence responsibility, in their order-processing group. This is a logical solution to an ongoing customer service problem caused by the inherent nature of the products sold. By contrasting two different aspects of the benchmarked data, the sponsoring firm can assess their relationship to each other, and it can look for patterns in the processes and management structures used by other firms (in the order-processing area, for example).

A further example is the data analysis recently completed in a benchmarking study of a major corporation's order-processing group; Figure 19.4 suggests one further elaboration of the data analysis process. In this figure, one specific facet of the total

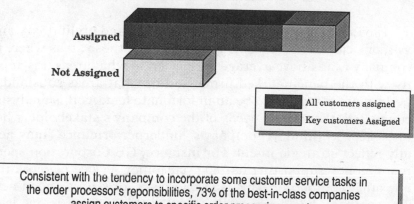

Figure 19.4   Sample data analysis.

order processing function is explored: whether or not customers are assigned to specific order-processing agents. What the study discovered is that 73 percent of the excellent companies did assign agents to specific customers. The graphic display of these data indicates that there is some variation in how this is accomplished: some best-practice firms hold to this approach across all customers, regardless of size. Others focus these "special services" on key customers only.

Thinking back to the information provided by the Avon Products case (see Chapter 5), Avon had also determined that its top customers required special services. It assigned key customers to specific customer service representatives and even went so far as to provide an enhanced level of service to its "top-performing" agents. The personal touch and increased referential knowledge about customer tastes provided by this service alternative obviously pays off. Best practice means top performance against all stakeholders' expectations (including profits).

Determining Parity

> Production is not the application of tools to materials, but logic to work.
>
> Peter Drucker

Having completed the cross-tabulations and preliminary analysis, one can complete some general lists of those areas where the company is an above-average performer, in what areas it is at parity with the benchmarked firms, and in what areas substandard performance appears to be an unfortunate fact. As this analysis is completed, the unique needs of the company's stakeholders have to be kept in mind. A company's "underperformance" may actually reflect strategic intent. For instance, GE Corporation spends more money supporting its "800" customer service network than any other competitor. This isn't bad news for GE; it's good news. The company has deliberately targeted this service as one leg of its service strategy. The information that it is spending more than everyone else says it is achieving its objectives.

What's Right, and What's Wrong?

> For of course the true meaning of a
> term is to be found by observing what
> a man does with it, not by what he
> says about it.
>
> P. W. Bridgman

Determining what a company does right and what it does wrong is not a simple process. Within a benchmarking context, right and wrong practice is relative—what was originally intended? Did the company pursue the right things the wrong way, the wrong things the right way, or one of the other alternatives noted in Figure 19.5? Obviously, value-added performance means doing the right things the right way. And the more important those "things" are to competitive success, the greater their impact on the ultimate "bottom line."

What is "right" for one company can be exactly the wrong thing for another. The key to this dilemma is the diverse needs of stakeholders. For a not-for-profit foundation, the goal is to deliver maximum service at the minimum price. Giving more for less is not a marketing slogan for them; it is their underlying objective. Take the same service (for example, running a hospital) and place it in a for-profit mode, and these goals change significantly. Service is provided at whatever level is required to ensure maximum profitabilty. Obviously, profits are a function of the quality of care delivered, but the hospital may well omit some services that don't pay their own way and expand on those that do. In the former case, the objective is to provide a full menu of services; in the latter, it is to specialize in those areas where profits can be earned. The same type of organization, faced with a different set of stakeholders and expectations, can pursue radically different strategies.

In areas where the benchmarked firm is underperforming the identified best-practice firms, then further analysis is needed. Is the difference by intent or not? If not, is the performance shortfall important enough to warrant immediate attention, or can it be set aside while other areas are addressed? Significant aspects of the

BENCHMARKING

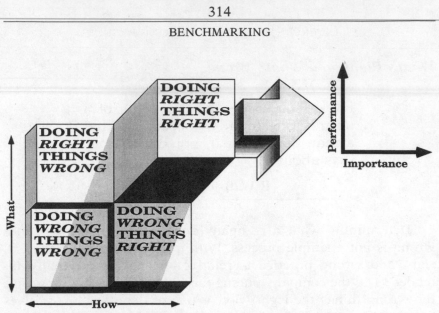

Figure 19.5 Interpreting benchmark results.

interpretation of benchmarking results are the identification of performance gaps and prioritization of the problem spots, based on relative value to stakeholders, cost of improving the service, and potential for change.

Recapping the Analytical Process

Once the benchmarking firm has obtained valid responses from benchmarking participants, it begins to integrate the information gained during its internal assessment with the responses gathered from the field. The objective is clear-cut: to identify those areas where the company is performing well and those where immediate change is needed. The analysis is bound by the degree of comparability between the benchmarked firms and the sponsor; low levels of comparability don't necessarily mean the data are useless. In fact, key structural differences may end up separating top performers from lesser players.

Reviewing the steps in the data analysis phase (see Chapter 17), the benchmarking firm should do the following:

1. Compare benchmarking data against original performance drivers and note similarities and differences for its firm and the benchmarking participants.
2. Classify and analyze the quantitative data.

3. Review qualitative data (interview comments) to identify innovative concepts and unique approaches.
4. Confirm findings where needed.
5. Reanalyze the quantitative results in light of the anecdotal information (interview comments).
6. Develop a straw man model of best practice for the area under study.
7. Communicate the basic findings to all benchmarking participants and internal staff.

Once preliminary data has been cross-classified, they should be provided to the benchmarking participants. There is no reason for the company to provide its own analysis of the data; instead, the simple tabulations of the data are adequate. It is equitable also to include comparative data for your own firm in the summaries. Since other firms have provided this level of information to you, it is reasonable for them to expect you to be equally honest.

The summarized data should not include the name of participating firms. Even if these are known, it is a leap of faith to assume that these companies would be willing for everyone to know these details about them. Unless a company has specifically stated that it would like its data to be publicly disclosed, confidentiality should be observed. If it's not, it can quite likely cause downstream problems for anyone trying to gain participation from the firms who feel their trust has been "betrayed." With the increase in interest in benchmarking, it is safe to assume that participation in a study is not a one-time event for a company—unless, of course, someone has muddied the waters enough to turn the company's management against further sharing (and, unfortunately, learning).

QUALITATIVE DATA AND STRAW MAN MODELS

Man does not live by words alone, despite the fact that sometimes he has to eat them.

Adlai Stevenson

> We should have a great many fewer
> disputes in the world if words were
> taken for what they are, the signs
> of our ideas only, and not for things
> themselves.
>
> John Locke

So far the data analysis discussion has focused on the quantitative, measurable data collected from the benchmarking firms. Carefully screening, analyzing, and comparing these measures is a valuable part of the learning process. What accelerates the learning process, though, are the interview comments, or anecdotal evidence, gathered from the benchmarking participants and industry experts. It adds depth to the level of understanding of why and how companies actually organize and manage their work processes.

Irv Kraus, the facilitator for the research and development study described earlier [see Chapter 16], commented about the role of qualitative data in the benchmarking process:

> When we did a set of interviews, we would carefully record the answers, because the anecdotal information is as important as the quantitative information in reaching a clear understanding of existing, and best, practice.

If quantitative analysis provides the skeleton of the best-practice straw man, anecdotal information is its flesh and blood. Numbers may seem more reliable, but they can hide as much as they reveal. In fact, Americans' love of numbers is often cited as one of their primary cultural shortcomings. Numbers are not inherently better than words; they may be easier to put on graphs or factor into an equation, but the measures obtained in benchmarking study are based on assumptions, estimates, and the perceptions of one individual out of the many employed by the target firm. Are they reliable? Perhaps, but they are just one side of the "truth."

19: INTERPRETING BENCHMARKING RESULTS

Qualitative data (such as the interview comments) can provide the clues to a puzzling result. And because they tell the story in the participant's own words, they can reveal nuances and omitted variables that redefine the quantitative measures. Best practice may not be a measurable event at all; instead, it may be an attitude, a cultural nuance at the best-practice firm: a vision inspired by leadership and enacted through the multiple interactions between the company's employees and its external customers.

When analyzing benchmarking results, then, make sure that every shred of evidence, whether verbal or numerical, is utilized to its fullest extent. If a chart is developed around a set of quantified measurements, append the respondents' words directly to it. Juxtapose the verbal insights against the numbers and look for inconsistencies. People are seldom careless in their use of words. Should the words used by the respondent paint a different picture of the processes, structures, management, and critical success factors for the function or role under study, step back from the numbers and think through the implications of the words.

It's possible that the individual answered the questions, because you asked him or her to, but didn't really have any relevance to how the organization functions. Since benchmarking targets best practice, it is the real practices that have to be examined. They may or may not correspond to the original model pieced together by the benchmarking team. If they don't, that's not only a finding—it may provide the clue to leapfrogging the continuous improvement cycle.

Creating and Using Straw Man Models

After the analytics are completed, it's time to turn the team's attention to refining and applying the lessons learned. The straw man, or best-practice result, is the basis for evaluating current performance inside the organization and for prioritizing improvement efforts. It can also serve as an effective communication tool for conveying the benchmarking message to top management and to other parts of the organization. At AT&T, the world-class CFO results are being shared with CFOs in other parts of the company. Driven by a realistic concern for maintaining the integrity of the financial community at AT&T in the face of ongoing changes in the corporation's structure and strategy, Jim Meenan is hoping to solidify the role of financial services as a strategic weapon. In the emerging "competitive team" structure, the effective performance of the financial function is not an option.

The straw man, or model of best practice, is the final product for that round of the benchmarking process. Once it is developed and communicated, it becomes a tool for action, not a topic of discussion. Benchmarking is an action-generating sequence that starts with a recognition of a performance shortfall. Where does it end? With the next round of data collection and the refinement of the company's knowledge of best practice as identified by the benchmarking process. The process of getting better never ends; it simply is refocused onto the next hot spot, the next opportunity for improvement.

TURNING STRAW MEN INTO REALITY

The question is not whether to adjust or to rebel against reality but, rather, how to discriminate between those realities that must be recognized as unalterable and those that we should continue to try to change however unyielding they may appear.

Helen Merrell Lynd
On Shame and the Search for Identity

Where benchmarking ends, real change begins. If the results of a benchmarking study are discussed and then tucked away inside of someone's desk drawer, they are worse than useless. The study consumed resources that could have been applied somewhere else; it wasn't free. Yet this may be the first response once the data are all in. Few managers happily face the reality that their performance is lagging short of best practice. They deny, rebel, and mourn the loss of illusion that is stripped away in the benchmarking process.

After allowing the shock to wear off, the benchmarking team has to expand its horizons and move toward developing plans that will change the status quo and improve the company's performance. Implementation of change is a challenging task in any situation. Thankfully, there is mounting evidence that managers are more readily convinced to undertake change when facing a crisis. Benchmarking can create exactly the level of creative anxiety required to get everyone moving. If no one manages to discredit the results, there really is no viable alternative left: change, or painful decline may become a reality.

The way the message is delivered by the benchmarking team can soften the blow. Rather than running about pointing out the sky is falling, it is more prudent to note the identified opportunities for improvement, to note the benefits (in terms of decreased costs, increased profits, or improved performance against stakeholder expectations) of pursuing the various paths, and to proactively encourage everyone to move forward in a positive manner. Action is the objective, not paralysis and fear.

Identifying areas that will yield rapid performance improvements is a second way the implementation process can be accelerated. Motivated by positive results, people more easily buy into the change process. The improvements should be measured, celebrated, and expanded as the company begins learning how to use the lessons from other companies in redefining its own work.

Get Everyone Involved

Benchmarking and the continuous improvement process are not an individual effort. They are team-based, participative events that unify and direct the activities of diverse groups and individuals across the firm. Individuals will more rapidly buy into changes they helped define and design. The benchmarking team should, on an ongoing basis, communicate with everyone in their group about the progress of the study, the information being obtained, and the findings which emerge. This communication process doesn't start when the straw man is constructed; it begins the day the decision is made to benchmark in the first place. People implement change, not companies.

Each affected group should be actively recruited in the process of establishing long-range improvement goals, to create action plans to achieve parity with the benchmarked best-practice firms, and to enhance the learning process. While the benchmarking team may be closest to the data, that can be as much of a hindrance to insight and intuition as a benefit. Often a fresh set of eyes and an open mind, uncluttered with the facts, can spot an opportunity or risk that others have overlooked. Every individual in the organization brings knowledge and perspectives to the problem that can support a creative breakthrough. Rank does not define wisdom—a fact that General Custer seemed to overlook.

Reinforce, Learn, and Change

Any good implementation sows the seeds of discontent with existing practices as part of the process of convincing the settlers to move into uncharted territory. But unlike farmers moving into the Midwest with the intention never to leave again, successful benchmarking encourages everyone to become a gypsy. No destination is final; each stop along the way is a temporary respite taken to regain momentum and chart the path ahead. Successful benchmarking, then, is benchmarking that is never complete, that never lets the organization rest on its laurels, and that constantly raises the level of acceptable performance.

Can people adjust to constant change? A multitude of books and psychologists suggest that they can't, but the world is not going to stand still because of them. The only constant factor in life is change, a fact well recognized by Heraclitus (a Greek philosopher, circa 540 to 480 B.C.) long before "future shock" was even a recognizable combination of sounds. In his own words: "Nothing endures but change." While some may suggest that the pace of change is accelerating, it is a fact to be accepted, not fought.

Benchmarking helps create the learning organization: a group of dedicated individuals who actively pursue excellence, growth, and knowledge. If the experts are right (Rosabeth Moss Kanter, Peter Drucker, Tom Peters, and Peter Senge, just to name a few), only those organizations that can quickly learn from and master their environments will survive into the twenty-first century. Objective information can help trigger the transformation to the continuous improvement philosophy, but it can only do so if it is continually reapplied and reinforced. Benchmarking sets the framework for excellence; attaining it depends on the actions that are taken once the results are in.

If I had given you any parting advice, it would, I think, all have been comprised in this one sentence, "To live up always to the best and highest you know."

Hannah Whitall Smith

20: LESSONS LEARNED AND THOSE THAT LIE AHEAD

> How to become conscious? ... It means
> that you will suffer still more–that's the
> first thing to realize. But you won't be
> dead, you won't be indifferent.... You
> will want to understand everything,
> even the disagreeable things. You will
> want to accept more and more—even
> what seems hostile, evil and threaten-
> ing.
>
> Henry Miller
> *The Air-Conditioned Nightmare*

Benchmarking raises the consciousness of the organization. It drives everyone toward improvement as the only escape from the harsh reality that current practices simply aren't good enough. Benchmarking results sound an alarm that lets everyone know that there's danger ahead; hopefully it also helps move everyone toward higher ground. It is a tool for generating action and for creating the learning organization.

In describing the learning organization, Peter Senge[1] suggests that it means more than copying the practices used by others. Identifying and learning from best practices does not institute learning as a separate event inside a company; but when everyone's feet are stuck in concrete, a push of major proportions is needed to get them moving. The first step in the path to excellence is the acceptance that change is needed.

20: LESSONS LEARNED AND THOSE THAT LIE AHEAD

To achieve excellence, a company has to experiment in every part of its business, fostering a critical eye toward internal activities. Everyone, from top management on down, has to be willing to dig in and get his or her hands dirty, poking in corners for answers and constantly asking, "Why?" (Five times will not be enough.) The role of benchmarking in this process is to provide insights and creative ideas for combining existing resources, and to show a path that has worked for others in gaining improvements.

Benchmarking, then, is a class on learning how to learn. The first few lectures are simply to get your attention. Once the groundwork is laid, the pace of change accelerates, as every individual begins to accept the fact that the status quo is a dangerous bedfellow. As novel approaches to organizing internal work are uncovered and measurements are derived to support them, attitudes change. People can become accustomed to change. In fact, change can become exhilarating. The final exam for the class is conducted by the market; those companies that embrace change and strive for constant improvement will survive into the twenty-first century. Those that remain mired in tradition will get failing marks, perhaps even flunk out of school.

Benchmarking is an applied discipline. It can't be learned from a book or a seminar. It is practiced in the trenches and mastered on the field of battle. The global marketplace may not be the battlefield of choice for a company, but it is only there that the battle can be joined. By applying benchmarking concepts a company can identify its weakest zones of defense and redeploy resources to strengthen them. Successfully managing a corporation is, at its heart, a military campaign with no apparent end; continuous skirmishing; and an intense need for flexible, but well-planned and -executed, strategies.

TAKING OFF THE BLINDERS

I sometimes react to making a mistake as if I have betrayed myself. My fear of making a mistake seems to be based on the hidden assumption that

> I am potentially perfect and that if I
> can just be very careful I will not fall
> from heaven. But a "mistake" is a dec-
> laration of the way I *am*, a jolt to the
> way I intend, a reminder that I am not
> dealing with the facts. When I have
> *listened* to my mistakes I have grown.
>
> Hugh Prather
> *Notes to Myself*

The benchmarking process described in this book has been focused on achieving one mission: removing the blinders that prevent organizations from improving. The cases describing how different companies have employed benchmarking have one thing in
common: reality was a jolt that was responded to with growth,
not denial. In each case, a change agent or leader emerged to
keep everyone moving toward the goal. Yet once momentum was
gained, the need to push evaporated. The organization began to
look for its own ways to implement new methods and learn from
the field.

Benchmarking is composed of four distinct phases. Phase I is
an internal assessment of existing practice. It provides the framework for subsequent work, details the key constraints and performance drivers that define the organization, and develops a set
of primary measures or constructs for the study. Internal assessment can also turn into an *internal benchmarking* study. Internal
benchmarking is the comparison of multiple groups within a corporation that are performing the same task. It is applicable in any
decentralized or divisionalized company.

Internal benchmarking gets the entire organization on level
ground. It is also an excellent way to convince people of the
need to change. At Avon Products, the improvements in the customer service system have been significant. Through a careful use
of internal competition, management is steering the diverse geographic regions toward common practice: common and excellent.
The driving force in the Avon study was the desire to improve the
service delivered to the company's primary stakeholders: the independent agents who sell their products. Change began to occur

before the ink was dry on the final report. It was a benchmarking success.

Phase II of the benchmarking process entails data gathering. It starts with a clear definition of what the project will attempt to discover, moves on through the development of the survey instruments and other information sources, and includes the identification and joined participation of target companies. Phase II is the meat of the benchmarking process. How it is finally structured within any one study will depend on the questions being asked, the time frame around the study, and the resources available. Phase II, then, is the "do" in benchmarking.

Phase III begins where data collection ends. It is the careful and creative sifting of the collected information, which results in the creation of a straw man model, an identification of performance gaps, and their prioritization. In Phase III a company begins to discover what it does right and what it does wrong. It is the time of denial, mourning, and final acceptance. The more shocking the results, the more lengthy the analysis will be. In Phase III, then, the real process of learning begins; concrete walls are broken down and movement is begun.

The final phase of benchmarking is *action*. Finding out the score is not the objective; changing it is. Mastering best practice is the goal; achieving it, a journey. The methods used to implement change in the aftermath of the benchmarking study are the same as those used in any change process. Communication, a clear set of objectives, measurements that track improvement, and the active participation and perceived value of each participant are the essence of any successful change. Benchmarking, though, is not a terminal event. It is iterative, adaptive, and continuous, because it is about continuous learning and the search for excellence.

Benchmarking Approaches

While the underlying process that constitutes benchmarking is fairly consistent across different settings, the targeted learning, or approach, can vary widely. Four different "versions" of benchmarking were explored in the preceding pages: internal, competitive, industry and best-in-class. Internal benchmarking, as suggested above, is focused on the improvement and standardization of internal operations. It is usually used as the first step in an external benchmarking project, but can also be a free-standing event.

Competitive benchmarking was defined by its concern with global measures of performance for a representative sample of companies competing in the same product arena. Out of all the approaches described, competitive benchmarking is the least concerned with discovering process or structural facts about the competition. Instead, it attempts to discover, in a broad sense, the relative deployment of resources in certain parts of the business, as well as the effectiveness of those resources. It yields a scorecard, but that scorecard is not the end product. Competitive benchmarking naturally leads to industry or best-in-class studies, because it prioritizes those aspects of the business that are underperforming the competition. Janssen Corporation used it to examine its administrative overhead area. The study spanned several functional areas (all those reported below the gross margin line on the income statement), looking for differences in the way resources were deployed and their relative productivity.

When the focus of the study shifts from the measured distribution of resources to a concern with *how* those resources are structured and managed, it is *industry benchmarking*. Industry benchmarking looks for trends or patterns in the way specific resources are deployed for a specific *industry*. While a function is usually the target of the analysis, the study remains defined within a broad band of competitive firms. For Exxon Chemical, the objective was to understand industry best practices in managing information system applications because of their increasing use as a strategic weapon.

The final benchmarking approach, *best-in-class*, moves beyond traditional competitive boundaries. BIC benchmarking, by definition, is focused outside of the sponsoring firm's industry. Concerned with the relative performance of one specific function or role, BIC studies reveal innovative practices used in diverse settings to manage the technologies and resources of an organization. AT&T is using this approach to move its financial function toward world-class performance. BIC benchmarking is giving them insights into how to master these new challenges and to deploy its resources in the most effective manner possible.

A second BIC study was explored in Chapter 16. In this study, the question being raised was "What practices are used to gain effective commercialization of R&D projects?" Competitive success is increasing a function of getting new products to market faster and cheaper. There's little time or slack for employing a strategy of "hope"—management hoping that R&D dollars will yield new products. The BIC study helped identify the key structural and philosophical differences in companies that are world-class managers of their R&D function and those that aren't.

Best-in-class benchmarking, then, is a focused study of the *roles* performed, those "soft" organizational issues that separate top performers from the pack in any discipline, any industry. It assumes that "best practice" is not confined to what is done within one specific industry, but rather in a global sense, across the varied corporate landscape. It is gaining increasing attention as the means to quantum leaps in performance, providing innovative ways to combine and utilize resources.

DEFINING FEATURES OF BENCHMARKING

Opinions have their upsets and all is well. But once a cataclysm takes place among a man's convictions, the outcome is more than well—it is supreme experience.

Henry S. Haskins
Meditations on Wall Street

Several messages or themes have been reiterated throughout this discussion of benchmarking (see Figure 20.1). They are continuous improvement, stakeholder interests, and change. Briefly summarizing these points, benchmarking is a tool for enacting change, as defined within the philosophy of continuous improvement. The measure of success in the change process is defined by the creation of value in the stakeholder's eyes. Benchmarking is externally oriented and seeks to gather information about creative

BENCHMARKING

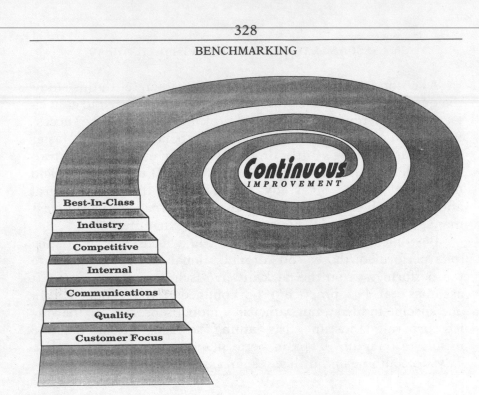

Figure 20.1   Continuous improvement.

ways to restructure the processes and resources of a company to better serve its varied stakeholders' needs.

To achieve these changes, benchmarking studies have to meet a defined set of criteria, defined in terms of comparability, objectivity, adaptability, and continuity. If benchmarking firms do not exhibit high levels of comparability with the sponsoring company, as defined and measured by key performance drivers and constraints, the study cannot hope to yield usable findings. The dimensions critical to this matching process shift as different benchmarking approaches are adopted. In each case, though, the benchmarking team has to carefully choose, and then validate, that the organizations or functions included in the target sample bear enough resemblance to them to support further analysis.

The analysis undertaken and methods employed in an effective benchmarking study are *objective*. While intuition and gut-feel have merit in certain settings, the power of benchmarking stems from its uncontestable relationship to "truth." In designing a benchmarking study, then, the measures chosen, the design of the instruments, and the analysis and reporting of the results have to be free of bias. Objectivity comes from sound execution of the benchmarking process. If shortcuts, personal elaborations of the facts, or other related events unfold, the benchmarking study will fail. Why? Because the first response most people have to benchmarking results is rejection; they'll seek to discredit the findings to avoid listening to the message. Faulty execution and the loss of objectivity will doom a benchmarking study before it starts.

Adaptability in the benchmarking process means that learning is not mimicking the actions of others but, instead, the adaptation of what others are doing to your own setting. Best practices may be definite items, but how they are translated in each company is radically different. Implementing benchmarking results doesn't mean doing exactly what everyone else is doing; this approach is unlikely to lead to a competitive advantage. Instead, the information obtained should be juxtaposed against the strategic objectives of the firm, its critical success factors, and its current areas of excellence to craft an implementation plan that will transform the "best practice" into a unique competitive weapon.

Finally, benchmarking is a process without an end. Each time lessons are learned and improvements made, they highlight the next area needing attention. This sequential, systemic approach to organizational problem solving is at the heart of the continuous improvement philosophy. It is reflected in the bottleneck concepts, or Theory of Constraints, so vigorously promoted by Eli Goldratt in *The Goal* and related materials. Learning and the changes it brings are not alien to people; in fact, we are all consummate students. Benchmarking merely drives this point home in a company setting.

Effective learning means arriving at new power, and the consciousness of new power is one of the most stimulating things in life.

Janet Erskine Stuart

Dropping the Chains of the Past

History is a great teacher; it shows you everything that has worked, and hasn't, with equality. Inside an organization, though, history can be a prison preventing growth and learning. Traditions and culture are blinders that screen reality and buffer the organization's senses. Institutionalized rituals of success are repeated, but in an everchanging world, they become less and less relevant. Any company that believes it has all the answers, and can learn nothing from others, has none.

Benchmarking is one way to cut the ties of the past. By carefully revealing reality to the organization in digestible pieces, it inserts new views, objectives, and models into the murky waters of the past. Once gathered, benchmarking data do not go away, even if placed in a locked safe or shredded. Every individual who came in touch with the message is forever changed; they will never again see the organization in the same light. These individual revelations can build toward internal revolution, even while the security system is reporting that all is well. Change cannot be prevented or contained once it begins. A failure to recognize that fact has been the downfall of many a tyrant.

In putting benchmarking to work, then, keep in mind that change will occur once the process is begun. By its very nature, it will cast new, and strange, light on accepted practice. It will reveal the strengths and the weaknesses of the organization. Where problems are uncovered, the immensity of the performance gap will be overpoweringly displayed. Benchmarking forces a clear recognition of a company's actual abilities, performance, and shortcomings. Laid out in objective fashion, these messages are undeniable forces for change.

If you want to maintain the status quo, then, don't benchmark. If you want to remain where you are, secure in the knowledge that you're doing the best you can, don't benchmark. If reality checks are not your cup of tea, don't benchmark. Benchmarking will open the organization to change, and to humility. Finding out your real "rank," your comparative competencies, is a sobering lesson. Without it, the performance illusion so carefully crafted by the organization can be maintained; with it, reality will replace illusion. Benchmarking instills creative tension, and perhaps anxiety, into the staid practices of an organization. Benchmarking provides the stones for building a path toward competitive excellence and long-run success. The outline of that vision has been sketched; applying these concepts will make it a reality.

I think that unless in one thing or another we are straining towards perfection we have forfeited our manhood. Our perfection is in being imperfect in something whose perfection to us is the highest thing in life.

Stephen Mackenna

The rung of a ladder was never meant to rest upon, but only to hold a man's foot long enough to enable him to put the other somewhat higher.

Thomas Henry Huxley

NOTES

Chapter 1   Benchmarking—The Competive Edge

1. R. Camp, *Benchmarking: The Search for Industry Best Practices That Lead to Superior Performance* (White Plains, NY: Quality Resources, 1989), p. 10.

2. R. Schonberger, *Building a Chain of Customers: Linking Business Functions to Create the World Class Company* (New York: The Free Press, 1990), p. 1.

3. Alfred Rappaport, *Creating Shareholder Value: The New Standard for Business Performance* (New York: The Free Press), 1986, p. 12.

4. William A. Band, *Creating Value for Customers* (Toronto: John Wiley & Sons, 1991), p. 19.

5. M. Dertouzos, R. Lester and R. Solow, and the MIT Commission on Industrial Productivity, *Made in America: Regaining the Productive Edge* (Cambridge, MA: The MIT Press, 1989), p. 137.

6. An excellent discussion of the problems with traditional control systems can be found in K. Merchant, *Control in Business Organizations* (Marshfield, MA: Pitman Publishing, 1985).

7. This is a quotation from the jacket cover of the book *Kaizen: The Key to Japan's Competitive Success*, by Masaaki Imai (New York: Random House, 1986).

8. Ibid., p. 3.

Chapter 2 The Many Faces of Benchmarking
1. Michael Hammer, "Reengineering Work: Don't Automate, Obliterate," *Harvard Business Review* (July–August 1990): 105.

Chapter 3 The Benchmarking Process
1. The company providing this diagram asked not to have its name included in the text. Because the example represents a common activity chain within a company, it serves well without the name of the firm attached.
2. Alan Kantrow, *The Constraints of Corporate Tradition* (New York: Harper and Row, 1987), pp. 95–96.

Chapter 5 Avon Products: Putting Internal Benchmarking to Work
1. J. Heskett, W. Early Sasser, Jr., and C. Hart, *Service Breakthroughs: Changing the Rules of the Game*, New York: The Free Press, 1990, p. 42.
2. Ibid. p. 11.

Chapter 6 Continuous Improvement: The Underlying Goal
1. Imai, *Kaizen*, p. 6.
2. This sentiment appears in Rosabeth Moss Kanter, *The Changemasters: Innovation and Entrepreneurship in the American Corporation* (New York: Simon and Schuster, 1983), p. 18.
3. Alan Kantrow, *The Constraints of Corporate Tradition: Doing the Correct Thing, Not Just What the Past Dictates* (New York: Harper and Row, 1984), pp. 177–78.
4. Imai, *Kaizen*, p. 21.
5. Paraphrased from R. Stasey and C. J. McNair, *Crossroads: A JIT Success Story* (Homewood, IL: Dow-Jones Irwin, 1990).
6. Imai, *Kaizen*, p. 6.
7. E. Lawler, III, "Achieving Competiveness by Creating New Organization Cultures and Structures," in D. Fishman and C. Cherniss, eds. *The Human Side of Corporate Competitiveness* (Beverly Hills: Sage Publications, 1990) pp. 69–101. Noted section appears on pp. 93–94.
8. This quotation was obtained while putting together the material for the book *Crossroads: A JIT Success Story* with Robert Stasey. It reflects his personal opinions as implementer of JIT, rather than a corporate strategy or commitment.

Chapter 7 Looking Outward: The Basics of Competitive and Industry Benchmarking

1. "Fad or Fundamental? A chat with Bob Camp of Xerox, the man who wrote the book on benchmarking," *Financial World*, September 17, 1991, pp. 34–35.
2. This information is available in many places. The source for this discussion is R. Camp's book *Benchmarking: The Search for Industry Best Practices that Lead to Superior Performance*, 1989.
3. James B. Kobak, Jr., "Application of Antitrust Laws to Joint Research, Development," *New York Law Journal*, December 10–11, 1984.
4. Alexandra Biesada, "Benchmarking," *Financial World*, September 17, 1991, p. 29.
5. Ibid., p. 30.

Chapter 9 Value from the Customer's Perspective

1. R. Schonberger *Building a Chain of Customers: Linking Business Functions to Create the World Class Company* (New York: The Free Press, 1990), p. 34.
2. John G. Kammlade, Pravesh Mehra, and Terrence R. Ozan, "A Process Approach to Overhead Management," (reprinted from the *Journal of Cost Management*) in Barry Brinker, ed., *Emerging Practices in Cost Management* (New York: Warren, Gorham, and Lamont, 1990), p. 195.
3. Ibid., pp. 193–198.

Chapter 10 Qualitative vs. Quantitative Benchmarks

1. D. Curtis, *Management Rediscovered: How Companies Escape the Numbers Trap* (Homewood, IL: Dow Jones-Irwin, 1990), p. 7.
2. Peter F. Drucker, "Controls, Control and Management" in Charles P. Bonini, Robert K. Jaedicke, and Harvey M. Wagner, eds. *Management Controls: New Directions in Basic Research* (New York: McGraw-Hill, 1964), p. 294.
3. This list is detailed in *Competing in World-Class Manufacturing: America's 21st Century Challenge*, published by the National Center for Manufacturing Sciences (Homewood, IL: Business One Irwin, 1991), on p. 184 as a paraphrasing of E. Goldratt's *The Goal*.

Chapter 11   Looking for Trends: Industry Benchmarking at Exxon Chemical

1. This is the thesis of James R. Beniger in his book, *The Control Revolution: Technological and Economic Origins of the Information Society* (Boston: Harvard University Press, 1986).

Chapter 12   The Basics of Best-in-Class Benchmarking

1. Gary Jacobson and John Hillkirk, *Xerox: American Samurai* (New York: Collier Books), 1968, p. 230.
2. These stages were initially noted in the book *Death and Dying* by Elizabeth Kübler-Ross (New York: MacMillan, 1969).
3. Peter M. Senge, *The Fifth Discipline: The Art and Practice of the Learning Organization* (New York: Doubleday Currency, 1990), pp. 142, 151.

Chapter 13   Identifying Performance Drivers

1. "Fad or Fundamental? A chat with Bob Camp of Xerox, the man who wrote the book on benchmarking," *Financial World*, September 17, 1991, p. 35.

Chapter 14   Using Best-in-Class Benchmarking to Gain Focus: AT&T and the World-Class CFO

1. These quotes originally appear in the FERF (Financial Executives Research Foundation) Study, *Changing Roles of Financial Management: Getting Close to the Business*, by Patrick J. Keating and Stephen J. Jablonsky, completed under the auspices of, and published by, the Financial Executives Research Foundation, New York, 1990, p. 167. Due to ongoing pressures at AT&T, Mr. Meenan requested that his comments be excerpted from this study. Whenever this occurs, a footnote will be used around his comments. For those cases when the quotation has been revised or replaced by Mr. Meenan during the review process, the footnote notation will be dropped.
2. Ibid.
3. Ibid., p. 7.

Chapter 15   People Issues in the Benchmarking Process

1. Mike Parker and Jane Slaughter, "Behind the Scenes at Nummi Motors," *New York Times*, Sunday, Dec. 4, 1988.
2. Kanter, *Changemasters*, p. 18.

3. Schonberger, *Building a Chain of Customers*, p. 24.

4. The discussion of OAP presented here is from David K. Carr and Ian D. Kittman, *Excellence in Government* (Arlington, VA: Coopers & Lybrand, 1990), pp. 217–219.

5. Elting Morison, *Men, Machines, and Modern Times*, (Cambridge, MA: MIT Press, 1966), p. 42. Quoted in Kantrow, *Constraints of Corporate Tradition*, p. 178.

Chapter 16   Excellence in Research and Development:
A Benchmarking Story

1. The study described here was spearheaded by Irv Kraus and John Lin of Meritus. The authors gratefully acknowledge the insights and knowledge provided by Mr. Kraus, as well as the sponsoring firm's agreement to allow this study to be presented.

2. This term, as well as a general description of what it means, is detailed in Philip Roussel, Kamal N. Saad, and Tamara J. Erickson, *Third Generation R&D: Managing the Link to Corporate Strategy* (Boston: Harvard Business School Press, 1991).

3. Ibid., p. 1.

4. The firm sponsoring this study agreed to allow the details of the project to be described in this book, but has asked that its identity, as well as those of the participating firms, be kept confidential. Given the broad-based focus of this study, this anonymity does little to impair the message the results convey or the knowledge about how to use BIC benchmarking in an effective way to assess best practice.

5. The team consisted of the external facilitator for the benchmarking project, the facilitator's staff, and key management players at the sponsoring firm. Confidentiality was deemed to be the primary concern for all involved. To ensure that it was maintained, the facilitator conducted the external benchmarking study and did not reveal the target sites to the sponsoring firm.

Chapter 18   Designing and Using Questionnaires

1. Floyd J. Fowler, Jr., *Survey Research Methods* (Beverly Hills: Sage Publications, 1984), p. 99.

2. Ibid., p. 101.

3. Bob Camp suggests this approach in *Benchmarking*, p. 91. It is also noted by Fowler, but with reservations as to its necessity, in *Survey Research Methods*, p. 103.
4. Fowler, *Survey Research Methods*, p. 103.
5. Ibid., p. 97.

Chapter 20   Lessons Learned and Those That Lie Ahead
1. Peter M. Senge, *The Fifth Discipline*.

INDEX

INDEX